Rosita,

I pray God's blessing
on your children. This is
a God inspired book. I pray God
Blesses us as we as as His will
to train up the children in
Blood us with!

Love
FINA
813-39?-0780

# Are You a Candidate to Read This Book?

Take our quiz to find out. Simply mark Y for Yes or N for No on the line before each entry.

## About You

___ Do you expect the best of your child?

___ Do you mean what you say?

___ Do you follow through on what you say?

___ Do you hold your child accountable for his or her actions?

If you're 4 for 4 with all "Y" answers at this point and are feeling pretty good about yourself right now, you may not need this book. But if you have nothing better to do, finish the rest of this quiz just for fun.

___ Do you yell at, scream at, threaten, or cajole your children to do simple, routine things like get up for school, get dressed, eat, do homework, or perform a chore?

___ When you say no to your child and your child cries, are you overcome by guilt? Do you find yourself giving in to the original request of your child—saying yes to what you had just said no to?

___ Do you engage in long conversations with your child, defending why you said no to a certain request?

___ Are you worried that your child doesn't feel good about himself or herself?

__ Are you bothered that your child doesn't seem happy?

__ Do you plan over-the-top birthday parties?

- Seven-year-old Rosa's parents chartered a bus and took her and multiple friends to a city 115 miles away so they each could "Build a Bear"; then they celebrated with cake and ice cream at an ice cream parlor.
- Five-year-old Mikey's parents rented the stadium club that overlooked an athletic field.
- Marti, a single mom, spent a whole month's income on her 10-year-old daughter's birthday party.

__ Are you concerned about your child not keeping up with the success or achievements of other children?

__ Have you ever wished another child would fail so your child would look better?

__ Do you have a difficult time saying no?

__ Do you have a hard time saying to your children what you really feel as a parent?

__ Are you frustrated most days?

## About School

__ Are you overly involved in your child's life? Do you fear that something terrible will happen if you don't chaperone every school field trip?

__ Do you complete your child's school assignments and projects?

__ Do you require a full explanation from your child's teacher when your child doesn't receive a superior grade?

__ Do you make excuses for your child not having completed his or her assignments on time? ("Oh, it was our fault. We had to go to _____ and we had _____ to do.")

__ Does a simple homework assignment take the whole family's energy for an entire evening? Are the end results lots of tears and frustrations—and an assignment that either never gets done or doesn't get done right?

__ Do you check and correct homework on your child's behalf?

## About Your Children

__ Do they have to be asked to help around the house on a daily basis?

__ Do they disrespect you and not value what you have to say?

__ Do they fuss about obeying you?

__ Do they lack for nothing?

__ Are they engaged in one or more extracurricular activities?

__ Do they need to be reminded more than once to do something?

__ When they slam the door in your face, do you write it off as "just the way kids are"?

__ Is bedtime a battle zone?

If *any* of these topics resonated with you and you marked even one "Y," you need to not only *read* this book but *carry it around with you*. Keep one copy in your car and another in your home.

This book will scratch where you itch.

I promise.

There's a conspiracy going on, right in your own home.

The ankle-biter battalion and the hormone group each have a game plan guaranteed to drive you up the wall. *Have a New Kid by Friday* is an action plan that will take your sails out of your child's wind and set him or her on a different course.

*It's the miracle turnaround you're looking for.*
*I guarantee it.*

# Have a
# New Kid
*by Friday*

## How to Change Your Child's
## Attitude, Behavior & Character
## in **5 Days**

# Dr. Kevin Leman

### Revell
Grand Rapids, Michigan

© 2008 by Kevin Leman

Published by Revell
a division of Baker Publishing Group
P.O. Box 6287, Grand Rapids, MI 49516-6287
www.revellbooks.com

Twelfth printing, September 2009

Printed in the United States of America

Library of Congress Cataloging-in-Publication Data
Leman, Kevin.
    Have a new kid by Friday : how to change your child's attitude, behavior &
character in 5 days / Kevin Leman.
        p.   cm.
    Includes bibliographical references and index.
    ISBN 978-0-8007-1902-9 (cloth)
    ISBN 978-0-8007-3276-9 (pbk.)
    1. Discipline of children. 2. Child rearing.  I. Title.
HQ770.4.L43  2008
649'.64—dc22                                                    2007041883

Scripture is taken from *The Living Bible,* copyright © 1971. Used by permission of
Tyndale House Publishers, Inc., Wheaton, Illinois 60189. All rights reserved.

To protect the privacy of those who have shared their stories with the author, some
details and names have been changed.

To my son,
Kevin Anderson Leman II

You have always been a great son.
We're so proud of what you've accomplished in life
already. Winning two Emmys isn't too shabby.
I have to admit that it's taken a little while
to get used to people coming up to me and asking
me if it's true that I'm Kevin Leman's father,
but it's a role I'm going to continue
to enjoy as the years go by.

What really means the most to Mom and me,
though, is the young man you've become.
We appreciate your kind, considerate, thoughtful nature.
We couldn't love you more,
and I pray that God will continue to
richly bless your life.

Love,
Your semi-famous father

# Contents

# Thursday

But What If I Damage Their Psyche? (Uh . . . What's a Psyche?)    67

*Let's debunk a major myth right now. Kids need Acceptance, Belonging, and Competence—the pillars of self-esteem. But there's a big difference between praise and encouragement, and your kid is smart enough to know it.*

# Friday

The Doc Is In . . . and It's You    79

*Today you review the principles and your action plan. Your mantra: "I can't wait for that kid to misbehave, because I'm ready to go to war." And she's not going to know what hit her. Remember, no warnings!*

# Ask Dr. Leman

A to Z Game Plans That Really Work

*Straightforward advice and gutsy plans of action on over 100 of the hottest parenting topics. Flip through A to Z or consult the quick index at the end of this book.*

Shh! It's a Secret!    93

# Epilogue

Fun Day    275

*Today's the day you launch your action plan. Sit back and watch the fun . . . and the confusion on your child's face. I guarantee you're going to hit payday if you never, never give up. (Old Winston Churchill was right.) The stakes are high, but you can do it. The power of your follow-through will reap benefits that will withstand the test of time.*

# Acknowledgments

To my editor, Ramona Cramer Tucker: It's been a tough year for you, and I want you to know how much I appreciate your ability to hang in there and get the job done in such a professional manner. My heartfelt thanks for your invaluable contribution.

To the other woman in my life, my Revell editor, Lonnie Hull DuPont: I love the secure feeling as an author that you, Mama Bear, have your ever-watchful eye on this carefree cub and keep him in line.

# Introduction

*They're Unionized . . . and Growing Stronger*

Your kids have a game plan to drive you bonkers . . . but you don't have to let them call the shots.

I've got news for you. Since the beginning of time, kids have been unionized, and they've got a game plan to drive you bonkers. Don't believe it?

Take a look around. You tell me what you see in malls, stores, restaurants, and even your own living room.

What about the toddler who cries until she wears her mother down and gets to go not only *once* but *three times* on the carousel?

The teenager who yells, "Bleep you!" at his dad and stalks off?

The dad who allows his overweight 12-year-old to fill the grocery cart with Twinkies, Oreos, Coke, and Salerno Butter Cookies, then simply shrugs when the boy downs two packs of Twinkies as they stand in the checkout line?

The 7-year-old who gives his mom the "I dare you to do anything about it here" steely glare as he pushes the broccoli off his plate and watches it fall to the floor at the restaurant?

The 16-year-old who flips off her dad for not giving her money for a movie, then demands the car keys for the evening?

The 14-year-old dressed in all black who has "attitude" written all over her and gives every sign of going the wrong direction?

The 3-year-old who spends his day screaming, to make sure his parents appease his every whim?

It all goes to show that in today's society, children even shorter than a yardstick are calling the shots. They're part of the entitlement group—they expect anything and everything good to come their way, with no work on their part, just because they exist. In their eyes, the world *owes them*—and owes them big time. Some hedonistic little suckers of the ankle-biter battalion have even graduated to emeritus status and are holding down the hormone group division. Then there are the already-adult children who return home to your cozy little nest and stay and stay and stay. . . .

You know all about that too. If you picked up this book, you did so for a reason. Have you just about had it? Do you want to see some things—or a lot of things—change in your house? It isn't always the big things that wear you down. It's the constant battles with attitudes and behaviors like eye rolling, talking back, fighting with siblings, giving the "silent treatment," and slamming doors. It's the statements like, "You can't make me do it!" and "I hate you!" flung into your face as your child retreats once again to his bedroom. It's the exhaustion and stress of dealing with children who start swinging from the minute they get up.

Maybe your child's behavior has embarrassed you (you could have done without your son's all-out tantrum in the mall or your daughter's belly button and nose rings, which she revealed for the first time when you had a business associate over for dinner), and you know it's time to do something. Maybe you've been held hostage from certain activities because of your children's actions ("Well, honey, I don't know if we should go out to dinner with the Olsons; you know how the kids get"). Or maybe you're seeing active signs of disrespect and rebellion, and you're worried about where your child is headed next.

I'll be blunt. You've got a big job to do and a short window in which to do it. I know, because I've raised 5 children—4 daughters and 1 son—with my wife, Sande. The years go far too quickly.

*It isn't always the big things that wear you down. It's the constant battles.*

If you believe that you, as a parent, are to be in healthy authority over your child, this book is for you. If you don't believe that you, as a parent, are to be in healthy authority over your child, put this book down right now and buy another. You won't like what I have to say, you won't do it, and you'll complain about me to your friends.

But let me ask you something first: how do you feel after an hour of yelling at your kids to get up in the morning in time to catch the school bus? Could there be a better way?

What if you did something different? What if you *didn't* wake them up this morning? What if you did nothing at all?

"But, Dr. Leman," you're saying, "I can't do that. They'd be late for school. And I'd be late for work."

Now you're catching on.

*How do you feel after an hour of yelling at your kids to get up in the morning in time to catch the school bus?*

How do you feel after listening to your children bicker constantly over who gets the bathroom first? Over who wore whose shirt and left it in a heap on the floor?

How do you feel after listening to your children bellyache over what you packed them for lunch?

What if you didn't intercede in the sibling battles? What if you didn't play peacemaker or rush to wash your daughter's favorite shirt in time for her to wear it to school? What if you didn't pack any lunch at all?

Ah, now you're getting it.

There *is* a better way, and you're holding it in your hand.

Did you know that your job as a parent is not to create a happy child? That if your child is temporarily unhappy, when he or she does choose to put a happy face back on, life will be better for all of you?

When your child yells, "You can't make me do it!" he's right. You can't *make* him do something. But if he chooses not to be helpful, you don't have to take him to the Secretary of State to get his driver's license either.

You see, nothing in life is a free ride. The sooner children learn that, the better. Every person is accountable, regardless of age, for what comes out of his mouth. And homes should be based on the cornerstones of mutual respect, love, and accountability. There is no entitlement. If you play the entitlement game in your home, you'll create BratZ—with a capital Z. You'll create children who think they are in the driver's seat of life's car. Who think that their happiness is what's most important in life, and that they are "entitled" to not only what they want but anything and everything they want, when they want it.

> *Nothing in life is a free ride. The sooner children learn that, the better.*

Many of us have unwittingly done this to our kids. We've spent far too much time snowplowing our child's road in life—making far too many decisions for her, giving him too many choices, letting him off the hook or making excuses when he's irresponsible, ignoring the little and big ways she disses us. After all, you want your child to like you, don't you? No wonder kids think they're in charge, and parental threats and cajoling don't work!

Many moms in particular tell me they feel like slave dogs, doing whatever their kids want them to do. And they're exhausted by the end of the day. (If you're saying, "Amen, brother!" read on.)

There are all sorts of experts who talk about boosting a child's self-esteem. They promise that if you praise your child for this and that and smooth his road in life, you'll land in the wonderful world of Oz and live happily ever after. But I'm here to tell you, after nearly 4 decades of helping families—as well as parenting 5 kids with my lovely wife—that often the opposite is true with that approach. Far too many families have landed on a stretch of road where they wish they had never gone.

You want your child to emerge as a healthy, contributing member of your family and society, right? *Have a New Kid by Friday* is a game plan guaranteed to work. *Every time.* It'll help to produce the responsible adult you'll be proud to call your son or daughter now and down the road. It'll ratchet down the stress level in your home and give you freedom you've never experienced before in your parenting. It'll even provide some chuckles along the way. (Just wait until Fun Day! More on that later.)

If you're thinking, *This sounds too good to be true. There's got to be a catch*, you're right. There *is* a catch—you. *You* are the key to changing your child's thinking and actions. For this to work, it requires you to become the kind of parent you want to be. It requires your decision to stand up and be a parent rather than a pushover. So give me 1 week to change *your* thinking and actions, and you'll be amazed at the results!

There will be times in this book when you're going to squirm because you're not going to like the suggestions. But I can offer you a 100 percent guarantee: if you follow the simple strategies in *Have a New Kid by Friday*, in just 5 days you'll have a good kid on your hands. A kid who has figured out that life isn't all about him. That other people do count in life. A kid who says thank you for the things you do for him. You'll have a new atmosphere of mutual respect, love, and accountability in your home. And you just might find a smile creeping onto your face far more often than you could have imagined.

How can I guarantee that your relationship with your child can change so dramatically in just 5 days? Because I've seen this transformation in hundreds of thousands of families *every time* these strategies are followed!

*Have a New Kid by Friday* isn't just any old book. It's a game plan that *really works.* Even better, anyone can do it. It doesn't take a PhD in rocket science. Want to have a great kid? Want to be a great parent? Take the Leman 5-day challenge.

> *If you're thinking,* This sounds too good to be true. There's got to be a catch, *you're right.*

On Monday, I'll reveal what your kid's life strategy really is—and why he continues to do the things that drive you bonkers.

On Tuesday, we'll talk about the 3 most important things every parent wants for their child—and how to teach them in a way the child will never forget.

On Wednesday, we'll take a look down the road. Who do you want your child to be? What kind of parent do you want to be? You can get there with my time-tested "3 Simple Strategies for Success."

On Thursday, we'll identify the 3 pillars of true self-worth and learn how to develop them in your child.

> *Want to have a great kid? Want to be a great parent? Take the Leman 5-day challenge.*

On Friday, you get to be the shrink. We'll review the principles and the action plan you've been developing since Monday and get ready to launch it upon your unsuspecting children.

The "Ask Dr. Leman" section provides practical advice on over 100 of the hottest topics in parenting. Read it straight through A to Z or use the index in the back of the book for a quick find.

Then there's what I call "Fun Day." It's my favorite day of all. After launching your plan, you get to sit back and watch the fun . . . and the confusion on your child's face. It's a parent's best entertainment.

If you don't give up, I guarantee you're going to hit payday. I know. I've seen those benefits in my relationship with my own children, who span the ages of 15 to 35. Sande and I are proud of them. They've all done well in school and life in general. Unlike me, they haven't been to traffic court and driving school. The interesting and wonderful thing is that they really love each other. They all make tremendous sacrifices to be together. And check this out: they love and respect Sande and me. They even like hanging out with us. Even our 15-year-old daughter's friends acknowledged to her the other day that her parents were "cool."

In *Have a New Kid by Friday*, I've taken nearly 4 decades of marriage and parenting experience—including my clinical experience as a psychologist, my personal experience as a father of 5, and the many stories I've heard as I've traveled around the country, bringing wit and wisdom to family relationships—and combined it all into one little book. I've done this because I care about *your family*. I want to see you have the kind of satisfying relationships in your family that I see in my own. I want you to experience a home where all family members love and respect each other.

*After launching your plan, you get to sit back and watch the fun . . . and the confusion on your child's face. It's a parent's best entertainment.*

Your children deserve that.

You deserve that.

And nothing would make me happier than to see it come to pass.

# Monday

*Where Did They All Come From?*

Why do your kids do what they do . . . and continue to do it?
Your response has a lot to do with it.

Four-year-old Matthew was in a bad mood. His mom could tell
that as soon as she picked him up from preschool. All he wanted
to do was argue with her. Then he delivered the vehement kicker
from the backseat as they drove home: "I hate you!"

If you were his parent, how would you respond?
You could:

1. Let the kid have it with a tongue-lashing of your own.
2. Ignore the kid and pretend he doesn't exist.
3. Try something new and revolutionary that would nip this
   kind of behavior in the bud . . . for good.

Which option would you prefer?
If you responded with a tongue-lashing of your own, both of
you would leave that car feeling ugly and out of sorts. And what

would be solved in the long run? You'd feel terrible the rest of the day. Your son would go to his room and sulk. One or both of you would eventually end up apologizing (probably you first, since your parental guilt would reign; then, because you would feel bad for losing your temper, you'd probably end up liberally dosing the child with treats).

If you ignored the kid and pretended he didn't exist, it might work for a while—until he needed something from you. With a 4-year-old, that lasts about 4.9 seconds since there are so many things he can't reach in the house (like the milk in the refrigerator on the top shelf). The problem is, if you don't address the behavior, you'll spend the rest of your day steaming under the surface . . . and kicking the dog.

This mom decided to go out on a limb and do something revolutionary. She was very nervous; she wondered if it would really work. She'd read all the discipline books and tried so many methods. None of the other techniques had worked. And Matthew was . . . well, getting to be a brat. She couldn't believe she was actually thinking that about her own child, but it was true.

She sighed. *Desperate times call for desperate measures.* But this new technique she'd heard about made so much sense. It had worked for three of her girlfriends. They said all it required was her standing up and being a parent, using consistency and follow-through in her own actions, and not backing down. She knew that would be the hardest part. She was a wuss when it came to Matthew. When he turned those big, blue, teary eyes on her, he always got what he wanted.

But today things were changing, she determined. She was going to give this new method her best effort. She had to do something. Matthew was driving her crazy. Just last week he'd thrown a temper tantrum in the mall; he'd bitten the neighbor girl when she wouldn't give him a toy of hers that he wanted; and the preschool had told her she needed to do something about Matthew's aggressive behavior toward his classmates.

Once she and Matthew got in the house, she didn't say a word. She went about her business, putting away the shopping bags from the car. After a few minutes, Matthew wandered into the kitchen. Usually chocolate chip cookies and milk awaited him there. It was his routine after-preschool snack.

"Mommy, where are my cookies and milk?" he asked, looking at the usual place on the kitchen counter.

"We're not having cookies and milk today," she said matter-of-factly. Then she turned her back on the child she'd pushed 11½ hours for and walked into another room.

Did Matthew say to himself, *Well, I guess I'll have to do without that today*? No, because children are creatures of habit. So what did Matthew do? He followed his mother to the next room.

"Mommy, I don't understand. We always have cookies and milk after preschool."

Mom looked him in the eye and said, "Mommy doesn't feel like getting you cookies and milk today." She turned and walked into another room.

By now, Matthew was like an NFL quarterback on Sunday afternoon—scrambling to get to the goal. He followed his mom into the next room. "But, Mommy, this has never happened before." There was panic in his voice. He was starting to tremble. "I don't understand."

Mom now knew that Matthew was ready to hear what she had to say. It was the teachable moment: the moment when reality enters the picture and makes an impact on the child's mind and heart. It's the time when a parent has to give her child the straight skinny.

> *"But, Mommy, this has never happened before." There was panic in his voice. He was starting to tremble. "I don't understand."*

"We are not having milk and cookies today because Mommy doesn't like the way you talked to me in the car." Again, Mom turned to walk away.

But before she took three steps, Matthew had a giant meltdown. He ran toward his mother and grabbed her leg (after all, he is part of the ankle-biter battalion). He was crying profusely. "I'm sorry, Mommy! I'm sorry. I shouldn't have said that."

Time for another wonderful opportunity. The mom accepted Matthew's apology, gave him a hug, and reminded him that she loved him. She also told him how she felt when he talked to her like that. Three minutes later, things were patched up, and she let Matthew out of her embrace. She began again to go about her work.

What did she hear next from Matthew? "Mommy, can I have my milk and cookies now?"

It was the moment she feared. She steeled her courage and said calmly, "Honey, I told you no. We are not going to have milk and cookies today."

Matthew was stunned. He opened his mouth to argue, then walked away sadly.

Let me ask you: will that little boy think next time before he disses his mother?

### Why Little Buford Misbehaves . . . and Gets Away with It

Why is it these days that so many children tend to diss their parents, to act disrespectfully? Why are so many parents caught in the roles of threatening and cajoling and never getting anywhere? What's going on here?

Kids do what they do because they've gotten away with it!

It all comes down to who is really in charge of your family. Is it you or your child? Today's parents often don't act like parents. They are so concerned about being their child's friend, about not wounding their child's psyche, about making sure their child is happy and successful, that they fail in their most important role:

to be a parent. They snowplow their child's road in life, smoothing all the bumps so the child never has to be uncomfortable or go out of her way. Why should she? She's used to having things done for her. Mom and Dad have become mere servants, doing the whims of the children, rather than parents, who have the child's long-term best in mind.

Parents today are also great excuse makers, and they tend to put themselves in blame positions—"I couldn't get her homework done because I had a business dinner"—rather than calling a spade a spade: "My daughter didn't get her homework done because she was too lazy to do it." They spend more time warning and reminding than they do training.

> *Kids do what they do because they've gotten away with it!*

As a result, today's kids are growing more and more powerful. They're all about "me, me, me" and "gimme." They are held accountable less and less and have fewer responsibilities in the family. To them, family is about not what you can give but what you can get. Fewer children today consider others before themselves because they've never been taught to think that way.

Every child is a smart little sucker, and he has a predictable strategy. In the daily trial-and-error game designed to get the best of you, he's motivated to win because then you'll do anything he says. That means if he tries something, and it works, he'll try it again. But he'll ramp up the efforts a little. Instead of simply crying when he doesn't get his treat, he'll add a little kicking too. If slamming the door causes you to go trotting after your teenage daughter to hand over the car keys like she wanted, she'll be more dramatic the next time she wants them. Children are masters at manipulation. Don't think they're not manipulating you.

That's why your child's behavior has everything to do with you. If you allow your child to win, your child's smart enough to try the behavior again next time. *Have a New Kid by Friday* is designed to give you a whole arsenal of tools to use without shooting your kid down. But it'll also accomplish something else if you follow the principles: it'll help you be the kind of parent you want to be so you can have the kind of child you want.

> *Children are masters at manipulation. Don't think they're not manipulating you.*

These principles work with 4-year-olds, 14-year-olds, and even CEOs of million-dollar companies. Just try them and watch them work. The basic principles may seem hard-edged, and some of you may be squeamish at first. But you came to this book because you want to see changes in your home, and you want to see them fast. Well, I'm that kind of guy. If you want me to hold your hand for 1½ years while you talk through all your problems over and over but don't really want to do anything to change them, you've got the wrong guy. But if you want to face life square on and do things differently for your entire family's welfare, you've got the right guy. People are astonished at the changes that happen in their homes in just 5 days. Teens have gone from mouthy and rebellious to quiet, respectful, and helpful. Screaming, tantrum-throwing toddlers are now saying "please" and "thank you."

So give this book a chance. Think about where you'd like to be. I can help you get there.

## Attention, Please

Did you know that everything your child does is for a reason? This is called in psychologist speak, thanks to Dr. Alfred Adler, the "purposive nature of the behavior." When your child misbehaves, he's doing it *to get your attention.* All children are attention getters. If your child can't get your attention in positive ways, he'll go after your attention in negative ways. That's because a child's private logic (the inner dialogue that tells him who and what he is and will inform his entire life) is being formed *right now.* And children naturally think, *I only count when people notice me or when other people are serving me. I only count when I dominate, control, and win.*

Here's the good news: what children learn, they can unlearn. Author Anne Ortlund has said, "Children are like wet cement— moldable and impressionable,"[1] and she couldn't be more right. Children are malleable—up to a point. But as they grow, their "cement" hardens. That's why the earlier you can start addressing your child's Attitude, Behavior, and Character, the better. (More on this in the "Tuesday" chapter.)

The problem with training is that it takes time, and parents today don't have time and don't make time. Some kids spend most of their days in what I call "kiddy kennels" (day care), then they spend their late afternoon and evening time in multiple programs: gymnastics, choir, baseball, etc.

When I used to teach at the University of Arizona, I worked with classes of 300 students—including graduate students, medical doctors, and nurses—in an auditorium. I'd bring in families and problem solve with them. Then I'd ask the students basic questions:

1. How do you think this child learned his behavior?
2. Why is he misbehaving?
3. What are the parents doing about it now? Why doesn't this work?
4. How did the parents say they feel about this behavior?
5. At what level is this child's behavior—stage 1 (attention getting) or stage 2 (revenge)?
6. What do you think these parents should do?

One family who was struggling with the behavior of their son told me all the activities he was involved in. Other than school, that young man had something every single night of the week, and he was only 10! My advice to the parents was, "Cut the extracurricular activities. All of them. Instead of taking your son to counseling, stay home and spend time together. The behavior you are seeing is because your son wants and needs your attention. He's desperate for your attention. And no coach is going to replace the role you have as parents in the life of your child."

When your child is acting up or acting out, what is he really saying? "Pay attention to me, please!"

If you don't pay attention to your child in the right way (we'll talk more about that in the "Thursday" chapter), your child ups the ante to the next level: revenge. "I feel hurt by life, so I have a right to strike out at others, including you." If your child is at this level, you really need this book. Many children who proceed to the revenge stage are headed toward the beginning of a rap sheet.

## Power Struggles

When you choose to do battle with your children, you'll never win. You have much more to lose than they do. Your teenage daughter couldn't care less if her shirt is too tight, but you care, and she knows it. So what is she implying as she flounces down the stairs, dramatically crosses the kitchen, and bounces out of the door with a backward look? "I dare you to say anything!"

You'll never win in a power struggle, so don't go there. Instead I'll teach you a different way, a better way. A way in which you can establish your authority in the home.

## Creatures of Habit

There was a classic study done in which researchers conditioned pigeons to peck 3 times in order to receive their reward, a pellet of food. Then, after the birds were trained, the researchers changed the reinforcement schedule. Birds got a pellet every 97 pecks, then every 140 pecks, then every 14 pecks. Those pigeons were so confused, they didn't know what to do. They had learned their behavior so well that they continued, day after day, to peck 3 times to get their food.

Children, like pigeons, are creatures of habit. If you don't believe that statement, just try leaving out one thing in your bedtime routine as you're tucking your child in. Listen to what happens: "Uh, Mommy, you forgot to rub my cheek. You always rub my cheek." Remember Matthew, who was used to the routine of milk and cookies after preschool? It was only when his routine was broken that he was ready to listen to his mother and learn to behave differently.

> *When you choose to do battle with your children, you'll never win. You have much more to lose than they do.*

Children learn a behavior, then keep pecking at it to get their reward. That's why those of you who have younger children will have an easier time—your pigeons have had less time to peck for the reward. If you have a child 12 years old or older, he has had a lot more time to peck for those pellets. It will require more effort on your part. But you can still do it by Friday if you stick to your guns. If you want your child to be responsible, I'll show you how to get there. If you want him to be teachable and listen, I'll show you how to get there. It's what you both deserve.

So how do you effect change in your relationship with your child? You retrain your pigeon. You use consistency and follow-through to make your point, never wavering from the goal.

### How Does It Work?

Let's say your child wants McDonald's at the mall, but you don't have money for

**Think about It**

What is your #1 challenge with your child right now?

In that situation, think of how you could use the following principles:
1. Say it once.
2. Turn your back.
3. Walk away.

McDonald's. He pitches an all-out flailing temper tantrum, and you're terribly embarrassed. What do you do?

"Mark, we're not getting McDonald's."

Then you turn your back on your child and walk away.

"But, Dr. Leman, wait right there," some of you are saying. "You don't mean you should leave a 6-year-old alone at a mall, do you? How could you just walk away?"

Ah, but here's the key. Your child doesn't want you to go away. He won't allow you to get very far. He just wants to do battle with you. He wants to win.

As soon as that child takes a look at your retreating back in the crowd, all of a sudden his fit isn't so fun anymore. Winning the battle isn't so important anymore. Finding and following Mommy—his safety zone—is.

Let's say you see your 3-year-old purposefully knock over his 18-month-old sister, who's just learning how to walk. Are you angry? Of course. That was downright mean, and you're not going to stand for it. Not to mention the fact that 18-month-old Caroline is now crying. But first you take a breath and think through your strategy. Then you call Andy over to you.

"Andy, do you need some attention today? If you need a hug, all you have to do is say so. Just come on over and ask me for a hug. You don't have to push your sister over to get it. That kind of behavior is not acceptable."

You took the fun out of that behavior by naming the purposive nature of the behavior for the child. By doing so, the child knows that you know exactly what happened and why he did what he did. You're the one in control, not him. He doesn't have a reason to do it the next time.

Let's say your teenager throws you some choice words because you're having chicken for dinner—again—and she says she hates chicken (even though a week ago she asked to have it). When it's time for her to go to Miranda's to "study," you say, "We're not going to Miranda's." Then you turn your back, walk away into the next room, and start folding clothes.

Just like that 4-year-old who wanted his milk and cookies, your 14-year-old will pursue you. "What do you mean we're not going to Miranda's? You always take me to Miranda's on Tuesdays."

"We're not going to Miranda's because I don't appreciate the way you talked to me earlier."

You turn your back and walk away. No matter what pleading, what tantrum, what apology happens, you don't take her to Miranda's. She has to be the one to explain to Miranda why she can't come. Of course, she might present a different take on the situation than you would, but what does that matter? You've made your point, and your daughter will think through her words more carefully the next time.

If you want your child to take you seriously, say your words once. Only once. If you say it more than once, you're implying, "I think you're so stupid that you're not going to get it the first time, so let me tell you again." Is that respectful of your child?

Once you've said it, turn your back. Expect your words to be heeded. There's no peeking over your shoulder to see if the child is doing what you say. There's no backtalk, no argument. You've said your words calmly, and they're over.

Then you walk away and get busy doing something else.

Will your children be mad? Shocked? Confused? Will you have a few days of hassle? Oh yes!

But let me ask you something. How do you feel after you get into a skirmish with your child? Angry? Bad? Guilty? Do you yell

> *If you want your child to take you seriously, say your words once. Only once. If you say it more than once, you're implying, "I think you're so stupid that you're not going to get it the first time, so let me tell you again."*

and then beat yourself up the rest of the afternoon for doing so? Do you "should" yourself ("I should have done this; I should have done that")? Are you the pigeon running through the maze, trying to get the reward of making your kids happy? Do you really want to live like that?

How do you deal with your 16-year-old when you discover a *Penthouse* magazine under his bed? With your 2-year-old who kicks you in the stomach when she's riding in a cart at the grocery store? (I once had a child kick me at a restaurant, and I didn't even know the kid. Talk about an embarrassed parent.) How do you handle the "I hate you/I love you" every-other-minute switches in your adolescent? The phone call from the principal letting you know your fun-loving son went a little too far this time?

What's normal (or is there normal?) and to be expected? What should you major on and what should you let go? In the next chapter, we'll talk about the 3 things most important to parents nationwide: Attitude, Behavior, and Character.

Remember, children are like pigeons. They need to work a bit for their rewards. Because they are creatures of habit, they need consistency and follow-through or they'll get lost in the maze. They also need to know they don't have free reign to run all over that maze and still expect a reward at the end of it.

> **What to Do on Monday**
>
> 1. Observe what's going on in your house. What areas in your relationship with your child really bother you?
> 2. Think about how you'd like things to change.
> 3. Decide to take the bull by the horns.
> 4. Expect great things to happen.

Suppose you and I went through life following our feelings for the next 30 days. We said exactly what we thought, did what we wanted, didn't do what we didn't want to do. What would life be like at the end of those 30 days? A mess! We wouldn't have a job because we would have dissed our boss. Our friends would have said, "Forget you." And someone would have shot us on the expressway.

Today's children need guidance. They need accountability. They need to be taught that there are consequences for their actions (or for their inaction). Otherwise their lives will run amok.

The other day, when my daughter and I were at the airport, we watched 3-year-old twins slugging each other. What was Mom doing? Talking on her cell phone. What was Dad doing? Reading the newspaper. I told my daughter jokingly, "Those are the kind of kids who will make your dad a wealthy man."

Parent, it's time for you to step up and be a parent. Your child needs to know that you mean business—what you say is what you will do. You are not to be dissed, and if you are, there will be consequences. Immediate consequences. And you will not be talked out of giving them.

Critics will say, "But won't you make your child feel bad and guilty?" I hope so! It's important to have a little guilt in life. And feeling bad can accomplish a heap of good.

Just wait and see.

Uh-oh, caught me. But I'm sure glad you did. I thought I was such a great mom. My parents were so authoritarian that I said I'd never be like them. I didn't realize that I'd gone the entirely opposite way. I hardly ever say no to my kids. I've been running ragged just to make them happy, and they're still not happy. Everybody tells me how much I'm doing and what a great mom I am for doing all this stuff, but I know the truth: I have a hard time standing up for myself. No more. A week ago I adopted your principles of "Say it once, turn your back, and walk away." They really, really work. I'm stunned. My son willingly took out the garbage yesterday, even without me asking him, and my daughter brought bread home from the store just because she noticed we were low. I can't believe the change!

Millie, North Carolina

I attended your seminar about changing a child's behavior last week, and it was even more powerful than I realized! My week has been so peaceful and easy with my 3 kids (14, 8, and 6)! My children have responded wonderfully. And I've changed too. Not only am I setting limits for them, I'm doing it with compassion. No yelling at all, and for me that is just too wonderful not to let you know.

Delighted in Georgia

I love listening to you—especially your humor and personal stories (like the one about hawking a gob out the window and your son copying you). They make me laugh. But they also helped my wife and me come to a very important decision. I had just lost my job and didn't see anything on the horizon in our immediate area. My wife has had a job and loved it for years. So now I'm a stay-at-home dad for our son . . . and loving every minute of it. It's the best decision we ever made, and it saved us a lot in day-care costs too.

Stephen, Michigan

I've cried, I've prayed, I've thrown up my hands, but nothing worked . . . until now. Your "B doesn't happen until A is completed" has turned around my relationship with my children. The first three days I used the principle I felt terrible, because I wasn't used to being consistent on anything. But when I saw the changes in just three days, that spurred me on to finish the job. I now can take my 2 toddlers to my girlfriends' without fear of embarrassment or having to listen to them scream. My 3-year-old walked up to me and asked yesterday, "Mom, may we have a snack?" This coming from the girl who would have ordered me a week ago, "Get me a snack!" It *works*! It's the answer to my prayers.

Kendra, Texas

# Tuesday

## Disarming the Dude (or Dudette) with the 'Tude

Want a kid with real character who isn't a character?
Here's how.

My wife, Sande, always prayed for a man with character. And she got a character all right. Me.

That's what many children are today—characters. Perhaps that's why numerous studies show that the top 3 long-term concerns of parents have to do with a new kind of ABCs:

- Attitude
- Behavior
- Character

When the rubber meets the road, these are the things that matter most. These are the things that will continue into adulthood and make your child someone worthy of trust . . . or not. Someone who acts with kindness and respect toward others . . . or not. Someone who is honest . . . or not.

### It's All in the Attitude

Attitude is the entrée into a child's head and heart. What your child thinks about herself—how she views herself and what happens to her—speaks loudly through her behavior.

Did you know, Mom and Dad, that one child just *looking* at another sibling can be a criminal offense? Consider these family felonies:

- "He *looked* at me!"
- "She wore my jacket and ripped it—on purpose!"
- "You never yell at him. He gets away with *everything*."
- "How come she gets to go? You never let me go."
- "Hey! How come her piece is bigger?"

Attitude can speak loudly—even if your child says nothing. Attitude screams in the "silent treatment." You know what I'm talking about.

A negative attitude shows itself through many behaviors: the rolling of eyes, talking back, stubbornness, poor manners, being a know-it-all, whining, the "me, me, me" syndrome, defiance, throwing a tantrum, choosing not to cooperate with family members, showing disrespect, etc.

But where does attitude come from?

> *Who do you butt heads with the most in your family? Is that child the most like you or the least like you?*

### Who Do You Butt Heads With?

If you have more than one child, you know that all the little foxes in the den can be completely different. Some children will be easygoing by nature; others will be wired for sound.

Who do you butt heads with the most in your family? Is that child the most like you or the least like you?

The answer, in all probability, is the child who is the *most* like you. Kids who sport attitudes have parents who sport attitudes. Attitudes are caught, not taught.

Sometimes the parents don't even know they are sporting an attitude. But what you think reveals itself in your actions toward your child. So if you have a "This is what's best for you, and this is what you're gonna do—and God help you if you don't" attitude, you're just asking to butt heads with any child who has a strong temperament. He will arch his back even at 18 months old. He'll be resistant to your hovering.

> *The key to changing your child is changing your attitude.*

The key to changing your child is changing your attitude.

Let's say you give your child a simple request: "Please take out the garbage."

"I'm busy," your child throws back in your face and proceeds to read her novel.

Ask yourself, *What would I usually do in this situation?*

If the kid is 6 years old, you could probably physically force her to do it. If the child is 10, you may get a little more forceful with your words. You repeat your command, a little more loudly. "I *said*, take out the garbage. *Now.*"

"I don't want to."

What happens next? Your angry attitude kicks in. *Just who does this kid think she is, anyway? After everything I do for her, how dare she?*

You raise your voice more. "Young lady, I said to do it NOW, and you're going to do it NOW! Or else . . ."

Your daughter doesn't even look up from her book. Why? Because she's heard your threats before, and they don't go anywhere.

But what if your attitude changed? What if you remained calm? What if you didn't pester her further after you'd asked her once?

What if you just walked away and expected her to do it? No reminders, no raised voices, no anger on your part.

"But, Dr. Leman, what if she doesn't do it? I mean, my daughter wouldn't."

Simple enough. Just have another sibling do the job, pay him, and take the money for the task out of your daughter's next allowance. If you do it yourself, pay yourself out of your daughter's allowance. The point is, someone else is doing the work she should be doing.

What's next? Your attitude remains calm. You remain in charge. Later she says to you, "Okay, I'm ready to go to the store to get shoes now."

Your matter-of-fact response? "We're not going to the store."

"But, Mo-om, you said you'd take me to the store."

"I don't feel like taking you to the store." Then you turn and walk away.

No guilt. No anger. No explanation. You're calm and in control.

## Just a Phase?

How do you know what's normal, or "just a phase," and what's an attitude to be dealt with?

Almost 100 percent of the time parents *know the difference* between respect and getting dissed, but they choose to ignore it. Why would someone do that? Because many parents today want to be their child's friend. But this never works in the long run.

If your adolescent daughter says to you, "Mom, that outfit looks kinda dumb. Are you sure you want to wear it?" her attitude will show in the way she says those words.

> *Almost 100 percent of the time* parents know the difference *between* respect and getting dissed, but they choose to ignore it.

If your 2-year-old gets in your face and screams, "I don't want to!" it's not about the "terrible twos." It's about attitude, and he's testing you to see how much you'll put up with.

So don't fall for the "just a phase" thinking. You know your child. You know when he is being rude and disrespectful and when he is simply asking a question to understand. It's clearly all in the body language and the tone of voice.

When you launch out with this new method of "Say it once; turn your back on your child; walk away," let your child work for the answer a little bit. Don't just tell him why you're changing your behavior. Let him figure out, sooner or later, that your new, consistent behavior has something to do with the big chip of attitude he's carrying on his shoulder.

In the meantime, take a look at your own attitude. Is your attitude escaping, even when your words are pleasant? It's kind of like what a wife might say to her husband: "Oh, honey, you can go ahead and play golf, and I'll stay here with your *mother*." The words might be pleasant on the surface, but what's the attitude behind them? Translation: "I hope you have a stinking, rotten time. How dare you leave me with your mother! You're a chump! And I hope you lose your 9 iron!"

Your attitude has everything to do with how you live your life. It has everything to do with how you behave. And it has everything to do with the character you develop.

How loudly is your attitude speaking?

## It's Not What You Say, It's How You Act . . . or Is It?

You've seen it. You've experienced it in your own home. Hitting. Spitting. Interruptions when you're on the phone. Sibling rivalry. Punching holes in walls. Stomping out of the room. Slamming doors. Screaming. Bed-wetting. Fights in the car. Fights regarding curfew. Fights over messy rooms. Purposeful disobedience.

Put-downs. Struggles over getting up on time for school. Struggles over eating. Kids who don't stay in bed but pop out like the Energizer Bunny. Carelessness with money. Lying. Not completing a project.

Did you know that behavior is learned? And that children will model their behavior after the things they see you say and do?

Think how many times you've said, "I'm never going to do what my father did to me. I'll never speak to my kids the way my mother did to me." Then you find yourself using the same words *and* the same inflection your parents did.

Think about that little "white lie" you told your boss: "I'm not feeling very well today. I think I need a day to rest." And then you took the kids to the beach.

Or what about the time you promised your children that you'd take them out for ice cream . . . then you got busy with work and didn't get home until they were already in bed?

That's what I mean. Your attitude can't help but slip out through your behavior, and children are always watching. That means if you want to see your child change, you have to change yourself. If you yell when you get angry, should it surprise you when your 7-year-old does it? If you give others the silent treatment, should it surprise you if your 13-year-old isn't talking? Do you break your promises? If so, you need to start honoring your promises—or not making them in the first place. My personal view is that you should never promise your children anything. Promising them is saying that (1) your car will never break down, (2) every day will go exactly as you've planned it, (3) you are perfect, and (4) it won't rain.

Misbehavior is going to happen. Kids are kids. Just accept the fact that they will say and do the dumbest and most embarrassing things you can imagine. I'll never forget what our pediatrician told us when we had Holly, our firstborn. "You have to safety-proof your house because kids are really dumb when it comes to putting things in their mouths." Kids will pull a dog's tail and get bit, they'll

42

play in electrical outlets, they'll run into the street, they'll stick a finger in their sister's eye, they'll barf all over the place when they get sick—just as you're getting ready for a big evening.

The problem comes when we, as parents, *ask* for the behavior. We expect it. What happens just before you walk into a public place? Let's say you're going to the grocery store. What do you say to the kids? "Remember, no fighting. Keep your hands to yourself. And if you don't, there won't be any treats for you. Mom just needs to get a couple things, then we'll go home."

What are you saying? "Kids, I expect you to misbehave, and you better not." You're actually teaching your kids to make trouble.

*Kids are kids. Just accept the fact that they will say and do the dumbest and most embarrassing things you can imagine.*

That's why so many children can be perfect angels with Grandma but turn into little devils when they get home to Mama. Why do they misbehave around you? Because you expect them to, and the only way they can get attention from you is by misbehaving!

How could things go so wrong? Take a little trip back in time. Remember when you first found out your little cherub would be in your life? Maybe you were blessed with 2 births in 18 months. Here's what's interesting. Even though Americans are supposedly the most educated people in the world, most of us fly by the seat of our pants when it comes to parenting. We follow our parents' example.

So if you grew up in a home that was a "don't touch that, you'll get hurt" kind of home, you'll be overly cautious with your own kids. You'll be constantly telling your children no.

If you grew up with an abusive parent, you'll find yourself yelling and lifting your hand to your child.

If you grew up with parents who gave you the silent look for discipline, you'll find yourself giving the same look to your child.

But after a while, the words and the looks no longer work if there is no consistency, no follow-through, no consequences. Then a chasm develops between parent and child that can follow them for years into the future.

When your children are giving you a run for your money, it's always important to ask yourself three questions that will help you view the behavior in the most helpful light:

1. What is the purposive nature of the behavior you're addressing? (In other words, why is your child doing what he's doing?)
2. How do you, as the parent, feel in this situation? (What you think about the situation and the emotions you generate have everything to do with the way you respond to the situation.)
3. Is this a mountain (something that will matter in the long run) or a molehill (the situation will take care of itself or is a small concern in the grand scheme of what you're trying to accomplish in your child's life)?

For help on specific topics, look up the behavior and what to do about it in the section "Ask Dr. Leman."

We parents so want our children to be perfect (like us, of course) that we are masters at making mountains out of molehills. "But, Dr. Leman," you ask, "how can I know for sure which thing is a mountain and which is a molehill?"

Try out your skills at deciding with the "Mountain or Molehill?" quiz.

Every child will fail, make mistakes, and embarrass you. But you don't need to hold those failures over your child's head for a lifetime. Correct the behavior and move on. What is most important, in the long run, is your child's character.

**Ask Yourself**

1. What is the purposive nature of the behavior?
2. How do you, as the parent, feel in this situation?
3. Is this a mountain or a molehill?

 # ▲ Mountain or Molehill ▲?

Is this situation a mountain or a molehill? Circle your answer, then write your reason(s).

▶ **Randy is 17.** His baggy pants, earring, and shaggy nonhaircut nearly drive his mom up the wall. But he always helps his mom carry in the groceries, makes mostly Bs at school, and plays guitar in the worship band at his church.

 ▲ Mountain or Molehill ▲?

▶ **Sam is almost 13.** He's a quiet, shy boy who has always spent a lot of time alone in his room, reading. But lately his grades have taken a nosedive, and he's turned almost surly. Is it just adolescent hormones or something else?

▲ Mountain or Molehill ▲?

▶ **Jennifer is 3.** Her parents wonder how on earth she can survive on what she eats. They've tried everything, but they can't seem to coax her to eat anything other than Cheerios and chicken nuggets from McDonald's.

▲ Mountain or Molehill ▲?

▶ **Mandy is 9.** When her parents divorced last year, she began spending weekdays with her mom and weekends with her dad. Now every time she comes back from her dad's, she mouths off to her mom, goes into her room, and slams the door.

 ▲ Mountain or Molehill ▲?

For Dr. Leman's answers, see p. 291.[2]

## Character Is #1

Character is what really counts. It's who you are when no one is looking.

Character is caught from those you grow up with, namely your parents. It's also taught through life lessons. The action-oriented discipline I'm prescribing in this book will go a long way toward helping a child save his character. Good character can be reinforced in a very natural, positive way: "I'm so glad you helped that girl. You saw she really needed help, and you helped her." Negative character traits need to be dealt with: "I overheard you talking to your brother. What you said was unkind. You were being a bully. That is not acceptable in our home. You need to apologize to your brother immediately."

Part of being human means realizing how imperfect you are. Having character doesn't mean you are perfect. It means you have an inner standard that cares about others more than yourself. Sadly, character is lacking in contemporary America. Surveys say that most people admit they would cheat to get ahead, and they wouldn't necessarily feel bad about it. High school students and college students are cheating in bigger numbers each year.

When I was an assistant dean of students at the University of Arizona, a Chinese student was caught in an immoral situation. I was the one who had to handle the case. Frankly, I felt sorry for the kid. The circumstances revealed made me fairly sure the kid had been in the wrong place at the wrong time and really wasn't a Peeping Tom, but he had been charged with that crime. So I gave him the name of an attorney whom the university hired to help students, and I encouraged the student to call him. That student was so ashamed that he phoned the attorney from a phone booth at 8 a.m. the next morning. When the attorney finally got around to returning the student's call at 5 p.m. that afternoon, the student was still waiting at the phone booth. The outside temperature that day was close to 100 degrees.

That student stuck out physical discomfort because the worst thing he could do was shame his family. He was a smart kid, an A student. A person of character caught in a tough situation. And his character won out in the end.

What happens these days when movie stars get into trouble? When they get caught driving drunk or beating someone to a pulp? Their publicist releases a warm-fuzzy apology: "Oh, he's so sorry. He's checking himself into rehab. . . ." But does the behavior really change?

If someone is truly a person of character, they will go to the person they have wronged, offer a heartfelt apology, and ask what they can do to make things right.

Is your child respectful of you, of others in the family and outside the family—including teachers—and of your faith? Does your child have good phone manners? Does she tell the truth? Is she self-motivated to do homework (or does she wait for you to jump-start her)? Does he care about being on time? Is she bothered when others cheat on a test, or does that seem "normal" to her? Is he a "gimme gimme" child who has a Christmas list the length of the expressway? Is your child kind? Does he stick up for others smaller or weaker than himself on the playground, or is he the bully? Is she respectful of her older sister's special things? Does your child take your no for a no or push until he gets what he wants? Does she use language that your grandmother would have approved of? Is he the kind of young man you would hire to work for your company?

> *Character is not only everything, it's the only thing in the long run. It is the foundation for your attitude and behavior.*

Character is not only everything, it's the only thing in the long run. It is the foundation for your attitude and behavior.

### 3 Simple Strategies for Success

If you want your child to have a respectful, kind Attitude, to have Behavior that you'll want to write your grandma about, and to have Character that reveals itself as true-blue even when you aren't watching, follow these 3 simple strategies for success.

*1. Let reality be the teacher.*

Reality discipline is a term I coined in 1984. Basically it means to let nature take its course. And when nature doesn't take care of the problem, you help nature along. Don't rescue your kids from the consequences of failed responsibility.

If your son is supposed to do a project for chemistry and doesn't complete it, don't stay up until midnight doing it yourself. In fact, don't do anything about it at all. Don't even mention it. Just wait for reality to hit when he stands in front of his stern chemistry teacher, who tells your son in no uncertain terms what he thinks of incomplete projects.

> *If the doctor says, "You responded to your medication," that's good. If the doctor says, "You reacted to your medication," that's bad.*

If your little girl goes into her older sister's room and gets into her makeup, don't intervene in the situation and help her clean it up before her sister gets home. Unless she thinks to clean it up herself, don't bother. Just wait to see what her older sister is going to say, and let the two of them work it out.

Parents have a tendency to rub their child's nose in what he does wrong. In most cases, letting reality be the teacher is enough discipline in itself.

There's also a tendency to be a bone digger—digging up the situation long after it's over and hitting your child over the head with the "bone." Just remember, you've done wrong things and have been forgiven. How would you feel if someone kept reminding you of your failures?

### 2. Learn to respond rather than react.

Parents are good at shooting themselves in the foot. Often we react instead of respond. Our emotions get the better of us, and we speak or act without thinking first.

What's the difference between responding and reacting? If the doctor says, "You responded to your medication," that's good. If the doctor says, "You reacted to your medication," that's bad.

While you're driving, your little girl says out of the blue, "Mommy, I want a pony."

"What?" you say. "That's the stupidest thing I've ever heard of. There's no way we could get a pony! We live in a two-bedroom apartment in Baltimore. And we're barely making ends meet. There's no way we could afford a pony. Are you out of your mind?"

That's reacting. Answering without thinking in the situation.

This is responding: "Oh, a pony." (Pause, to show you're dreaming and thinking about it too.) "Can you imagine having your own pony? Getting up in the morning, saddling him, and riding to school as the other kids walk to school? Can you imagine waving to those kids as you go by? I can see the pony now. He's black and white. Wow, wouldn't that be cool? At lunchtime, all the kids would go to the cafeteria, but you'd go outside and check on your horse first. . . ."

Sure, you live in a two-bedroom apartment in Baltimore. But why shoot your child's dream out of the water? Your child will eventually realize that a pony wouldn't fit in your home.

There's a way to stick to your guns without shooting yourself, or your children, in the foot. Instead of reacting, respond by saying, "Tell me more about that."

*3. B doesn't happen until A is completed.*

You never have to change this strategy. It works every time, with every age. If you've asked your child to do something and it's not done, you don't go on to the next event—no matter what that event is.

> *There's a way to stick to your guns without shooting yourself, or your children, in the foot.*

Let's say you've asked your 8-year-old son to mow the lawn, and it's clearly not mowed. Two hours later your son wants to go to the pet store to get the fish you promised him. If your son is 16, he'd probably want to head to his buddy's to shoot pool. He wouldn't care about the pet fish. But no matter what the activity is, simply say, "We're not going." Then turn your back and walk away.

If your child follows you, don't announce your strategy. It works better if the child has to figure it out for himself. It comes down to this: seeing the changes you want implemented is more about *you* than it is about your child. It's more about you changing *your* Attitude, Behavior, and Character than him changing his Attitude, Behavior, and Character.

### What to Do on Tuesday

1. What is your attitude toward your kids?
2. How does your behavior reveal your attitude?
3. What changes do you need to make in your behavior toward your children?
4. What kind of character do you want to be known for? How can you get there?

Here's a caveat: when you start applying these techniques, often Attitudes and Behaviors will get worse for a time. But that's actually good news—it means you're on the right track!

The most important thing is that you use consistent action, not words. You don't embarrass the child on purpose; you correct the behavior. You keep the tennis ball of responsibility in his court, not yours. There is no harassing, no threatening, no warning. There's no reminding, no coaxing. There are no put-downs, because no one wins with put-downs. In today's democratic society, if you have the right to put me down, guess what right I have? No one wins in such a situation. Your relationship breaks down. But as you work together on Attitude, Behavior, and Character, you can work your way toward a relationship that's mutually satisfying.

Your principle of "Let reality be the teacher" really hit home. I've been rescuing my young-adult son for far too long, I'm embarrassed to say. No more being a wuss. I'm starting today.

Hank, New Hampshire

I felt like a failure as a parent for over 7 years. Often at night I wondered if I should ever have become a parent. Why was I so frustrated all the time? Then my husband and I started to homeschool this past year (not a smart plan when you're already frustrated with your kids), and I knew for sure I was a failure. Our house was completely chaotic. Then I found your principles. They have transformed our home. I can never express how thankful I am for the wise instruction, humor, and down-to-earth reality. My 2 children are still far from perfect angels; in fact, some days they do still resemble "hedonistic little suckers," to quote you, but the ankle-biter battalion has come a long, long way. Thank you, thank you.

Laura, Nova Scotia

It's been a week since I started applying your parenting principles, and my home is a completely different place. My 4 kids, who wouldn't give me the time of day unless they were mouthing off, are now respectful. They used to demand that I be their personal chauffeur. Now when they want to go somewhere, they approach me and say, "Uh, Mom? Would it be all right with you if I went to Hannah's tomorrow? If you could get me there between 6 and 7, I can get a ride home." That little example, in itself, shows the difference in our home. I'm now a free and appreciated woman.

Maryann, Tennessee

# Wednesday

*Show Me a Mean Teacher,
and I'll Show You a Good One
(It's All in the Perspective)*

Take a look down the road a few years.
Who do you want your family to be?

I'll never forget the day that our firstborn, Holly, came home from eighth grade and talked about Old Lady So-and-so and how mean a teacher she was. She had me picturing a stereotypical librarian (the stern lady with her hair in a bun who shushed you with a finger to her mouth if you made a whisper) or the old schoolmarm who rapped your knuckles with a ruler if you didn't follow the rules. I imagined her in black-tie shoes with a one-inch heel—the kind my teacher used to wear.

Then I met Holly's teacher. She was a 24-year-old hottie, 2 years removed from her bachelor's degree. I couldn't help but think, *This is the old lady Holly talked about? You've got to be kidding!*

You see, it's all in the perspective. And perspective changes based on your age and emotional maturity. What doesn't change is the fact that you have a big job to do and little time in which to do it. As the famous quote says, "Time waits for no man." Children grow up so fast! How often have you said to your spouse or a friend, "I can't believe Anna is already 15! Where does the time go?"

Life is speeding by like sand draining through an hourglass. You can't afford not to take advantage of the time that you have. Sometimes your job will be tedious and boring (like doing the laundry and ironing the same clothes over and over). Other times the pace will be breakneck, especially when your children are young, are apt to get into danger, or are involved in a lot of activities.

> *What your children think about you at any one particular moment isn't necessarily what they will think about you for life.*

But here's the important thing to remember: what your children think about you at any one particular moment isn't necessarily what they will think about you for life. If you are calm, you are consistent, and you always do what you say you're going to, you will earn their respect and trust. But it won't happen with a snap of your fingers.

### Taking the Long View

Take a look down the road 5, 10, 15, 20 years. Who do you want your child to be? What do you want her work ethic to look like? What about the way she views herself? Her relationships with others? Your relationship with her?

Bestselling author and business consultant Stephen Covey has a great perspective. If you want something, start with that end in mind, he says.

In other words, if you want your child to be kind, teach your child to be kind now. If you want your child to be a responsible adult, teach him responsibility now. If you want your child to enjoy spending time with you, start now in setting aside nonpressured time to spend with her instead of getting caught up in the rat race of constant activity.

Do you think the parents wanted or planned for these situations?

> **What's Important to You?**
>
> What 3 qualities do you want your child to have?
>
> What steps can you take now to encourage these qualities in your child?

- Henry is 17 and just went into drug rehab.
- Miranda was arrested for shoplifting and spent a night in jail.
- Tony bit another child and was kicked out of kindergarten.
- Amanda went thrill riding on a friend's motorcycle, and both of them ended up in the morgue. They were trying to dash between two cars, and they lost the race.
- Keri is 15 and weighs only 88 pounds. She has struggled with anorexia for the past 2 years.
- Jason, who is 21, lost his third job for back talking his supervisor.

Did these situations "just happen"? Or did little things happen along the way that led to these bigger things? Here's what these parents said as they looked back:

"Henry was the kind of kid who always overdid everything. We caught him smoking a joint with a friend when he was 11, but he just shrugged off our concern. He gave me the old, 'But Dad, I was just curious. I won't do it again.' Dumb me, I believed him. I should have followed up. Now I know that he kept smoking marijuana, then moved to meth. I thought he was saving up money for a car. He was using the money from his job for drugs."

"We never confronted Miranda when she took things from her sister's room. When I found out she took 20 bucks from my purse,

I let it go because she said that she needed to pick up some things at the store. But I should have pursued it."

"Tony was an out-of-control 2-year-old, but I thought it was just because he was 2. You know, the terrible twos thing. I figured he'd grow out of it. But then he proceeded into the independent threes and threw even more fits. Two of our babysitters quit. I should have had a clue that something major was wrong. But I just figured they were pushovers. Now I realize it was me who was the pushover. I gave him everything he wanted. When he ran into someone who wouldn't, he just bit them. He'd bitten the babysitters too."

"Amanda was always a free spirit and really social. Everybody liked her. She had lots of friends. But when she was a junior in high school, her friends changed. They were more of the partying, thrill-seeker type. I figured it was just a phase and Amanda would get over it."

"Keri has always been concerned about the way she looks. When she was 9, she was a little chubby. A favorite uncle commented to her about seeing her 'big fat belly' in her swimsuit when we were at the pool one day. After that, she made a lot of comments about how fat she was. She started eating less at meals and ate a lot of veggies. I thought it was a good turn—eating veggies is good for you, right? Then she hit 11 and really slimmed down. She looked great. When she started getting thinner, I just figured she was going through a growth phase (you know—kids puff out, then get tall and skinny, then gain weight and grow taller again). It wasn't until a friend mentioned that she thought Keri had a problem that I talked to her about it. Keri has been in counseling and a program for anorexics for the past 2 years, but it is a hard battle to fight. Even though she's terribly thin, she always sees a fat person in the mirror. I wish I would have paid attention to the little things along the way."

"Jason was a mouthy kid. He had something to say about everything. His dad and I would just roll our eyes and say, 'Someday he'll learn.' I don't think he has yet . . . and he's back home living with us because he just lost his income."

If you want your child to be a healthy, well-adjusted adult, you need to realize just how important you are in the picture. Your child needs not only your attention but also a relationship with you.

> *Your child needs not only your attention but also a relationship with you.*

## What Kind of Parent Are You?

So often I hear people say, "I never wanted to be like my parents. I hated the way they parented. But then I open my mouth and sound just like them. And I act like it too." This just goes to show that what parents model sticks—and sticks well. That's because every child wants to please his parent. Every child longs for parental approval and can't stand it when he doesn't get it. There's nothing worse than knowing you've disappointed your parent. If that disapproval is continual, the child will rebel—the old "oh, yeah? Forget you" syndrome.

There are three types of parents, and who you are as a parent has a lot to do with the way your child responds to you. I've talked about this in depth in other books (*Making Children Mind without Losing Yours* is a great resource for this topic), so I'll just summarize here.

### "Buford, have you chosen to go to bed yet?"

Do you want to make sure your child never fails? Are you continually doing things for your child that he could do for himself? Are you your child's best friend at every turn? Do you find it hard or impossible to say no to him? Are you always cajoling him into doing something? Promising a reward if he does what you ask?

A permissive parent:

- Is a slave to the child.
- Places the priority on the child, not on his or her spouse.
- Robs the child of self-respect and self-esteem by doing things for her that the child can do for herself.
- Provides the child with the "Disneyland" experience; makes things as easy as possible—does homework for the child, answers for her, and so on.
- Invites rebellion with inconsistent parenting.

Does this sound like you?

### "You go to bed right NOW!"

Are you always right? Do you bark out orders to your kid and threaten him with warnings if he doesn't immediately do what you say? Do you tell him how to do life in no uncertain terms?

An authoritarian parent:

- Makes all decisions for the child.
- Uses reward and punishment to *control* the child's behavior.
- Sees himself as *better than* the child.
- Runs the home with an iron hand; grants little freedom to the child.

Does this sound like you?

### "Let me know when you've brushed your teeth, and I'll come tuck you in."

Do you ask your children the facts about a situation and what they think about it before you jump to conclusions? Do you give them age-appropriate choices? Do you look out for their welfare, yet allow them to experience the consequences of their behaviors?

An authoritative or responsible parent:

- Gives the child choices and formulates guidelines with him.
- Provides the child with decision-making opportunities.
- Develops consistent, loving discipline.
- Holds the child accountable.
- Lets reality be the teacher.
- Conveys respect, self-worth, and love to the child and therefore enhances the child's self-esteem.[3]

You as the parent are in the position to leave an indelible mark on your child. And you do it often without even being aware of it. The truth is, both extremes (permissive and authoritarian) will cause children to rebel. With a permissive parent, there are no guidelines, and children flounder. With the authoritarian parent, everything is heavy-handed. The wise parent finds the middle ground.

Let's say you are sitting down for dinner, and your child isn't crazy about your food choice of pork chops.

The permissive parent would say, "Oh, honey, do you want a cheeseburger instead? I'll get up right now and make it." (While your spouse is looking at his pork chop and wondering what's wrong with it.)

The authoritarian parent would say, "Eat it. Pork chops are good for you. And you better clean your plate."

The authoritative parent would say, "I know pork chops aren't your favorite, but that's what I made for dinner tonight. If you want to make yourself something else afterward, that's fine. But thanks for sitting with us at dinner anyway. Dinner as a family is important."

# Parent Check

In your parenting style, are you:

___permissive

___authoritarian

___authoritative or responsible

Why did you label yourself as you did?

What kind of parents did you have?

Do you follow your parents' parenting style, react to it, or respond to it? What's the difference?

What makes the difference? The authoritative parent is majoring on the relationship and minoring on everything else.

### It's All about the Connection

If you don't have a connection with your child, why should she care what you think? If your child doesn't feel your love and acceptance for her—no matter what she does—there will be no relationship.

You can't run a family by rules if there is no connection between family members. If you try to, you'll always have an adversarial relationship. Your children will know that no matter what they say, do, or look like, you'll be playing judge and jury. If that's the way your home is run, no wonder you get knee-jerk reactions every time you try to talk to your kids.

Note that I said "talk to your kids," not "ask your kids questions." There's a big difference. Asking questions puts your child on the defensive. Instead, make open-ended statements (even in response to stupid or out-of-the-blue comments) such as, "I've never thought about it that way. Tell me more." Let's say your child wants to listen to her music in the car, as all teens do. I've got news for you: you won't like her music. (But your parents didn't like your music either.) Instead of wincing, say, "That's an interesting beat. I like that beat."

Such comments are respectful of your children, and they set the paradigm that you are open to talking with your children about anything. Talking with your children about the little things means that they will be more likely to talk with you about the big things.

Your children need to know that you are on their team—that no matter what they do, you love them. You may not like what they do, but that doesn't change your love for them. Many children don't experience the connection, but they experience the pressure. They are bullied into submission, called names, ordered around, told they have to do better in school—and then the next day parents act like none of that happened.

That's why parents need to address their own behavior before they expect their children to change. Many parents create a home environment that is not a fun place to be. Their kids are like robots with no choice (until they choose to act in rebellion). Yet you worked hard to have this child. Some of you went to fertility clinics, held your legs up after sex when you were trying to get pregnant, or went through myriad paperwork for adoption. Is it too much to ask that you show your child some attention and appreciation 3 years or 15 years down the road? To take the time to find the middle ground in your parenting style? Rules don't work without a relationship.

## You May Not Have Much, Mama, but It's All You Need

You don't need a PhD. You don't need to have a lot of money. You have all you need. You know the biggest secret of all: your child wants to please you. She can't stand it when she knows you're unhappy with her. She wants to know you are a team. Yes, all this is true, even if she sometimes gives you the eye roll and wants you to walk 10 feet behind her because you're embarrassing her.

*Every once in a while, slip your child a commercial.*

What's most important is your relationship, and that is based on respect and unconditional love. So much has to do with you and how you treat your children.

Every once in a while, slip your child a commercial. I love to do that. The other day my youngest, Lauren, was in the backseat of the car when I was telling Holly, her 35-year-old sister, "I can't wait to see what Lauren is going to be someday. I know it's going to be something special." I wanted Lauren to hear what I was saying. I wanted her to know that I like the person she's become, and I look forward to our future together. Most parents talk very little to kids. I want to talk *to* my children and also tell good gossip *about* them.

Parent, you hold all the aces. You've got the bank account, the car, the house, the groceries, the power. Children have nothing except what you give them and what they'll someday inherit.

What kind of legacy are you going to leave for them? If you want them to be healthy, independent thinkers who are kind and giving to others, *now* is the time to start. And you can start by changing yourself.

If you tend toward being authoritarian, work on giving your children age-appropriate choices. Children need to develop the ability to make good life decisions. After all, you're not going to be in the same house with your child, making her decisions when she's 32, are you? It's not likely. When you release your children to the world, you want to know that they will be all right on their own. That they will be standing on a firm foundation of love, acceptance, and understanding.

So give age-appropriate choices. There's nothing wrong with saying to your child, "Which would you rather have for breakfast? French toast or scrambled eggs?"

However, you also need an understanding of your child's age and stage. If you say to your 4- to 6-year old, "Oh, honey! Your birthday is coming up in six weeks. Why don't we go to the toy store and get an idea of what you want?" you've created a scenario in which you are going to lose. Children his age live for the moment. Tomorrow is too far away. Six weeks is a lifetime. He's not emotionally mature enough to wait. So parent, use your head. Provide age-appropriate choices that will not frustrate your children.

> *Being happy all the time isn't real life, and you're not being fair to your child if you're providing a continual Disneyland experience.*

If you are a permissive parent, you need to stand up and be a parent instead of trying to be your child's friend and make her happy. Being happy all the time isn't real life, and you're not being fair to your child if you're providing a continual Disneyland experience. Without accountability for her actions, your hedonistic little sucker will grow up to be a teenage brat and then an adult who back talks and can't hold down a job. Will your children always like you? No. But did you become a parent so you could be high on the likeability scale? If so, you are the one who needs a reality check.

The stakes are too high. You cannot back down.

The goal of every parent should be to raise independent thinkers who have a healthy respect for themselves and others. This is extremely important in today's permissive society, as shown in the following commencement speech. The speech was given by J. Neusner at Brown University in 1981, but it is even more applicable today:

> **What to Do on Wednesday**
>
> 1. What kind of parenting style do you have?
> 2. How does your child respond to this parenting style?
> 3. How can you adapt your parenting style to be more balanced?
> 4. In what ways can you emphasize relationship in your home?

We the faculty take no pride in our educational achievements with you. . . . With us you could argue about why your errors were not your errors, why mediocre work was really excellent, why you could take pride in routine and slipshod presentation. For four years we created an altogether forgiving world, in which whatever slight effort you gave was all that was demanded. When you did not keep appointments, we made new ones. When your work came in beyond deadline, we pretended not to care.

Why? Despite your fantasies, it was not even that we wanted to be liked by you. It was that we did not want to be bothered, and the easy way out was pretense: smiles, and easy Bs.

Few professors actually care whether or not they are liked by peer-paralyzed adolescents, fools so shallow as to imagine professors care not about education but about popularity. It was, again, to get rid of you. So go, unlearn the lies we taught you.[4]

Parent, how much do you care? How much do you want to be bothered? What kind of foundation are you building for your children? What kind of lies are you teaching through your parenting style? How are you preparing them for the future?

Start with the end in mind, and keep the focus on your relationship, not on rules.

> I have friends on all sides of the issue—from permissive to authoritarian—and boy, are you right! Authoritative is the only way to go. I saw the fruits of the other two methods in my work at a public welfare agency for 20 years. I'm glad that I chose the balanced perspective with my own kids. I'm proud of them. They're now grown with families of their own. And I'm close to my grandchildren. It truly *is* all about the relationship.
>
> Belle, Texas

> You're right about taking the long view. I can't believe how fast the time goes. It seems like yesterday that my 3 children were babies, and soon my oldest is going to graduate from high school. Now that I have teenagers in my home, I found your advice about not asking questions extremely helpful. I'd been getting "the grunt," but now that I've shut my mouth, they're opening theirs. Thanks!
>
> Sharon, Nebraska

> Boy oh boy, did I need a reminder of the long view. My wife got pregnant a lot earlier than we'd planned, and we now have twins under the age of 2. Our home went from quiet strolls in the evening to the chaos of toddlers. I was, I admit, an "escapee father." A month ago it hit me, after listening to you speak, that's exactly what my father was—an escapee. And when he was home, he was always ordering me around. I didn't want to be like him, so I didn't do anything. I've now apologized to my wife and told her that I want our family relationship to be a priority. And I've asked for her help on that. Thanks for being the reality check I needed.
>
> Jay, Illinois

I've been known to say that parenting 6 children (what were we thinking?) is kind of like herding yowling cats. But after listening to your principles, I think our home could become manageable chaos. This was the first time my husband and I ever agreed on any parenting principles, so this is a biggie. Your no-nonsense approach and personal examples won him over since he thinks most behavior specialists are, to quote him, "a crock." I'm the permissive parent; he's the authoritarian parent. Neither of our approaches was working. Now I've got a backbone and determination, and my husband's goals are being approached in a manner that isn't as severe.

Susan, Kansas

My husband left me a year ago for another woman after 13 years of marriage, and I have full custody of our 2 boys. Every once in a while, I get in the pit of depression, feeling like I'm not there for my kids enough (I have to work full-time now) or that I'm too strict on them (they come home from their dad's house full of too much sugar and exhausted from late bedtimes). Your talk on "You May Not Have Much, Mama, but It's All You Need" was exactly what I needed to remind me what I do have and how important I am to the kids. Thanks. It's the encouragement I need to raise my boys.

Tamara, New Mexico

I've read so many statistics about how children raised by a single mom are doomed that I felt doomed. Then I heard your parenting principles and thought, *Hey, I can do that, with or without a spouse.* You lightened my burden by pointing out that my relationship with my kids is the most important thing. I can't give them everything, but I can give them my time and attention. That was exactly what I needed to hear (and I loved your 3 simple strategies for success too). I felt like you were cheering me on.

Lily, Iowa

# Thursday

## But What If I Damage Their Psyche?
## (Uh . . . What's a Psyche?)

There's praise, and there's encouragement.
Your kid is smart enough to know the difference.

I knew a kid who was a real live wire and a comedian. He got thrown out of fourth grade because he put his hand down his pants, stuck his finger out his fly, and wiggled it at the girls. He got kicked out of Cub Scouts at age 11 for "unpredictable behavior." He got thrown out of consumer's math (the math the "dummies" took so they could at least buy groceries when they graduated) as a senior in high school. He was the kind of guy everyone laughed at, but only his mother really believed he'd grow up to count for something.

Until Vincent Stearns, a high school English teacher, stepped in. He took no crap from anyone and made his expectations very clear. Well, this child had barely done homework in all his years of school—but he did homework for Mr. Stearns. For the first time he rose to the challenge, because guess what? Mr. Stearns had such positive expectations of the young man's abilities that even a flunky would take notice.

What made the difference?

1. The expectations were clear. There was no wiggle room for miscommunication.
2. The adult expected the best . . . so he got it.

It didn't matter that the kid's academic records were at the bottom of the scale. It didn't matter that the kid was known to get his kicks from clowning around and drawing attention to himself. That teacher gave the young man a second chance.

## Expect the Best, Get the Best

These days, parents are overly concerned with a child's self-esteem. "I want Johnny to feel good about himself," a mother says. So what does that mother do? She goes out of her way to clear life's roads for her child, to do things for him that he should be doing for himself.

> *Many children are "mommy-deaf"—and for good reason. When rules change with Mom's hormones, why should they bother to follow them?*

She thinks she's helping him with his self-esteem, but what is she really doing? She's sending a negative message: "I think you're so stupid that you can't do it yourself, so I'll do it for you."

It's similar to saying things one time only. If you remind children more than once, you're saying, "You're so dumb I don't think you're going to get it, so I'll say it again." Actually, saying it once consistently increases your chance that you will be heard and your instructions followed. Many children are "mommy-deaf"—and for good reason. When rules change with

Mom's hormones, why should they bother to follow them?

Doing things your children should do is not respectful of them. Expecting the best out of them—realizing that "the best" differs based on the activity, the age of your children, and their specific talents—is respectful. Every child lives up to the expectation you have for him.

Don't be afraid to set the bar high (many children can do far more than you could dream), but don't expect the world either. If your D-student son comes home with mostly Cs and 2 Bs because he's been working really hard, that's something to celebrate! If your 4-year-old decides to clean her room on her own, although things are not quite as clean as you'd like, tell her you appreciate her thoughtfulness in cleaning her room (and don't follow behind her, cleaning it further).

Does that mean you should never help your child? No. You are the captain of the *Good Ship Family* on the sea of life. Like all good captains, you need to be in charge of your boat and aware of where the hidden rocks are, and you have to have a port of call to know where you're going. There will be times when some of your passengers will fall off your ship, but you don't have to let them drown. They will need a life jacket and a rescue.

> **How to Respect Your Children**
> - Never do for them what they can and should do for themselves.
> - Don't repeat your instructions.
> - Expect the best of them.
> - Don't praise them.
> - Encourage them.

*Every child lives up to the expectation you have for him.*

## Self-esteem or Self-worth?

There is a big difference between children "feeling good" about themselves (self-esteem) and true self-worth. Many parents today are so concerned about their child's self-esteem that they are raising feel-good children: they have to feel good about themselves and everything they do. You wouldn't want any waves on their ocean of life, now would you? Nothing to cause the little darlings to have to swim for it.

Making a child feel good is easy. Just give him everything he wants, when he wants it. But if you do, that hedonistic little sucker takes over and turns into an adolescent big sucker. He'll give you a run for your money with his expectations. That run for your money can often last way into a child's twenties and thirties. Interestingly, 2 of the 10 moms who talk about mother stress at my seminars are older parents who have a child college-age or older living with them. "Boomerang kids," I call them. The kind of children who felt good about themselves because Mom and Dad always took care of things for them. Now Mom and Dad are seemingly stuck in that role even when the child is an adult and should be stepping up to the plate.

> *Making a child feel good is easy. Just give him everything he wants, when he wants it.*

Part of the art of parenting is knowing when to draw the line and when your children need a push. Adult children who are still living at home definitely need a push out into the real world.

Did you know that your job, as parent, isn't to make your child happy? In fact, an unhappy child is a healthy child. Look at it this way. If you're happy and everything is going well, are you motivated to change? It's when things aren't going well that you start evaluating. *Hmm, that didn't work so well. Maybe I should try something different next time.* That same thinking is true for your child. When a child is unhappy (it could be because of something she has done wrong or simply the fact that you are not heeding her wishes), she's motivated to do something different. That's again why the "B doesn't happen until A is completed" principle works so well.

What she gets away with . . . or doesn't get away with . . . depends on how closely you adhere to the principles in this book.

Feeling good is a temporary thing. It's based on feelings, and those change from moment to moment. A child can feel good about getting a toy he wants, but true self-worth is established when the child works hard for a toy, earns that toy, and truly can call it his own, thinking, *I did that myself. Wow. This is how it works.* By providing the types of experiences where children pull their weight and learn responsibility and accountability, you are establishing a healthy self-worth.

## The Pillars of Self-worth

We've already talked about the ABCs of Attitude, Behavior, and Character and how important they are in your child's life. But there are also a second group of ABCs:

- Acceptance
- Belonging
- Competence

These ABCs are the 3 pillars of self-worth for any person.

### Acceptance

Remember, children long for your approval. Your unconditional acceptance of your child means everything in her development. A child lives up to the expectations you have for her. If, by your words and actions, you are portraying the thought, *You are the dumbest kid I've ever seen*, your child will have very low self-worth and won't feel like she can accomplish anything. If, by your words and actions, you are portraying the thought, *Hey, kid, go for it; I know you can do it*, you're establishing a healthy self-worth. Children fly sky-high for a long time on just one compliment. But note that the compliment has to be true—not a made-up one to make the child feel better (more on that later in this chapter). Otherwise every kid on the planet will see right through you. *Ah, I get it. I'm a real loser. And that's what Mom and Dad think too. Dad can't even come up with one good thing to say about me that's true.* And then that child will live up to your unwritten expectations.

If children don't find unconditional acceptance in your home, they will talk less (or not at all) to you, listen to CDs nonstop, use their iPods at dinner rather than communicating, and swap stories via IM with their friends about unfair house rules and stinkin' parents. You see, kids accept kids for who they are. They don't hassle them for their blue hair (they think it's kinda cool), their nose ring (they've got 'em too), or their baggy pants (give 'em all belts, I say!).

> *Your child is a lot more helpless than he seems.*

But the truth of the matter is, as important of an influence as peers are to your child, the peer group can't do diddly-squat for him. Think about it. If your 11-year-old has anything, you bought it for him—that includes soap and a toothbrush. Your child is a lot more helpless than he seems. That's why the method of "B doesn't happen until A is completed" works so well.

Does accepting your child mean accepting everything he does? No, because as we've said earlier, children can do dumb-as-mud things. There will be times when, frankly, you don't much like your child. But you can always extend unconditional love and acceptance. If you do, he'll be less likely to seek acceptance in his peer group.

### Belonging

Every child needs to belong somewhere. Will it be in your home or in his peer group? Gangs in South Central L.A. flourish because they provide a sense of belonging. There's a shared ID there, something those children do not get at home.

From the get-go, establish your home as a place to belong. Give family members a vote in decisions. Listen to what others think and say. Support each other in any activities you do. Instead of piling on a host of after-school activities, choose them wisely so you can set aside family time. Don't lose your family dinners or your family vacations. Friends will change, but family stays. Say through your actions, "We're a family. We belong together."

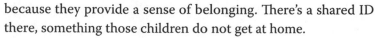

*Do your kids know who they belong to?*

When a new acquaintance approached 15-year-old Melanie to ask if she wanted a cigarette, she simply said, "No thanks. We Crayburns don't smoke." Because Melanie had a strong sense of belonging in her family, she didn't need that cigarette. She liked herself just as she was. Implanted deeply within her character were the pillars of Acceptance and Belonging, because her family had majored on family time and minored on outside-the-home activities. She knew who she was: a Crayburn.

Do your kids know who they belong to? If there is no sense of "belonging" in your home, there will be no relationship. Without a relationship, your rules, your words, and your actions mean nothing. The wedge between you and your children will drive them toward Acceptance and Belonging in a group outside your home.

### Competence

Want to empower your children? Give them responsibility. When your child takes the initiative to get the job done—whether it's feeding the dog, fixing his bike, making dinner—say, "Good job. Bet that made you feel good inside." (If used properly, you see, the temporary "feel good" can be an inspiration to a child to do something again.) And it did, because your child did something all on his own, and he should feel proud of that accomplishment.

When we as parents set up parameters for children to make, create, and excel at things, and then we stand back and say, "Good job," that's empowerment. What does that child think? *Hey, I can do this. My mom and dad believe I can do it. They're thinking the best of me. Let's see what I can do.*

> *Want to empower your children? Give them responsibility.*

Your child doesn't flourish when you do everything for him. He develops true self-worth when he contributes to a project or, even better, does it himself. Those "projects" could include a young child getting her own drink out of the fridge or making a PB and J, a 7-year-old making her own lunch for school, or a 16-year-old newly licensed driver picking up groceries for you. When you allow your children to be competent, they will be competent. And if they fail? They learn how to do things differently the next time. As their responsibilities increase, confidence in their own competence increases. That's how children get ready to move out into the adult world as healthy, functioning members of society.

Your children are longing for Acceptance from you. They ache for Belonging in a family. And they want to have Competence. If they don't get these from you, they'll seek them in their peers. You matter much more in your child's world than you think—which is why your parenting matters more than you think.

### My Child Is So Gifted, He Can Count Backward!

Ever heard one of those moms who just gushes out praise to her child?

- "Oh, Ethan, you're such a good boy! You got an A in math. Oh, that's just wonderful! I can't wait to tell your father. I'm sure he'll take you out for ice cream."
- "You're so smart. You built that Lego tower all by yourself!"
- "You're so cute when you do that. I can't wait to show it to the neighbors."
- "You look adorable in that skirt."

If I went out right now and asked any parent, "Is it good for parents to praise their children?" I bet every single one of them would say yes. But they're wrong.

Praise isn't good for kids. That's because most of the time it's false and drummed up to make them feel good, and your children are smart enough to know the difference. It's never a good idea to associate "goodness" or "cuteness" with how a child does a certain task. If the child did the task badly, would that make him bad or ugly?

Do you see where I'm going with this?

Praise links a child's worth to what she does. To a child's mind, that means, *Uh-oh, if I don't do something "good" all the time, then I'm not worth anything. And Mom and Dad won't love me.*

It goes back to the pillars of self-worth: Acceptance, Belonging, and Competence. Children need to feel unconditional acceptance no matter what they do, to know they'll always belong to your household, and to learn to be competent. All of these pillars will be knocked down by the falseness of praise.

Instead, *encourage* your child. Encouragement emphasizes the act and not the person. Here's a replay of the comments above, in the context of encouragement:

> *Praise links a child's worth to what she does. Encouragement emphasizes the act.*

- "Oh, Ethan, you got an A in math. I know you've been working extra hard in that area, and that work really paid off. You'll have to tell your dad about it. He'll be happy too."
- "I love what you built with your Legos. It's very creative and fun, and you did it by yourself. What are you going to build next?"
- "That's a fun cheer. Where did you learn it?"
- "When you went shopping yesterday, you did a great job. That skirt looks great on you. A wise choice."

See the difference? It may seem subtle, but it means the world to a child. When you encourage the act, you encourage the child to be competent and to try something else because he succeeded in that area. Little by little, your encouragements build a core foundation of solid self-worth that will last through any situation in life and even combat negative peer pressure.

So the next time your daughter plays the piano well in a festival, say, "Oh, honey, you must be happy with your performance. You worked so hard to get that piece just right. That was beautiful!" And the next time your child scores a goal in soccer, say, "I can sure tell you've been practicing hard. All that work paid off, didn't it?"

Don't praise your child by saying, "You're the greatest kid who ever walked the earth." What happens when she isn't? Besides, she can already look around and see she's not the greatest, so she knows you're lying to make her feel good. That sets up the disconnect in your relationship: *Hmm, can I trust Dad's word? He's snowing me now.*

Instead, encourage her in what she does: "I noticed yesterday that you helped your little brother when he was struggling to tie his shoes. Instead of doing it for him, you coached him and then encouraged him, saying it would get even easier next time. That was great, honey. I appreciate it. You have a very kind heart."

Such encouragement not only spurs your children on but further solidifies their 3 pillars of self-worth.

Remember the kid at the beginning of the chapter—the live wire and comedian whom only his mother believed in? The kid no one thought would go anywhere in life? Even though that kid was a goof-off, his parents provided a firm foundation of self-worth through the pillars of unconditional Acceptance (even though he tested it many times as he grew up, and his mother grew extra gray hair in the process) and Belonging (this baby of the family always knew that he was part of the family and had an important role there). His mother would sigh each time he failed a class, then encourage him in the area of Competence once again. It wasn't until that kid met teachers like Mr. Stearns, though, that he grew in the area of Competence. For his mother, it was a long wait . . . but she never gave up.

How do I know?

Because that kid was me.

> **What to Do on Thursday**
>
> 1. How can you show your child uncondi-tional Acceptance?
> 2. How can you empha-size Belonging in your family?
> 3. In what way(s) can you spur your child on to Competence?
> 4. Think about the differ-ence between praise and encouragement. What truly encourag-ing thing can you say to your child today?

I'm in my third year of teaching kindergarten, so when I heard you speak about your principles, I was excited as both a mom and a teacher. I can't wait to put your books on my first-day letter to parents as "Recommended Reads." I'm also going to explain about the 3 pillars of Acceptance, Belonging, and Competence and about the difference between praise and encouragement. Your books will give me a way to talk to parents about difficult things during the school year—especially since I already know 2 of my 20 children were known as "difficult" in the nearby preschool. I have this sneaky little feeling I know where they got being "difficult" from.

Tricia, Georgia

My daughter called yesterday. She felt so stressed with her 5 children (ages 10, 6, 4, 3, and 3 months) and just needed some encouragement. Based on your principles, I shared with her all the things she was doing right and encouraged her to take the long view . . . and a nice, long bath when her husband got home.

Harriet, California

I've been divorced for 1½ years, and I have 2 young children. Because I felt so bad that they didn't have a father, I was going out of my way to praise everything they did. Thanks for showing me the difference between praise and encouragement. From now on, I'm going to encourage my boys, not praise them. And I'm going to work hard on the ABCs instead of feeling guilty that I can't provide everything for them.

Janna, Arizona

Your words about Acceptance, Belonging, and Competence hit home for me. I've always internalized the image of myself held up to me by other people during my childhood. I didn't realize how much my permissive parenting had to do with the fact that I didn't feel good about myself. The few times I could remember my parents being kind to me had to do with praise. But I was never encouraged. Now that I know the difference, I'm going to go out of my way to encourage my daughter. I've been doing it all wrong, but now I'm going to do it right. Hearing you speak was a huge step of healing in my own life . . . and the encouragement I needed to look forward!

Marta, Alabama

# Friday

## *The Doc Is In . . . and It's You*

It's time to pull together your game plan.

Your mantra: "I can't wait for that kid to misbehave, because I'm ready to go to war."

For the past four days, we've been setting the stage for change in your home. You've done some evaluating each day about what you can do to kick-start that change. Today's the day you pull your game plan together. Fun Day is just around the corner!

But first let's review the key principles, because knowing them is the key to your success in this venture.

## MONDAY

In order for your child to know you mean business (and to keep you calm and rational):

1. Say it once.
2. Turn your back.
3. Walk away.

## TUESDAY

It's all about the ABCs:

1. Attitude
2. Behavior
3. Character

You now understand where your child's attitudes come from, and you've done a check in the mirror for your own attitude. You understand why it's important to be aware of the purposive nature of your child's behavior. You are determined to hold firm in directing your child's character.

You also have the 3 simple strategies for success firmly in your mind:

1. Let reality be the teacher.
2. Learn to respond rather than react.
3. B doesn't happen until A is completed.

## WEDNESDAY

You're taking the long view in this journey of parenting. You've evaluated what kind of parent you are:

1. Permissive
2. Authoritarian
3. Authoritative or responsible

You've evaluated how your parenting style influences the way your children respond to you. You are actively thinking of ways your Attitude, Behavior, and Character can be better balanced in regard to your children.

You've decided to focus first on your relationship with your child, realizing that without relationship, any rules will not be effective.

You've also decided not to make mountains out of molehills, and you're strategizing which areas really are important ones to address (you'll find the "Ask Dr. Leman" section helpful in this regard).

## THURSDAY

You understand the difference between self-esteem ("feeling good" about yourself) and true self-worth. You're evaluating how you can help your child develop the 3 pillars of self-worth:

1. Acceptance
2. Belonging
3. Competence

You're determined to move from praise (focusing on how "good" a person is) to encouragement (focusing on an action).

Okay, got all that in mind?

### What's Your Game Plan?

Today's the day you decide to go for it. You're going to launch your action plan on your unsuspecting children. Remember, there are no warnings, no threats, no explanations—only action and follow-through. Above all, there's no backing down, no caving in. Your child needs to know you mean business, or you won't accomplish anything. If it takes you longer than a week to change your child's Attitude, Behavior, and Character, then you need to revisit these key principles. Children who have been allowed to have their own way for a while can be extremely powerful. But look at it this way: if your teenager doesn't change, he'll have the most boring teenage years on record because he won't be able to do anything. Remember, B doesn't happen until A is completed. Not even a powerful child can hold out for long under such a principle. No matter what, the family comes first. So if there's a problem at home, you don't look at life outside the home until the problem is solved.

> *Children who have been allowed to have their own way for a while can be extremely powerful.*

Now is not the time to back down, so don't be a spineless jellyfish. Stand up and be a parent.

Will it be easy? No. There are days, and then there are *days*. You know what I mean. When you start applying these principles, your child's behavior is probably going to get worse . . . for a time. It's a little like fishing in a creek. When you hook a game fish, it will try to throw the hook out of its mouth by leaving the water and thrashing back and forth. You can expect that "fish out of water" syndrome with your children too. They'll come thrashing wildly out of the water and be very ticked.

However, if you talk to a fisherman, he'll tell you that in order to land the fish, you've got to keep tension on the line. You don't give that fish any slack. If you give it slack, not only will it jump out of the water, but it will scrape its jaw against the bottom of the creek to try to get rid of the hook. To catch that fish, you have to keep the line consistently taut. If you suddenly drop the pole toward the water, you've developed slack in the line, and you give the fish the opportunity to get off. Then it'll be pretty tough to catch that fish again.

The good news is, if your child is thrashing as he comes out of the water, you'll know you're on the right track.

## What's Up, Doc?

Now you get to play the shrink. Think about a situation that's currently going on in your home. Ask and answer the following questions as if you're the doctor in the house.

> *If your child is thrashing as he comes out of the water, you'll know you're on the right track.*

1. What's the situation?

2. How would you diagnose it?

3. What's the purposive nature of the behavior?

4. How do you feel about the behavior?

5. What would you normally do? Think it through.

6. Now what would you do differently? Whose problem is it? Have you left the ball in the child's court, or are you attempting to dribble it yourself?

## Consistency Wins Every Time

Remember that your child's behavior serves a purpose in his life. It draws your attention to him and provides a power base for him ("I'm going to show you"). As your child grows more powerful, his contempt for you will grow. After all, if he can control you, why respect you? You're not the authority figure any longer.

That's why it's so important to realize that your child is misbehaving for a reason. More than anything else, she needs a relationship with you. Consistency in your Attitude, Behavior, and Character breeds contentment in your child, whether she is 3, 13, or 23. She can know that the rules won't change based on your moods or life circumstances.

When you understand the basic principles in this book, you don't need a shrink, because you can be the shrink. In fact, instead of paying a shrink to "solve your family problems," take a trip together as a family. Too many parents pay psychiatrists to prescribe a label and then medicate their child when all the child needs is her parents' time and attention.

## Getting Ready for Fun Day

Want a new kid by Friday? Here's a Top 10 list of what it takes. (For a summary, see p. 289.)

*10. Be 100 percent consistent in your behavior.*

You can follow these principles nine times and blow it the tenth time, and you're back to square one. Think of it this way: you're trying to forge a new and different path in life. You're retraining your kid—and yourself—to behave differently. Your kid needs to know you mean business.

*9. Always follow through on what you say you will do.*

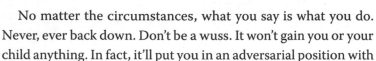

No matter the circumstances, what you say is what you do. Never, ever back down. Don't be a wuss. It won't gain you or your child anything. In fact, it'll put you in an adversarial position with your child, who will wonder, *Hey, when is she serious, and when isn't she?*

### 8. *Respond, don't react.*

Use actions, not words. Flying loose with your words will only gain you trouble. So close your mouth, think, and respond to the situation rather than reacting to it.

### 7. *Count to 10 and ask yourself, "What would my old self do in this situation? What should the new me do?"*

Let's say the siblings in your home have been going after each other for 9 years. What do you usually say and do? What will the new you do differently?

### 6. *Never threaten your kids.*

The problem with threats is that our children know we don't mean them, because we rarely follow through on them. Even more, our threats often don't make sense: "All right, no more candy for life!" "If you don't get off that chair, you're going to break your neck!" Even the youngest child can figure out when there's no action or truth behind the threats.

### 5. *Never get angry.*

As soon as you get angry, you'll be back at square one. I understand that there are triggers—things your kids do that make you angry. But you're the adult in the situation. You are the one who ultimately decides when you get angry. Don't let your children control your moods. If you get angry, an explosion of anger is like throwing up all over your child. The release in tension may feel good temporarily, but look what you've done to your child.

85

Okay, so you're human. If and when you get angry, apologize quickly. For example, "Honey, I'm sorry. I shouldn't have said that."

### 4. Don't give any warnings.

If you warn your child, you're saying, "You're so stupid, I have to tell you twice." Your goal is to get your children to listen, listen once, hear what you have to say, and act on it.

### 3. Ask yourself, "Whose problem is this?"

Don't own what isn't yours, and don't force the ownership on a sibling either. You need to keep the ball in your child's court. Don't take over what she should be doing herself.

### 2. Don't think the misbehavior will go away.

I've got news for you. Kids won't stop misbehaving on their own. They gain too much by it. You have to intercede and administer loving and consistent discipline.

An old CEO of a major airline told me that at one time the airline gave the employee at the counter 100 percent discretion to make decisions about passengers. "Kevin," he said, "because too many ticket agents took liberties, we lost millions." That airline learned the hard way that they can't just give a ticket agent carte blanche. Nor can you as a parent give a child carte blanche. You are responsible for informed guidance.

Let's say you're going shopping for fall clothing. You say to your child, "This is the budget we have to spend on your clothes this fall. You can spend it any way you want, but we cannot go over this amount." That still leaves the child with the freedom to decide what kind of clothing she will purchase with that money. But if you see her going the way of buying twelve T-shirts, you might want to say, "Those T-shirts look great, but you might need a sweater and some jeans too." You are giving your child informed guidance. If she chooses not to follow it, she may end up washing the same pair of jeans every night for the next school year. And if your child insists on buying clothing that does not fit your standards (i.e., too tight, too low), then your informed guidance should say a firm no.

If informed guidance could save your child a lot of grief in the small things, like clothing choices, then why would you, as parent, not offer informed guidance in the more important issue of misbehavior?

> *"You need to go on strike."*

Simply said, you can't let the prisoners run the asylum. They'll get themselves in too much trouble. In such cases, it's better to force a blowout than to face a slow leak, hoping your child will come to her senses one day.

*1. Keep a happy face on, even when you want to . . . do something else.*

## Get Ready, Get Set . . .

A woman came to my seminar and told me, "I'm so tired of the way things are done at my house. The kids treat me like a slave and a short-order cook. No one likes anything I make, and they complain about it all the time. It's been this way for years, but I'm sick of it."

This poor woman was at marine training camp, and she'd been cleaning and licking boots for years. Her family expected it. But no longer.

Here's what I told her: "Lady, you need to go on strike. Don't cook dinner at all. For a week. Go out for dinner each night, get a bite to eat by yourself. If your children ask where you're going, just say, "Out." When you come home, don't do the laundry, don't wake them up for school, don't make breakfast or lunch. Get their attention. You are not their slave; you're their mother. When they

**What to Do on Friday**

1. Review the key principles.
2. Identify the mountains you want to address.
3. Think through how you usually respond and how you'll respond now.
4. Get ready, get set . . . go!

ask, simply say, 'I'm done doing things for you. Until I see effort on your part, I quit.' And just watch the shock on your kids' faces."

You see, oftentimes you're too good a mother. You're too good a father. You do way too many things for your children. On Fun Day you need to level the playing ground, using the "B doesn't happen until A is completed" principle.

It isn't rocket science. Any parent can do it. Your kids need you to step up to the plate so life in your home can be what it should be—a place of love, respect, and accountability for actions.

Now launch your plan. Stick to your guns. Your mantra should be, "I can't wait for that kid to misbehave, because I'm ready to go to war."

Just do it!

> I have been struggling with my daughters, ages 7 and 4, for some time now, and I have felt such frustration. I've felt like a total failure because I find myself constantly yelling at them, then feeling incredible mommy guilt afterward. The amount of junk food in our home shows how guilty I've felt. You have given me practical and easy-to-follow principles that I can really use. I know it won't always be easy, but I'm determined to stick to it.
>
> Robin, Ontario

> I'm launching my action plan today. I can't wait for Fun Day. I've already decided that I'm taking myself—no kids—out for ice cream when it's all over. Your advice is priceless and exactly what I needed. I felt a connection and an understanding that I haven't

felt with any other parenting expert. Your humor and personal testimonies were reassuring to an average guy like me.

Mark, Ohio

My life has completely changed. My relationships with my kids have changed. And, okay, I admit my relationship with my husband has changed since I'm no longer stressed out due to the kids. Thank you so much! My husband says thank you too.

Melissa, Illinois

For the first time in 2 years, since Elizabeth turned 13, I have hope and an action plan.

Kara, New York

We have 3 children—4, 3, and 2. We couldn't see spending our lives the way things were going. Nobody would babysit for us, and people would stare at us in public (with good reason). Simply put, our children are monsters. Your principles have changed *everything* about our lives. I hope every parent on the planet hears you speak or reads your books. They *need* this approach. We certainly did.

The Nesbits, Montana

# Ask Dr. Leman

*A to Z Game Plans That Really Work*

Straightforward advice and gutsy plans of action on over 100 of the hottest parenting topics.

# Shh! It's a Secret!

A no-nonsense approach to having a great kid
and being a great parent.
Just look up the topic,
but don't tell your child what you're up to.
(Hint: There's a quick index at the back.)

If we had ten minutes together in person where no one else could overhear us, what's the one thing you'd most want to know about parenting? Why?

Over nearly four decades, it has been my joy to help families succeed. I want to see *your* family succeed too. So in this section, allow me to be your personal psychologist. I'll just perch here on the arm of your chair while you look up the topics you're currently facing for some timely and time-tested advice.

Then think about your own situation. Ask yourself:

1. What is the purposive nature of the behavior?
2. How do I, as the parent, feel in this situation?
3. Is this a mountain or a molehill?

The answers to these questions will help you formulate an action plan for your own family. If the issue is a molehill, a can of Raid might help. If it's a mountain, the ante is upped significantly. You must handle the situation well, because it will affect your family dynamics, your well-being, and your child's well-being.

So pick the topic that's hottest in your family right now. The topics are organized A to Z so you can find them easily, or you can check the index at the back of the book. If you want a Parenting 101 crash course, just read straight through the section. I've included over 100 of the topics that parents ask about most.

For additional help on specific topics, consult the resource list on pp. 299–300. You'll also find a lot of practical help at www.lemanbooksandvideos.com. Have a specific parenting question? Go to iQuestions.com, where I answer all sorts of parenting and marriage questions (and you even get to see my mug shot).

Above all, remember the secret: do *not* let your child in on what you're up to. What you're doing must remain your secret until Fun Day. There are no warnings in this system—and no wimps allowed either. Backing down once you launch your action plan will only get you pushed back into the corner you started in.

You *can* be a great parent. And you *can* have a great kid.

So go ahead—plunge right in. Fun Day awaits.

## Allowances

"I give Matt, our 14-year-old, an allowance every week. But he's always coming back to me the day after he receives the money, asking for more money for something he's just got to have. It's driving me crazy."

"Trey is only 3, but he seems interested in money. The other day he took some coins off the kitchen counter and put them in his pocket. He's so young that I don't think he had any idea that what he did, without asking, was stealing. But it made me wonder: should

I give him an allowance? How old should kids be before they get an allowance?"

"We give all three of our kids—who are 12, 14, and 16—the same amount of allowance every week. But our 16-year-old is constantly asking to borrow money from our 12-year-old . . . and getting it. Should we give more to the 16-year-old because he's older, or keep the amount consistent so we're fair to all 3 children?"

"Our 2 children, ages 11 and 13, are vastly different in personality. Jen, our older child, is a real worker. After she's done her regular chores, she always pitches in and does extra ones if she sees other things that need to be done. Mark, our younger child, has to be prodded from his PlayStation several times in order to get even his own chores done. I was raised with a brother, and everything was 'even Steven' in our home. But it always drove me crazy when I did all the work and got the same allowance as my younger brother. I don't want to make Mark feel inferior by giving him less money than his sister. Help! What should we do?"

Giving allowances is one of those areas that influence many other areas, so I'll spend a little more time on it than on some of the other topics. Why? Because the money a child has at his fingertips, how he has received that money, and how he views that money affect not only what he's able to buy or save but how he feels about himself.

What's an allowance for? In my view, an allowance is part of a family's recreational budget. It's one of the perks of being a member of the family.

This is a very different view than most of us grew up with. Remember the chore list on the refrigerator? We all groaned about it, but we did it (unless we could get our

> *An allowance is part of a family's recreational budget. It's one of the perks of being a member of the family.*

little sister to do it for us on the sly), because it was the only way we could get paid. The list went something like this:

Clean your room. 50¢

Set the table. 10¢

Feed and walk the dog for a week. 50¢

Clean out the garage. $1

Take out the garbage. 20¢

Doing those chores directly related to how much money we received in our allowance each week.

But here's what I'm suggesting: every family member should automatically receive an allowance from the family's recreational budget. That means everyone, as part of their "perk" for being in the family, has money to spend. I know some of you are thinking, *I can't afford an allowance.* The reality is that all parents spend money on their children, so "I can't afford it" doesn't fly with me. Just take what you'd spend on the child for lunch, clothing, etc., and lump it all together as the allowance money. That doesn't cost you any more money than you're already spending, and it will teach your child responsibility.

Some family members, due to age and abilities, will have more work to do than others. For instance, you wouldn't expect a 6-year-old to do the same kind and quality of work that you would expect from a 14-year-old. But by the same token, the older child also has some perks that the younger child doesn't have—for example, a later bedtime and the freedom to go out with friends.

I suggest that you start a child with an allowance around the age of 5. Give the child, say, 5 quarters ($1.25 per week). There's nothing more wonderful to a child than to have something of her own, and shiny quarters are like gold to a young child. Age 5 is also a good age at which to begin teaching the value of money—what a penny, nickel, dime, quarter, and dollar are worth and what they can buy. Go to the bank together and start a savings account for the child. Invest in a money market account or a stock, if you are able to do so. (It's amazing how small amounts can grow, and it's wonderful for a child to see this on a quarterly or yearly basis).

If a child wants to spend money on something above the cost of what he has in his allowance, *do not* pad his allowance money. Have the child wait to purchase that item until he has enough money to buy the item himself. Then he can experience that thrill of buying what he himself has earned—and also the dash of buyer's remorse if he accidentally breaks a plastic toy he purchased. Having "money of my own" gives a child some dominion over dollars and a growing understanding of how long it takes *you* to pile up the cash needed to buy certain things for your family.

As a child gets older, increase that child's allowance with respect to her age. The more money you give your older child in her allowance, the more the child can do with it, whether saving or spending.

Our Lauren, who is now 15, *loves* to save her allowance. Someday she'll be happy to have a little nest egg all her own for a special purchase. Little Kayla, who is 8, is also a saver. She puts every penny she receives into her buy-a-horse-someday fund. But last year, when she heard about a little girl who lost her home in a flood, she dipped into her allowance and sent that girl's family a special gift—from her very own heart and finances.

Kyle, who is 11, discovered quickly that money doesn't grow on trees and that what's hot among his peer group today may not be hot tomorrow. It took half a year's allowance to buy a skateboard. Three weeks after his purchase, his classmates laughed at his skateboard because it wasn't the latest and greatest anymore. Now Kyle tends to buy only things that *he* really wants—not items that he thinks will make him popular.

Children need to know that when the money is spent, it's spent. There's no free lunch in life.

If your child asks for more money because he's used up what he has, say, "Well, payday isn't until Saturday. I'm sure you'll make something work." Would it kill your son to pack a lunch for school instead of going out with his buddies to the local pizza joint?

Would you say to your boss, "Hey, I need more money to last me until Saturday"? Then don't allow your kids to manipulate you either.

But should you ever pay your children for specific jobs? Let's say that your daughter comes to you and says, "I'd like to earn some extra money this summer. Anything I can do around here?"

"Well," you say, "I've wanted to get the garage painted for 2 years. If you paint the garage, I'll give you $100."

Such a deal, which is beyond the norm of your child's usual responsibilities, is a great way for you not only to get a job done but also to allow your child the opportunity to earn additional money for a special project. And when the painting is complete, you can bet your daughter will look at that garage every day and be satisfied with her accomplishment.

Children need to know that upholding their end of the bargain as a family member is important. If they don't, there are consequences.

For instance, let's say your 14-year-old doesn't mow the lawn like he's supposed to. Instead of nagging or bickering with him about when he'll do it, what if you just quietly hired another sibling or someone from the neighborhood to cut the lawn? What if the money it cost to hire that person was taken out of your son's allowance the following week? Do you think you'd get the message across quickly?

Let's say that your older child always does everything you expect her to do. You can count on her jobs being done; you don't even have to check.

Then there's her younger sibling who hates to do a lick of work but is supposed to clean out his room. When he doesn't, what do you usually do? Rag on him, right?

What if, instead of saying anything at all, you asked his sister to go in and clean his room, and you paid her $4 out of your son's next allowance for doing so? Chances are, little brother isn't going to be happy that (1) he lost some of his allowance, and (2) his *sister* was in his room.

But do you think you got your point across that all family members are expected to pitch in, and when they don't, they have to pay someone else to do what was expected of them?

Allowances teach children how to manage money—and they also teach children firsthand about consequences. For example, I could run my car through the car wash and hand the workers $8. Or I could wash the car myself in the driveway and keep the $8 in my pocket. It's all a matter of choice.

If your child doesn't get around to a certain task, don't cajole her, remind her, or lecture her. Simply hire someone else to do that task and take whatever you had to pay that person from your child's allowance. There are no threats, no warnings—only action.

That action will speak much louder than any words you could use. I know, because it got swift results in my own home. Our teenage children were responsible to cook dinner for us one night a week in order to give my wife, Sande, a break. One night I arrived home from work, and there was no dinner cooking. So I decided it was a good time for a teachable moment. I took Sande out for dinner at one of her favorite places, where they serve food with real silver forks, not plastic picnic ware. When our children received their allowances the following week, the price of that dinner had been divvied up among them and taken out of their allowances. Do you think that ever happened again in our house?

Lesson learned.

## Anger

"Mike would come home from school, go into his room, slam the door, and start punching his pillow. I'd try to talk to him, but he'd always tell me to go away—that I was butting into his business."

"Shawnee pitched a fit—an honest-to-goodness screaming fit—every day when it was time to take a nap. I got so tired of it. *I* was the one who had to take the nap while she roamed the house freely."

"It doesn't take much for Tim to blow, and when he blows, it affects our whole house. Everybody gets really, really quiet and goes and hides in their rooms. It's like, to him, he's the only one that counts."

"Monica doesn't yell; she *seethes*. I'd rather she yell than give me the silent treatment."

What's the atmosphere like in your house? Is an angry person in control? Interestingly enough, a person can be loudly angry or quietly angry. Either way, you get the picture loud and clear.

> *Anger is an active choice to control someone else. It's projecting your thoughts and emotions onto another person in an attempt to change their behavior.*

When it comes right down to it, anger is an active choice to control someone else. It's projecting your thoughts and emotions onto another person in an attempt to change their behavior.

The children above have learned that being angry wins them something. They get attention, they get their way, people feel sorry for them, etc. They are angry because that purposive behavior puts them in the driver's seat in their home. Without it, they don't have the control they crave. So they create, in effect, a temper tantrum that says, "Pay attention to me!"

Guess how they learned this behavior? Probably from a parent (usually a mom) who is a people pleaser and likes the oceans of life smooth. In order to keep them that way, she'll do anything to avoid harsh words. The child is smart enough to know that regardless of age, throwing a temper tantrum will gain him exactly what he wants—everything from sympathy about a hard day to money for a movie to the car keys for the evening. Your child is a skillful manipulator.

How'd he get this way? Such maladies don't just appear. They fester over time. They start with an 18-month-old who feels misplaced when little sister comes home from the hospital, so he throws a fit to make sure his place is still secure. What do we as parents do? We try to squash the behavior quickly when, in fact, all that child is saying is, "Hey, I feel a little left out here. Will someone pay attention to me?"

What would most parents say in such a situation? "Stop it, Buford! You need to learn to get along with your new little sister. Things aren't going to be the same around here anymore, and you might as well get used to it." This sort of statement just ups the ante on the fear and displacement the child is feeling. But what if the parent said, "Come over here, Buford. Are you feeling left out? I know things have changed with having a little sister. But I want you to know that you are just as important to me as you always were. You don't need to throw a tantrum to get my attention. Just come to me and ask me for a hug, and I'd be happy to give you one."

Anger isn't always bad, either. Did you know that you can be *good* and angry? Bad things happen in life, and it's okay to be angry about things that are unjust. Like the teacher who doesn't believe your daughter didn't cheat on her exam and gives her an F. Or the coach who thinks your son was the prankster who removed the tires from his car and refuses to let him play for the big game. If your children were innocent and wrongly framed, they have every right to be angry.

So being angry in itself isn't right or wrong; it's *how* the anger is handled that is right or wrong. What should you do when your child explodes in anger?

Imagine that you have a balloon in front of you. Each time you get angry, you blow those bad feelings into the balloon. If no pressure is released after a while, the balloon will pop. But if you let a bit of air out, little by little, the balloon stays malleable, with no threat of it breaking.

That's the goal with children: to teach them how to handle anger. If children talk about what bothers them, it's like releasing the air out of the balloon. So give your children opportunities to talk about what is bothering them. Begin with open-ended statements: "You seem upset." "I can tell by your face that something's bothering you." "I'm ready to listen if you want to talk."

When the child finally does talk, it may be a terrible sound, like the squawk air makes when it comes out of the balloon. But remember your end goal: to keep your child malleable and less brittle.

Teach your child to use "I" statements rather than "you" statements. For example: "I feel like you don't respect me when you do this" instead of "You diss me all the time." Or "I feel angry when my sister goes into my room and plays with my things when she knows I don't want her to" instead of "She's such a jerk. She knows I don't want her to play with my things and she does anyway." Talking in "I" terms focuses on how your child feels about what's happening rather than pointing an accusing finger at someone else. This method models how to talk things out rather than strike out. It also works extremely well in solving sibling rivalry. (See also "Sibling Rivalry.")

## Attending Your Place of Worship

"Jeri always went to church with us with no complaints. But the Sunday after she turned 15, she said she was sick. The Sunday after that she claimed she was sick again. By the third Sunday she simply told me that she wasn't going to my stuffy old church anymore. That the only kids who went there were geeks and weirdos, and she didn't want to be pegged like them. Jeri's always been such a good kid. What went wrong?"

"When I remarried, I became a dad to Christopher, who was 13. He made it clear right off the bat that (1) he didn't need a father, and (2) there was no way he was going to spend a day at some old church when he could be at the beach nearby with his buddies. I know he's been through a lot of changes in the last couple years and his friends are really important, but it's important to me for us to go as a family to church. Should I push the issue and make him go? Or will that make him hate not only me but God? Should I just give him some time and hope it works out?"

There's a wonderful saying: "The family who goes to church together stays together." However, what that saying didn't add was, ". . . unless the teenagers in the family are kicking and screaming about going—in which case the family staying together is loud and not all that fun."

Far too many parents tread on their teenagers' feelings on this issue and ramp up this situation until it becomes a war. But before you get hot about what you *think* I'm going to say, hear me out.

First of all, don't deny your child's feelings. Let's be honest. There *are* a lot of geeks and weirdos in churches (after all, churches are made up of human beings, and we all have our quirks—some of us more than others). So if your child points out that the majority of kids in the youth group are weird, then tell the truth: "You're right. They are weird." By telling the truth and agreeing with your child, you'll: (1) surprise your child and get her to pay attention to your next words, and (2) get on the same playing field as your child, where you're seeing eye to eye.

What you say next is crucial: "Your mother and I only ask you to do a few basic things, and one of the things we expect you to do is go to our place of worship." Before the child opens her mouth again, say, "We know you don't want to be there, but we want you to know how thankful we are that you are willing to come with us out of respect for us. There are many things we as parents do for you that we don't really like to do. But we do them anyway out of respect for you. So please get ready for church."

Depending on the personality of your child, that may sway her into coming with you. But no matter what you say, some kids will throw these words in your face: "I'm not going."

If that happens, don't make a federal case out of it. Simply get ready for church and leave.

> *Don't make a federal case out of it. Simply get ready for church and leave. After church, do one thing different: don't come home.*

"What?" you're saying. "But, Dr. Leman—"

Let me finish. After church, do one thing different: don't come home. Make a day of it somewhere. Go out for dinner after church, go to a park or enjoy some shopping after that, see a movie. . . . In other words, take your jolly good time coming home. When you walk in after 5:00 that afternoon and your teenage son says, "Where the heck have you been?" simply say, "Church."

"But church is over at noon," he argues. "It's 5:15. When are we going to get some food around here? I'm starving!"

Simply rub your full stomach and say, "Food? Don't even mention that. The strawberry pie topped it off. . . ."

If your child continues to refuse to go to church the next week, do the same thing again. Make a day of it without the child. Then, after making your point, talk to him straight: "Frank, I realize you're an individual, and we're not all the same. You don't have to believe what I believe. I can't make you go to church. But I want to make it clear to you that I expect you to be with us next Sunday. Is that understood?"

All of a sudden the person in authority has changed, and your son is no longer in the driver's seat. In many cases, this is all the tough love that's needed. The next Sunday he'll be out in the car, ready to go.

Sometimes, though, a teen will still absolutely refuse to go, even after you've tried the previous steps of tough love. So you as a parent have a choice. You could:

1. Let him stay home in bed like a slug, shrug, forget about it, and not raise your blood pressure.
2. Let him stay home but assign him extra work to be done around the house since he now has idle time.

Of the two options, I'd definitely choose having him do some extra work while you're gone. Every family member needs to contribute. And part of that contribution is doing certain things together. If your teen decides he doesn't want to contribute in that way, ramp up what he needs to contribute in another area, even if it's something he's not crazy about. It's like the day the john backed up at my house. We all pitched in to clean up the mess because that was what life required of us. It wasn't pretty, it wasn't fun, but we did it as a family.

Don't let your child get off scot-free just because he doesn't "feel like" being a part of your family. Either he goes with you to your place of worship, or he pulls extra duty in another area of responsibility. (And here's a secret: because at the heart of every child is a longing to belong and be accepted, it won't be long, after using this technique, that your child will begin to feel lonely and want to be a part of the family again—including attending your place of worship.)

## Attention Seeking

"Last week we had my new boss and his wife over for dinner. We put our 8-year-old, Charlie, in bed, and I went to the kitchen to prepare dessert. Five minutes later I heard a heart-stopping crash from the living room. Charlie had sailed down our stair railing— something he knows he's never supposed to do—and landed smack in the middle of a table that has our Tiffany lamp on it. The lamp shattered in a bunch of pieces, and Charlie cut his hand. Instead of serving dessert, we ended up taking Charlie to the ER to get his hand stitched up. What would possess him to do that, when he'd never done anything like that before? I was shocked."

"Our 3-year-old twins, Kylie and Kari, always act extra silly and talk nonstop when my girlfriends come over to the house. I can never get a word in edgewise with my adult friends. It's like the Kylie and Kari entertainment hour."

"I was so mad yesterday. I just happened to be at the kitchen door when I saw Isaiah, my 7-year-old, bowl his 2-year-old sister over *on purpose.*"

"My daughter Annie wears really short miniskirts, and her T-shirts are way too tight. I swear she does it just to drive me crazy because she always gives me 'the eye' and waits for my reaction before she flounces out the door. It's like she's trying to prove that she's a big girl and can choose her own clothing. I don't get it. We've never fought about clothing, what she can wear or can't wear. But for the past year, ever since I went back to work, it feels like she's been trying to pick fights. I want my old girl back."

All children crave attention, and they will do just about anything to get it. If they don't get enough positive reinforcement from parents, they will seek attention through negative behaviors, doing things they know drive their parents crazy.

Charlie hated being left out and wanted his parents' attention, so he sailed right into the middle of the party. Kylie and Kari didn't leave the party; they simply decided to stay in the center of attention and let the world revolve around them. Annie created the attention by picking fights—wearing clothes she knew her mother would hate.

Some children demand that adults pay attention to them. They're the comedians, the entertainers, the crisis creators. They go out of their way to be noticed. I was that kind of kid, so I totally understand. (Oh, the things I put my mother through!)

How can you, as a parent, respond to such a kid? When younger children use negative behavior to get your attention, say, "I see you need extra attention today, don't you?" Such a comment generally takes the fun out of the behavior, which means the child isn't as likely to do it again. Then say to the child, "Honey, I'd be more than happy to give you attention. Do you want me to just sit and look at you? Would that be enough? Or do you want me to take time to read you a story and play with you for a while? I love you, and I can tell you need extra attention right now. But just so you know, I saw you push your little sister over. Was that part of your need for attention? If so, you don't need to push your sister over to get it. If you need a hug or a kiss, just come and tell me that, and I'm happy to do it."

> *Some children demand that adults pay attention to them. They're the comedians, the entertainers, the crisis creators. They go out of their way to be noticed.*

When an older child uses negative behavior to get your attention, the ante is upped. Let's say your teenage daughter flounces down the stairs wearing a skirt so short that you wince. In fact, you've never seen that skirt before. Did she borrow it from a friend? You wonder. . . .

You know that she's acting like this to get your attention, but she's also doing something else. She's building up her skill in the power game. *I'll MAKE you pay attention to me*, her attitude screams. *I'm not going to be what you want me to be.*

And then what does she do next? She sticks her hand out and says, "Where are the keys?"

Your response? "What keys?"

At her incredulous look, you say, "I can tell by the way you're dressed that you're not ready to go out."

Will you have a big blowout? Probably. But the fact holds firm: she's not going anywhere dressed like that.

Too many parents back down from this attention-seeking and power-driven behavior. They let things slide, thinking, *She'll come to her senses one day.* Don't wait. It's better to force a blowout than to suffer through the slow leak.

By saying or doing these things, you are telling the child that you know not only what he's doing but why he did it. And you're disclosing what you feel and see going on before your very eyes. You're also telling the child, without saying it in words, *Hey, kid, it's not all about you. You're not the only one who needs attention.* Such words get back to the purposive behavior. All behavior serves a purpose. When kids act out, they are seeking attention. Calling a spade a spade gets at the core of what the child needs and also dissuades him from more attention-getting behavior.

When your kid does something stupid to get attention, simply say calmly, "Oh, honey, do that again! You haven't done that in a long time. Oh, my, you must really need Mom's attention. Come on over here. Let's talk about that."

## Babysitting

"Friends ask me all the time if my 11-year-old daughter will babysit for their 3-year-old. I just don't feel comfortable letting Lexi do it since it feels like a lot of responsibility for a young child. What if something went wrong?"

"A girl down the block has always watched our 2 children. But now she's 17, and she always brings her boyfriend. I keep wondering who she's paying attention to: our kids or her boyfriend? Should we switch babysitters or just tell her she can't bring her boyfriend?"

Babysitting is a two-way street—choosing a babysitter for your children and deciding when your child can babysit other children, if she has interest.

When should you let your child baby-sit? Kids can babysit at age 10 or 11 if they are children who show a high level of responsibility in other areas of life, but I usually suggest no younger than age 12. Sure, the money they can earn may sound good, but they are also agreeing to a great deal of responsibility—especially if the child they are babysitting is younger than age 2 and can't express feelings and needs in words. Also, how many children would your child babysit? How well behaved are the children? A lot also depends on the personality of your child. Emily, for example, didn't start babysitting until she was 16. Before that, she wasn't ready for the responsibility, and she wouldn't have been able to keep track of more than 1 child. Jill began babysitting at 11. She had a natural affinity for younger children since she had 4 younger siblings of her own, and she was used to juggling multiple needs.

> *I usually suggest no younger than age 12. Sure, the money they can earn may sound good, but they are also agreeing to a great deal of responsibility.*

No child should be pushed to babysit children from outside her own family unless she wants to. If she has an interest, offer the opportunities in bits and pieces so she can develop the responsibility for babysitting without being overwhelmed or potentially getting herself and the children into danger. I know two families on the same block who have 11-year-old and 13-year-old girls who trade babysitting responsibilities for the younger children in their families. On two Fridays a month Stacey, the 11-year-old, goes out for a movie with friends while her parents also go out for a date night. Kendra, the 13-year-old, watches the 3 younger children from both families at Stacey's home, while Kendra's parents have a date night at their own home. The next Friday, the two girls and the two parents switch roles. This way both girls earn money for summer camp, yet both are just three houses away from a set of parents (the ones having the date night at home), should there be any concerns with the younger children. It's a plan that works well for all parties involved. And the emergency plan has been used only once—when all the power went out in the house because of a storm, and Stacey didn't know how to work the electrical panel to get the lights back on.

> *If your child is the babysitter, be careful about where you let her babysit.*

If your child is the babysitter, be careful about where you let her babysit. It's best, if possible, for you to personally know the family. Either way, make sure that *you* are the one who takes your daughter to the home and that *you* are the one who picks her up. Sadly, I've heard way too many stories of grown men—*fathers*—hitting on teenage girls when they take them home after babysitting. If we had a teenage girl or woman babysitting for our family, Sande always drove that babysitter home. Because it's easy for kids to make up stories about what adults do with and to them, Sande and I adopted this policy early on: I take boys home; Sande takes girls home. We've never deviated from that policy.

If your child is older and has a boyfriend, that can often add an interesting mix to the babysitting equation. My suggestion is that you have an agreement with your child that when she babysits, the boyfriend never comes along. That way she is free to focus on the children she's responsible for, and she's not sending a mixed message to the family she's babysitting for.

Before agreeing to any babysitter for your own children, think about these things:

1. Your child's physical safety and emotional security is in this person's hands. What kind of person do you want your babysitter to be?

2. What instructions do you need to give the babysitter about your child's care? It's always best to write them out and leave a copy with the babysitter so there is no confusion. This is especially important if there is any medicine to be given or feedings of infants/young children that need to be done.

3. How long do you want to be gone for the first trial run? Some parents decide to be gone only an hour and to go to a place no more than 10 to 20 minutes away from home if they have a new babysitter.

4. What expectations do you have for what will happen while you're gone?

5. Some parents suggest a schedule such as the following: Pizza for dinner at 6:00. Movie (handpicked by the parents and on the counter) from 7:00 to 8:30. Bedtime at 8:30, with a bedtime story already picked out to be read to the children. You and only you know the children's schedule. If you want your young children to be sleeping peacefully when you get home, tell the babysitter the schedule so things will seem normal for the children. If you're a parent who doesn't mind a free-for-all evening (and the resulting messy cleanup), that's fine too. Either way, make your expectations clear to the babysitter, including that she will clean up.

6. Make sure the babysitter has your cell phone number, knows when to expect you home, and knows how to call 911.

All of these things will help your child and you to have healthy babysitting experiences.

## Bad Language

I haven't given specific examples here, because every family will differ on some of the specifics of what they consider bad language. A lot of it has to do with whether you are a person of faith (i.e.,

Christian or Jewish) who honors the 10 Commandments or not. If so, then those commandments clearly say to not take the Lord's name in vain. But bad language isn't only taking the Lord's name in vain. It extends beyond that to words or phrases like Bleep you, the S word, A-hole . . . well, you get the idea.

Sometimes younger children will use bad language and not even know it. They hear it at school and just bring it to the dinner table as an experiment. Countless parents have been surprised by what's come out of their child's mouth in a matter-of-fact way.

One mom told me about a quiet family dinner she was having until her 6-year-old, Samantha, said very matter-of-factly, "Would you pass the bleepin' potatoes?" The following evening, Samantha's 8-year-old sister used the *d* word.

On both occasions, that mom just about dropped her fork. Her children just looked back at her serenely. On the second occasion, the 8-year-old simply said calmly, "What does *d—n it* mean?" Neither child had any idea what she was saying. They were just repeating what they'd heard out of another child's mouth.

After the mom's blood pressure slowed down from the shock, she took the experience a step further and decided now was the time for a teachable moment.

*The words you use reveal your character.*

"I know the words," she said. Then she proceeded to explain what the words meant and that they'd hear them come frequently out of other people's mouths in public places. "However, we as a family have chosen not to use those words because they are filthy words and not honoring to God."

Whether you are a person of faith or not, here's something else very important to consider: the words you use reveal your character. Just by listening to the words you use, others will assume things about you that may or may not be true. Is that the picture you want to portray to others?

The bottom line is that families need to decide whether they are going to use certain words or not. Then they need to stick with that decision and convey those values to their children.

## Bathing

"But I don't want a bath! I don't need a bath! I just had one last week!"

"It's none of your business. I'll take a shower when I want to. None of my friends rag on me about it."

How is it that bathing and basic hygiene always seem to turn into an all-out war between a parent and child? And it all seems to start at a young age. To young children, baths seem like unnecessary evils. They interrupt the fun your child is having and require him to take time out from what is so important to him.

From day 1, make baths routine at your house—just "what you do"—rather than a big deal. Some infants are afraid of water; others love water. There are all sorts of bath devices to assist with this, including little visors that allow you to shampoo the child's head without getting soap in her eyes. Use these when you need to make bath time more pleasant. But take charge. When it's time for a bath, don't let crying stop you. Remain matter-of-fact and calm.

> *Make baths routine at your house—just "what you do"—rather than a big deal.*

If your 6-, 7-, or 8-year-old refuses to take a bath, you need to get a little tougher. "It's bath time. Do you want me to give you a bath, or do you want to give yourself a bath?" No child on the planet—especially a boy—would want his mother giving him a bath at that age. So off will come the pants, shirt, and socks, and off your kid will march to the bathtub.

113

Bathing can become a real problem in the teenage years (especially with boys who tend not to mind the locker-room aroma) because many teens simply do not bathe as much as they should. When your teen is sweating or menstruating, and hormones are fully functioning, he or she should take a shower or bath every day. If your teen resists, simply adopt the "sniff test." You can take a whiff as your teen walks by to snag some breakfast before school, or even insist on the underarm sniff test. If there's anything smelly going on, you'll know. If so, simply insist that he go up and take a shower *now.* It doesn't matter if he's late for school. In fact, if you really want to clinch the deal so that he'll take showers from now on, write in the note to school the reason he's late:

> *Franklin is late for school today. He smelled, so I insisted he take a shower first. Feel free to do whatever you do to children who are late for school, and I will fully support you.*
> *Franklin's mom*

After that, do you think Franklin would miss doing his own sniff test before he even came down to the kitchen?

## Brushing Teeth

"It's so gross. I swear his teeth are turning yellow. Pretty soon they'll start growing mold. I think the last time he brushed was when I made him when he was 12."

"When I bugged her about brushing her teeth, she just shrugged. 'I chew gum, Mom. It's the same difference.'"

"He's often too crabby at night to brush his teeth, and I'm too tired to make him do it. Isn't once a day enough?"

Brushing your teeth is a basic hygiene action. No one wants to talk to anyone who has bad breath—at least not for more than a couple seconds past the first whiff. Not brushing your teeth also affects more than your social life. Studies from the American Dental Association show that there is a direct correlation between how healthy your mouth is and how healthy your entire body is. And just because you chew gum to make your breath smell "minty fresh" doesn't mean that you're getting all the fuzzies off your teeth that can cause cavities or make your body sick.

> *Brushing your teeth is basic hygiene that everyone should practice. Enough said?*

Adopt good teeth-brushing habits as soon as your child has teeth to brush. Even little ones can learn to be adept at teeth brushing. Brush 2 to 3 times a day (what all dentists suggest!) so that it becomes a routine, not a fight. Brushing after a sugary snack is a good idea too.

If your child forgets to brush his teeth or fights you on it, adopt a "breath check" in the morning. Before your child goes out the door to school, he has to breathe on you. (It's not the most pleasant job for a parent, but the results are effective.) If your child's morning breath could stop a moose in its tracks, the child turns around and goes back upstairs to brush his teeth. No fighting. No questions asked. Yes, even if he is late for school. In fact, if he's late, the better the lesson for him.

Brushing your teeth is basic hygiene that everyone should practice. Enough said?

## Bedtime Battles

"It takes us about 3 hours to get the kids to bed. By the time we get through the requests for snacks, juice, water, a bedtime story, and tucking them in—only for them to pop out 10 minutes later and come downstairs—I'm so exhausted I wish I could go to bed too."

"Aaron won't go to sleep without my husband or me lying down next to him. The problem is, by the time one of us lies down long enough to get him to sleep, we fall asleep too. I don't think we've had any 'couple time' for over a year!"

"I remember always seeing imaginary monsters at night when I was a kid, so I understand Anna's fears and I've tried to be patient. But lately she's been getting up so many times in the night, claiming to see monsters, that I'm starting to walk into walls. There has to be a better way."

I'll put it bluntly. As my pa used to say, "When it's bedtime, it's bedtime. Either you can walk under your own power or you can be ricocheted into bed." All of us kids knew that once we were in bed, there was no getting out of bed. Dad was absolutely firm about that.

The point is, every child needs a set bedtime. But that bedtime can vary, depending on the age and nature of the child. For example, a 2-year-old needs a different bedtime than a 14-year-old because that 2-year-old requires more sleep. Some children require more sleep than a sibling of the same age. The only children in a family who typically go to bed at the same time are twins and triplets. Does this mean that a child can't go to bed *before* her bedtime, if she's tired? Of course not! But it can mean an awful lot to your oldest child to know that she could stay up 15 minutes later than the other kids if she wanted to—a sort of birthright.

For many families, bedtime becomes a battle zone of:

1. going through the child's getting-ready-for-bed routines
2. getting the child into bed
3. getting the child back into bed when she pops out
4. making sure the child stays in bed

Children love routine, so here's a caveat: pick your bedtime routine very carefully. Once chosen, it will be difficult to change.

For example, if you have cereal as a snack or you read a bedtime story, your child, resembling a Philadelphia attorney, will *always require* that you do those two things before he can settle down to sleep. The more complicated the routine, the longer it will take.

Every child on the planet will push to lengthen that routine. My advice, from personal experience with 5 children, is to not let that happen. If you read "just one more story," you'll need to do that every night. The smart parent will make routines brief and simple. I remember taking Holly, our firstborn, to bed as a child. When she was 18 months old, she'd grunt and point at the things she wanted picked up. And I, like a trained monkey, was foolish enough to do it for her. After a while I had so much stuff in my arms that I could barely hold her. Was that nuts or what?

> *Pick your bedtime routine very carefully. Once chosen, it will be difficult to change.*

No matter what routine you come up with, when 9:00 (or whenever bedtime is) comes, once that child is tucked into bed, it's important that she *stays there.* When Holly was a toddler, I made the mistake of always getting her a drink of water from the *kitchen*, which Holly claimed always tasted better than the water from the nearby bathroom faucet, before she went to bed. By the time we got to Lauren, our youngest, any requests for water came from the bathroom, which was closer (by then I was smart enough to not let on to where the water came from).

> *Children have a huge arsenal of things to pull out to delay bedtime and to needlessly involve their parents.*

Children are adept at manipulating parents . . . especially once they are in bed. They can manipulate by "needing" water and a snack ("My tummy is so hungry it's rubbing itself raw"), seeing imaginary monsters ("Mommy, I'm scared"),

117

claiming that they don't feel good ("My stomach hurts"), or tattling on siblings ("Jason came into my room and scared me" or "Amanda won't let me have my toy"). Children have a huge arsenal of things to pull out to delay bedtime and to needlessly involve their parents in sibling battles.

But what's the purposive nature of the behavior? To get your attention. Is it working in your home? Probably, if you're reading this! So what can you do?

Establish a bedtime routine if you don't have one. The shorter and simpler, the better. Once that routine is established, follow it. Then, once the kids are in bed, insist firmly that's the end. The kids need to stay in bed.

Warning: Your kids know how to play the bedtime game really well. Some kids will go to bed just fine, and you'll heave a happy sigh. Then, a half hour later, you'll see little eyes peering out at you from the stairway. The children will insist they need . . . well, *something*. If this sounds familiar, try this tactic: without even turning your head or acknowledging the child, simply say, "It's bedtime. You need to go back to bed," and return your attention to whatever you were doing. There will probably be a hesitation, perhaps even a request again for a snack, for water, or to take them back to bed, but ignore it. Simply go about your business. As far as you're concerned, the bedtime routine is over. The bedtime job is done, and now you're on to something else.

What about the child who shows up in your bedroom at night? If your child slithers into your bed on occasion in the middle of the night, that's a molehill. If your kid slithers into your bed every night at 2 a.m., that's a mountain. Why? Because your child doesn't belong there.

With all respect to the advocates of the family bed, I believe wholeheartedly in the philosophy that every child needs a bedroom separate from their parents'. Children need a place to identify as their own space. And that's true of a husband and wife too. How can you and your spouse develop a solid, lasting foundation—one that will continue after the children are gone—if you don't have one place in the house where you can be with each other without interruption? How exactly can you get it on with two little bodies in bed between you?

If your child continually gets up in the middle of the night and crawls in with you, close and lock your door to keep the little disruption away. For those of you who are worriers, what's the worse thing that can happen? You'll wake up and find the little nipper curled up with her blankie or pillow outside your bedroom door.

Does that mean you should never comfort your child in the middle of the night? Certainly not. What I'm talking about is continual behavior, not the once-in-a-while behavior.

Thunderstorms will come and things will go bump in the night. Your child will get sick, wake up from a nightmare feeling scared, or be sad because of a real-life situation. As the parent, you are the psychological blankie for your child, and that child does need you sometimes. So here's what I suggest for those times: keep a sleeping bag under your bed. If your child is scared and wants to feel close to you, let her know she can pull out the sleeping bag and lie down in it next to your bed without waking you up. That way your child gets the psychological closeness she craves, and you can still function the next day because you've had a good night's sleep. You also retain your bed as your space in your child's perspective.

For those of you with young children, do not climb into your kid's bed to snuggle with her when you accompany her back to bed. If you do so, you're reinforcing the attention-getting behavior. And you're also violating the child's individual space that she needs to be solely hers. If you violate her bedroom space, why would she not violate yours?

Also, moms (who are especially tempted with this one), do not take naps with your child in his bed, or he won't be able to take naps without Mommy sleeping with him. Think about it this way: if you were little, would you rather go to sleep by yourself, watching that musical toy that goes around and around until you feel dizzy enough to fall asleep, or with Mommy, who has a warm body to snuggle up to?

Part of learning to grow up and be age-appropriately independent is having your own bed and your own little space. It's important for psychological development. That's why if siblings share a room, the room should be divided in some way that gives each child his own privacy and space.

Every child wakes up differently. Some children will wake up slowly, talk to themselves, and sing. They'll happily look through books for two hours. They'll relish time in their own "space." That's our Lauren. She was still in her crib at age 3 and would not have complained if she had still been there, reading books, until she was in seventh grade, when she was too old and too big for her crib. Other kids wake up ready to take on the world and insist (usually loudly) on getting out of their bed as soon as possible. That was our Holly, who pole-vaulted out of her crib when she was 18 months. She woke up with fire in her eyes. She was one determined little kid. Our family joke was always this:

*Some kids wake up with a happy face. Some kids wake up hard.*

"Lemey [one of my wife's pet names for me], you better go wake up Holly."

"I'm not going to wake her up. You do it."

"No, you."

The back-and-forth continued. You see, if you were smart, you didn't want to wake up Holly. Some kids wake up with a happy face. Some kids wake up hard.

Some kids go to bed easily. Some kids go to bed hard. And some kids naturally just don't stay in bed. They want water or a snack, they don't feel good, they're scared, they want to sleep with you, or they're feeling social—they simply want some friendly

3 a.m. conversation (ah, what a nice time to share your innermost thoughts and feelings).

Setting—and sticking with—a solid bedtime is a mountain, not a molehill. If you start bad habits in this area, everyone in the family will suffer. Everyone's actions and emotions just seem to work a little better when you've all had a good night's sleep. So be extra careful on this one.

## Bed-Wetting

"I've tried everything—the buzzer, the bell and pad—but he sleeps through it all. Nothing works. Help!"

"Andrea's been potty trained since she was 2. Then one day I got a call from the school to bring her a change of clothes. She'd wet her pants. I was stunned. Andrea's in second grade. What's up with that?"

"Jarrod's still wetting the bed sometimes, and he's 10. What am I doing wrong?"

Many parents go to the extreme on bed-wetting. They try all sorts of contraptions to stop their child from wetting the bed. There's the buzzer that, upon the first sign of wetness, buzzes and wakes up the child. There are the bell and the pad—when the pad gets wet, the bell goes off and wakes up the child.

But let's put things in perspective here. You can read a dozen books and try all the techniques. You can make sure your child doesn't drink a lot of fluids at dinnertime; you can have your child go potty before he goes to bed; you can talk about getting up to go to the potty immediately upon feeling a full bladder.

And your child will still wet the bed.

How does this make you, as the parent, feel? Many parents rack their psyches with angst. *Oh my goodness! I must not be giving him enough love and attention. I must be a terrible parent. He must be stressed in some way to cause him to do this. If any of his friends found out, he'd be so embarrassed. And what a mess! I hate cleaning those smelly sheets and changing the bed every morning . . . not to mention the mattresses he's ruined.*

> Children who wet the bed have deep-sleep patterns. The majority of children will eventually grow out of those patterns and stop wetting the bed.

But consider this: a research study indicated that children who wet the bed have deep-sleep patterns. The majority of children will eventually grow out of those patterns and stop wetting the bed.

So chill out! As the wise saying goes, "This too shall pass." Bed-wetting will stop by high school. I guarantee it. In the meanwhile, just use rubber sheets and install gutters on the bed!

You might also need to do some things behaviorally. For example, if your 7-year-old wets the bed, you wouldn't allow him to stay overnight at a friend's house. You wouldn't want to embarrass the child or inconvenience the friend's parents. But how do you explain that to your son? Do so matter-of-factly, so the child knows the reason he can't stay overnight at his friend's house. There should be no warning or punitive tone in your voice. Simply say calmly, "Honey, when you get this under control, we can do things like that. But for now, we can't."

If your child has an accident at school, call it an accident. Don't make a big deal about it. Bring your child a change of clothes. Do not, however, put an extra set of clothes in your child's backpack *in case* your child has an accident. That would simply be reinforcing the behavior.

In bed-wetting it's important to not embarrass your child—and to take the long-term view.

## Bullying

"I was incensed when my child told me what had happened to him on the playground. How could the playground monitor not have seen what was going on? Now Daniel doesn't even want to go back to school."

"I was so embarrassed when I received a call from the school that Ricky had called a little girl names and then pushed her into the bushes and scratched up her face. How could I have raised a bully like that? I mean, I know Ricky can be aggressive, but I never thought he'd be mean. Especially to a girl."

"Girls can be so mean. Seventh grade was an awful year for Crystal. In fact, so bad that we decided to switch schools midyear. A group of girls decided they didn't like her because she couldn't afford the right clothes and she wears glasses. They spent the first half of the year passing snotty notes about her, making rude comments about her body, and telling other girls that if they were friends with Crystal, they could never be part of *their* crowd. I must admit, I was more than a little tempted to smash those girls' faces in myself. For a while I tried to let Crystal handle it herself, but it got too bad. She would cry every day after school.

"Finally I decided to talk to two of the girls' mothers before I went to the principal. Sadly, their mothers are just like them. It seemed that everything was about being part of the popular crowd. One mom said she was late for an appointment with her personal trainer and didn't have time to talk; another one said she didn't see why her daughter should give 'a girl like Crystal' the time of day because she wasn't part of her daughter's group. . . . I knew I wouldn't get anywhere with the principal since those two mothers were big donors to the private school. So I gave up and switched Crystal to a different school. We both agreed that her crying every day after school wasn't worth it.

"After we left that school, I heard that the group of girls had turned on Jeni, the newest member of the group, and now were making her life miserable. Although Jeni had made Crystal's life miserable, Crystal still felt sorry for her . . . because she knew what it felt like to be picked on."

Is your child the bully or the child being bullied?

There's something very important to know about bullies. Bullies are insecure. They think that by putting others down (physically or emotionally), they'll feel better about themselves. They'll feel more powerful.

When I was growing up, bullies were those nasty boys who followed you home from school on their bikes and beat you up in the back alley. When you got home, your dad would take one look at you and tell you not to back down next time. He'd give you some tips about where to hit 'em (out of your mother's hearing, of course). When you came home a couple days later with a black eye but grinning ear to ear, he congratulated you because he knew that you'd faced the bully square on . . . and won.

> *Bullies are insecure. They think that by putting others down (physically or emotionally), they'll feel better about themselves.*

But today's bullies are different. They're more aggressive, and, sadly, many have parents who are physically absent, are emotionally distant, or simply don't care. You can no longer count on the *Leave It to Beaver* father and mother to carry out discipline in the lives of the bullies who are making your child's life miserable.

Bullying can take many forms. An adopted kindergartener was told by a bully girl in her class, "Your parents bought you off a shelf in China because nobody wanted you. Nobody wanted girls." The little girl had nightmares for months about being "purchased" and having a price tag on her arm. She kept wondering how much she was sold for. And she worried that if her adoptive parents could buy her, maybe someone else could buy her from them. When her mother approached the bully girl's mom to talk through the situation, the bully girl's mom just laughed and said, "Sometimes kids say the silliest things, don't they?" Clearly she didn't understand the impact of what had happened, nor was she willing to.

Another little girl had her arms squeezed so hard by a first grade classmate that she was terrified she couldn't get away. He was much larger than her and actually left bruises on her arms. When the mom told the teacher about it, the teacher said, "Oh, he was just trying to be friendly." But the mom pursued the issue with the principal of the school, since it was the third occasion on which the boy had squeezed her daughter. She was worried that the next time the boy would break her daughter's arm.

A fourth grade boy was told he was a "girly boy" because he didn't like to play football with the boys during lunch hour. The next day someone put a pink tutu in his locker and taped pink ballerina shoes and the word *gay* on the front of his locker. Ian was devastated. He's now in seventh grade, but he'll never forget that moment. He's wondered ever since if he is gay.

A second grade girl spent her recess hiding from two boys who liked to "play catch" by flinging her back and forth between them.

Bullies who are not stopped in their tracks merely become older bullies who are more dangerous. In some locales, today's bullies carry knives and guns, depending on the neighborhood and their age. (And not only gang members are bullies; bullies can be very clean-looking types too.) They're the kids in the back alley behind the school who catch other kids walking out and try to force them to smoke or do other drugs. They're the boys in the locker room who catch a boy who doesn't have a big penis, strip him down to his jockstrap, and force him to walk into the hallway in front of the girl he has a crush on. They're the girls who tell a new girl on the scene that to be cool, she has to have oral sex with one of the soccer players.

If such a thing happens to your child, go immediately to a teacher you trust. If you see no action from the teacher, go to the principal. Bullying is not anything to mess around with. It's a mountain to tackle *immediately*, no matter which side of the coin you are on.

If your child is the one bullying other children, go for the jugular. Confront your child forcefully, when you are the only audience: "Are you really that insecure that you have to bully other kids?" This will cut to the chase because no child wants to admit he's insecure. Or that he picked on someone younger and smaller just to feel better about himself. Ask your child why he did what he did. Explain how the other child felt about what happened, how you feel about what happened, and what kind of behavior you expect out of your child from this point forward. Insist that your child apologize as soon as possible to the child he wronged. It helps to cement the lesson if you are present to make sure this happens. In order to have emotional restitution, the bully must say, "I'm sorry for hurting you. It won't happen again."

But here's the important part. If your child is truly sorry, you need to allow him to move on. In other words, don't be a bone digger. We parents have the tendency to go back and whack our kids over the head with something they've done earlier. We love to constantly remind them of their failure so they'll be "good."

As embarrassing as it is to be the parent of a bully, keep in mind that, as a parent, you'll face lots of crises. Your job is to deal with them as best you can, then move on. Training children takes time. They'll make mistakes. You'll make mistakes. Remember the democratic society rule? "If you have a right to put me down, I have a right to put you down." This can be a hard cycle to break if you continually bring up the wrong things your child has done. By addressing bullying behavior and demanding immediate emotional restitution, you and your child can move on with life.

If your child is the one being bullied, report the behavior immediately to the child's teacher. If the teacher doesn't give you specific feedback, such as, "Thank you for letting me know. I will be on top of this and watching for it. Let your child know to come immediately to me if she feels threatened," then you haven't been heard and the teacher doesn't consider bullying behavior serious. The next step is to go to the principal. You cannot take bullying lightly, nor can you take the "wait and see" approach. Too many children get the tar beaten out of them by bullies. Although their physical wounds may heal, their emotions may not. Bullies don't stop easily, so you have to be vigilant. You have to put safeguards in the system to stop bullying behavior. The playground monitor, the teacher, the principal, and both sets of parents must be aware of the behavior and that it must stop.

In short, bullies and bullying should never be treated lightly.

## Carelessness with Money

"Every time Timothy gets money, he seems to lose it. So he's always asking for more."

"As soon as Jan gets money from her grandma, she spends it. And it's usually on things that I think are really—uh, how else can I say this?—stupid. How can I teach her the value of money?"

Let me ask you a question: where do your children get their money? If you haven't yet read the section on allowances, now's the time to do so.

If you started your child on an allowance at 5 years old and he seems to always be losing his money, perhaps he's too young to have an allowance. Maybe you should wait until he's 7 and can keep better track of his money. Every child is unique—and that includes the rate at which their level of responsibility grows.

But let's say your child loses his allowance the first week you give it to him. What should you do? The number 1 rule is: don't replace it. When you're at a 7-Eleven and he wants a Slurpee, say, "Sure, you can buy one with your allowance if you want."

"Uh, I don't know where my money is," he says.

Your response? "When you find your allowance, bring it with you next time we come, and you can buy a Slurpee."

Think that kid will keep better track of his money?

> *If your child tends to spend money carelessly, simply let reality be the teacher.*

If your child tends to spend money carelessly—always buying whatever he wants at the moment rather than saving up for something special—simply let reality be the teacher. When your son wants that new bike, say, "Sure, Jeff, you can buy that with your money." And when he gets that crestfallen look, knowing he's spent all his money on things that have already been eaten or discarded or broken, don't rescue him. When your daughter gets her ears pierced and wants to get diamond studs for her "new look," don't fall for her "Please, Mom!" If you let her save her money, you can bet she'll take much better care of those diamond studs.

## Cell Phones

"But, Dad, all my friends have them!"

"When Jason started playing football in junior high, we got him a cell phone. That way I knew I could work in the office until he called me from the locker room to say he was done. By the time he took a shower, I was there to pick him up."

Cell phone or no cell phone? At what age should you consider getting a child a cell phone?

You see it everywhere these days: kids walking down the street and even into school, talking on their cell phones. The other day

I walked into my daughter's school and saw a first grader talking on a cell phone . . . and it wasn't a pretend one either.

When our daughter Lauren was 14, she really wanted a cell phone. All her friends had one. So Sande cut her a deal that she'd get her one for her birthday in the summer if she continued to do well at school.

I'm not crazy about younger children having cell phones. Children don't need them and can't use them during school (at least in most schools). Yet 6- and 8-year-olds have them. That's crazy! In most cases it's only a vanity thing ("hey, look at me"). In my book, children should be at least 15 years of age—close to getting a driver's permit or license—before considering getting them a cell phone. On the other hand, if my son or daughter was driving a vehicle or out by himself or herself, I'd be the first one in line to buy a cell phone for safety reasons.

> *A cell phone should be a perk, not a given.*

If your child begs for a cell phone, consider these things:

1. Does she really need a cell phone to contact you? Or is it just to be "cool"?
2. How responsible is your child? Will she keep track of the cell phone or leave it somewhere?
3. Who is going to pay for the cell phone? If it's your child's, she should pay for not only the cell phone itself (that will tell you how badly she wants it, if it has to come out of "her" money) but also the monthly bill when she racks up too many charges texting her friends. If she needs to call you, you could pay for the flat rate but never for any charges beyond that. If she doesn't pay the bill, the cell phone is discontinued.
4. Having a cell phone encourages even more telephone time with friends. Is your child doing well in school? Is she getting her homework done? Is she a responsible family member, helping out when things are needed?

A cell phone should be a perk, not a given. With it comes extra responsibility.

## Cheating

"I was shocked when I got a note from Kent's teacher. She had given him an F on his biology exam because she caught him cheating with his cell phone. When I asked him if it was true, he admitted it. At least he was honest about that!"

Well, they say confession is good for the soul, so here goes. I would still be in Latin 1 if it weren't for a guy named Carl Maahs. When it came to exam time, I simply said, "Hey, Maahs, would you lower your left shoulder?" If not for his kind gesture, I'd still be in that class. I was taking it as a sophomore in high school, and I'd already flunked it twice.

*Let's be honest. Everyone has cheated sometime.*

Then there was my sociology class when I was a freshman in college. Some unnamed woman, God bless her, had a very natural slouch. That slouch helped me pass my final exam. During that class, we'd studied the Dobu Zuni and Kwakiutl Indians. Our teacher was one of those deep thinkers talking to the babbling brook. He might as well have been speaking in Arabic for all the good it did me.

Let's be honest. Everyone has cheated sometime. So when a child is caught cheating, it's good to come alongside her and establish what I call equality. Tell your child, "Hey, I've been there. There have been times in my life when I've cheated too. All I can tell you is that it doesn't make you feel good after the fact, and you end up paying for it. Sometimes you pay for it by having someone flunk you in their course or sue you for plagiarism. It's just not worth it. "

It's also important to own up to your own feelings about the matter. "Honey, I'm disappointed in what you did. I wish you wouldn't have done it." Note that there is a big difference between saying you're disappointed in *what they did* and saying you're disappointed in *who they are*. Your child needs to know that you love him no matter what—but sometimes you don't like what he does.

If a child repeatedly cheats, the smart thing for a parent to do is to put the ball back in the school administration's court. Let them pronounce a just sentence on your son or daughter. My experience has been that when a stranger or someone outside the family administers discipline, it usually carries a little more weight . . . and fear.

Cheating is a molehill, not a mountain—unless it's a repeated behavior. The smart parent doesn't hold a onetime event like cheating over their child's head. Just address it and move on.

## Chores

"Ah, Mom, do I *have* to?"

"I'm so sick of doing all the work around here."

Every household has tasks that need to get done, and every family member needs to pitch in and help. That means everyone from the youngest child to the oldest child to the parents. There are a lot of things young children can do, such as setting the table, washing the dishes, putting in a load of laundry, gathering garbage, sweeping off the porch, washing the car, taking care of pets. As children get older, they can help with more advanced tasks, such as cutting the lawn, running to the store for groceries, changing oil in the car, researching places on the computer to go for a family vacation, etc.

Every child will forget every once in a while. When a child forgets, it's not a mountain, so don't make it one. Simply say, "Honey, I know you must have hurried off to school because you forgot to walk the dog. I saw that Rosie was doing the potty dance, so I took her out myself." Much of the time, the child will respond, "Oh, thanks, Mom. I did forget. I'm so sorry!" and that's the end of it. The next day he'll remember.

> *Every household has tasks that need to get done, and every family member needs to pitch in and help.*

But if forgetting to walk the dog becomes a constant thing, you need to do something different to get your child's attention. The best thing I've found is to hit the child financially in the pocketbook. There are no warnings, no threats, no whining, no fighting. Simply pay someone else (or yourself, if there is no one else) for doing that task, then deduct the money from the child's allowance. Your message will get across, loud and clear. Family—and what the family needs to get done—must come first.

This mom's action reaped swift results:

"Jason is supposed to take the garbage out every week. When he didn't do it for the third week in a row, my girlfriend gave me an idea that she used with her teenage son to get the point across. She collected all the garbage from the house and outside garbage cans and put it in her son's room after he'd left for school. She closed his bedroom door and left the stinky garbage in his room all day. By the time he came home, it smelled really rank in there. I tried the same thing with Jason. Hey, a desperate mom's gotta do what she's gotta do! He got the picture, especially when his girlfriend just happened to walk home with him after school that day. That was 6 months ago, and since then he *always* remembers Monday is trash day. He's usually up a little early to get it out the door. When Jason found out I meant business, he stopped complaining about other things I asked him to do too."

## Christmas Gifts (the "Gimme Gimme" Syndrome)

"It never stops. Even before Thanksgiving, she's got a list of things she wants that's several pages long."

"My boss gave his son a motorcycle for Christmas. And his son is only 17!"

Children get far too many things these days, especially children in middle income and affluent homes. It's the smart parent who's able to discern the difference between what children need and what they want.

"I cringe every time I'm at my in-laws' for Christmas," Jill told me. "Everyone rips open presents all at once and it's over within 5 minutes . . . except for the complaining they do about the presents they didn't want."

In today's materialistic society, children see—and thus want—more and more things. But does that mean they should get them? These days, children tend to be less and less thankful because they receive so much.

> *It's the smart parent who's able to discern the difference between what children need and what they want.*

What does Christmas really mean to you? Do you want your children to think it's all about "gimme gimme"? Or do you want your children to understand what giving and sacrifice is all about?

I suggest to parents that they minimize the number of gifts that kids are given. The Billings family, for example, has 3 children. Each of the children receives a large gift, which has been thoughtfully considered for its long-term value, and a stocking stuffer. Their 9-year-old received a mandolin and lesson books and tapes, which she'd been dreaming about. Their 10-year-old got ice skates and a 6-month membership at the local skating rink. Their 13-year-old got a gift certificate for a week of horse camp the following summer. Such gifts show just how well the parents know their children and will value lasting experiences instead of spending money on plastic toys that will break or get lost.

One of the things we Lemans have always done as a family is to help a needy family at Christmastime. We provide the necessities of life—groceries, clothing, etc.—as well as some fun little surprises for the children of that family to open on Christmas. As our children have delivered these gifts with us throughout the years, they've developed tender hearts toward those in need. That's a character quality that will last a lifetime!

You can't always control the number of gifts your child receives since some of those gifts are from other people, but you can do this: whenever you open your gifts, have one person open one gift at a time so the children aren't just going from thing to thing, ripping packages open wildly and not even considering who gave the gift or how much sacrifice went into giving it. Many families also insist that before that gift is played with, the child needs to thank the giver (whether in person, by note, or with a phone call).

Let's face it. We all know children who are never thankful. No gift they receive is ever enough or good enough. A well-to-do father approached me a couple years ago, torn about what to do with his daughter. He admitted that he has a lot of money and that he has showered her with presents. Anytime she wanted to drive the posh family car, she got it. She was always going out with friends, shopping, going to lunch. Basically she was a wild hair doing whatever she wanted to do. She was mouthy, calling her mom "bleepin' b—h" and her father other choice words when she didn't get what she wanted.

This year she announced that she wanted an iPhone for Christmas. And the father didn't know what to do. He had always flooded her with designer this and that for her birthday, Christmas, and many times in between. But, to put it bluntly, she had turned into a brat.

I suggested to the father that instead of putting a Christmas present under the tree, he should put a letter that said this:

*Because we love you so much, your Christmas gift is this letter. There will be no iPhone and no other gifts this year. This is a year where you need to sit back and think about how you treat your parents, your sister, your brother, and your friends at school.*

*Love, Mom and Dad*

The father gulped and turned a little pale, but he did it. And that Christmas morning, he got the message across to his daughter that he loved her but that he would not tolerate her behavior any longer.

What do your children really need this Christmas? I'll answer that question with this little anecdote. I write a weekly column for a Tucson, Arizona, newspaper. One year they asked me to write on this topic: "What does your wife want most for Christmas?" My answer? "To be treated with kindness and respect all year long." Evidently that column had an impact because I received a lot of letters about it. An insurance sales guy even stopped me at a ball game to tell me what a great piece of advice that was and how much he needed it. "I make a lot of money," he admitted, "and I give my wife a lot of things. But I've taken too many liberties with her in too many areas. I have not respected her or treated her kindly. It took that article to make me realize that things really don't matter. My wife needs my respect, love, kindness . . . and time. You've opened my eyes."

What do children need way more than the "gimmes"? They need parents who will respect them, treat them kindly (and help them learn to treat others likewise), and give them the gift of their time. Those are gifts of a lifetime, not trinkets that will rust or break.

## Common Courtesy

This one doesn't need any examples, because you know exactly what I mean. Whatever happened to common courtesy these days? It always astounds and annoys me as a car-pool dad when I drive a child home in my car after an activity and don't even receive a "Thanks, Mr. Leman, for taking me home." *Isn't that basic manners?* I wonder to myself.

Contrast that with my little grandson, Conner, who, ever since he was 3, always thanks his grandma and me *without prompting from his mother* every time he comes over to play. He thanks us when we get him a drink or his favorite cookie. If a 3-year-old can remember to say thanks, why can't a teenager? Could it be that he simply hasn't been instructed at home as to what to do and say?

If you have a young child, start now by instructing him in what to say. Children don't learn how to say thank you without some prompting. It's not uncommon for a mom of a young child to say, "What do you say?" as a prompting when he receives a kindness. Then the child remembers, *Oh, I'm supposed to say thank you.* If a mom reinforces this over and over, by the time a child is 3 it should come out naturally, without a reminder.

> *If you haven't taught your children basic manners, it's never too late to start.*

In the same way, kids don't learn basic manners without teaching and prompting. So teach your child how to say please and thank you. If you haven't taught your children basic manners, it's never too late to start. Teach her how to put a napkin in her lap, which fork to use first if there is more than one, and how to hold her utensils. Teach her to cough into her elbow rather than into someone's face or into her hand before touching a doorknob. Teach him that belching and other bodily noises aren't polite behavior in public.

Why not turn learning manners into creative fun at the dinner table? Play the "Catch Someone Not Using Good Manners" game. Everyone loves it in our house. At the dinner table, put a stack of coins in front of each adult and each child (ages 6 through 10 works best). If you catch someone not using good manners, you get to take a coin off their pile and add it to yours. If you're a goofy daddy like me, you might chew with your mouth open, just so someone can catch you. You could order, "Pass the potatoes" and wait for someone to correct you with "Please pass the potatoes." You could even burp. Be creative with the ways you reinforce this. Your child will love it. They need a mom or dad to make a few mistakes along the way. So why not invent a few as teachable moments for the kids?

Let's say your child receives a gift. After the age of 3, your child shouldn't be prompted to say thank you. If he doesn't say thank you on his own, when you get in the car, what could you do? Simply say, "Honey, I noticed you didn't say thank you to Mrs. So-and-so for the gift she gave you."

"Oh, Mommy, I forgot," the child is likely to say.

"Okay, thanks for letting me know. I'll hold on to this gift until you are able to thank Mrs. So-and-so with a note or a phone call."

What are you really doing in this situation? You're not coming down on your child, beating him into the ground for forgetting to say thank you and embarrassing you. Instead, you're teaching your child to do the right thing by delaying gratification (which goes against the grain of a child who usually wants to play with that toy right away) until the task is accomplished.

### Communicating/Not Wanting to Communicate

"How was school today?"
"Fine."
"How did your test go?"
(Grunt.)
"What did you do today?"
"Nothin'."
"Where have you been?"
(Shrug.)
"What did you do with your buddies tonight?"
"Nothin'."

Every parent has received the silent treatment. The "fine." The grunt. The "nothin'." The shrug. There's nothing more exasperating than trying to communicate and having the other end of the two-way conversation not cooperating.

How are you trying to communicate? By asking questions. It works in most conversations, right?

Wrong. Most questions we ask our kids really are nonproductive ("So, how was your day at school?"), and kids are smart enough to know it. When an adult asks questions, children know what answers the adult expects. And that makes them more determined not to answer.

*If you want a child to talk to you, don't ask questions.*

"But, Dr. Leman, how will I ever know anything about what's going on with my child if I don't ask questions?"

Put yourself in your child's shoes for a minute. If, as soon as you opened your mouth, your parent turned into Judge Judy and gave you an edict, put your ideas down, and put *you* down, would you want to open your mouth?

Why not switch the paradigm? If you want your children to talk to you about anything, don't ask questions. Instead, get quietly involved in their world. Talk about what they're interested in— even if it's not what you're interested in.

For example, if your child likes a certain rock group you're not crazy about, say, "I was thinking about that group the other day. I wonder if those guys in that band get along, if that guy with the far-out hairdo is as weird as he looks, and who the leader of the group is."

If you meet your children on their interest level, they'll be a lot more willing to talk. They'll feel less alienated from you if you show interest in entering their world. By meeting them on their interest level, you're saying, "I love you. I care about you. What interests you is of importance to me too."

If your child makes a comment you think is shocking or ridiculous, instead of saying, "That's the stupidest thing I ever heard," which is probably your first inclination, instead say, "That's interesting. Tell me more about that."

By not asking questions, you'll learn a lot more about your child and your child's world.

## Complaining

"He always goes into my room and messes it up."

"Do we *have* to take her to the mall with us? She's so embarrassing."

"She took my sweater without asking. And now she can't find it."

"I hate that teacher. She's so unfair."

A long time ago, when I was assistant dean of students at a university, two secretaries complained nonstop to me about each other. Finally, I got tired of it. The next time one secretary complained about the other, I walked her, arm in arm, to that secretary's desk. It nipped the complaining in the bud and took away all the angles. It forced those two women to handle their skirmishes themselves, instead of involving others.

Another time I received a call from a student's parents. They were very upset because their son had phoned them about something he felt wasn't fair. So I said thank you, then called the student into my office.

"How's school going?" I asked.

"Great."

"Your social life?"

"Fine."

"Your classes?"

"They're fine."

"Well, that's interesting, because the reason you're here in my office is that I got a call from your mom and dad."

The student shifted in his seat. "Oh, don't worry about that. I just wasn't in a good mood last night. . . ."

Do you think that student was likely to call his folks anymore to blow off steam, knowing he could end up in my office again?

Not likely. He was forced to own up to his words.

Kids will always complain—about their brother, sister, other parent, teacher. In fact, children *love* to whine and complain about someone else. What they don't like to do is to confront the other person. So if your child complains, guide him toward the source of the complaint.

> *If your child complains, guide him toward the source of the complaint.*

Let's say your son comes in and complains about his older brother. The responsible parent will say, "Listen, did you talk to your brother about that?" Chances are the child will say no. Then take him by the hand, lead him to his brother, and say, "Tell your brother how you feel."

When I was in high school, when students got into a skirmish, the administrator would give them boxing gloves, take them to the gym, say, "Let me know when you're through," and walk out the door. But I never heard of anyone actually fighting. A couple of times I got collared and was brought to the gym. I never fought with anyone.

There was no "You started it" or "No, you did." No one even bothered to point the finger of blame.

Such an action—putting two skirmishers together—will take the wind out of your child's sails . . . or, more like it, take the sails out of your child's wind.

Kids will blow about one thing or another. It's a given. But if you guide your child toward the source of his complaint, you'll often end the complaining quickly, without involving yourself any further.

## Curfew

"My daughter is 16 and starting to hang out with guys. What curfew should I set?"

"Ryan ignores every curfew we ever set and comes home whenever he feels like it. I sit home by the window and worry until he gets home. My husband just gets mad and raises the roof once Ryan does get home about how irresponsible he is. Nothing seems to work."

Some states and cities have curfews, but, frankly, curfews don't make a lot of sense. Sande and I have raised 5 children, and we have never pronounced a certain "magic hour" when the children had to be off the streets and home. Instead, we've always put the ball back in their court. As soon as a teen is driving, she had better be responsible; otherwise she shouldn't be driving. (By the way, driver's education is good for teens, and it also saves Mom and Dad money for insurance.)

*Don't set a curfew. Instead, say, "Be home at a reasonable hour."*

So when a child says, "Dad, what time do you want me to be home?" instead of giving a curfew—"You better be home by 10 p.m. or else"—say, "Be home at a reasonable hour." This makes your teen think through his decision and be accountable for the time he chooses to come home.

Give your child the benefit of a doubt until he proves you wrong. If you have a 16- or 17-year-old who comes home at 4 a.m., I'd say that would be the last time he could borrow the car. In such a situation, you would say, "Coming home at 4 a.m. shows me that you don't have good judgment. I'm not interested in lending my car, which I'm responsible for and is registered in my name and insured with my money, to someone who comes home at 4 a.m. Let's cool it with the driving for a while and revisit this in 3 months."

It may feel good to you as a parent to say these things, and it's wise for you to take this tactic, but it also costs you. As soon as you uphold this important standard, you've impinged on your own life. That 16-year-old can no longer drive himself places. That means Mom or Dad will have to drive him.

But guess what? Parenting *is* an inconvenience. There are no two ways around it. You love your children, but sometimes—be honest—they are a pain in the neck (and other places too).

When you allow a child a 1- to 3-month time-out on driving, you're sending a strong message about how lucky he was to be driving the family car—and what he'll need to be doing differently next time. It's a lesson not easily forgotten.

Children will misuse their freedom sometimes, but the important thing is to keep the ball in their court so they are growing in responsibility and toward a healthy adulthood.

So don't set a curfew. Instead, say, "Be home at a reasonable hour." Chances are, when you do so, your child will be home even earlier than you expect.

When our daughter Lauren went to a birthday party in eighth grade, I asked her when the party was over.

"There's no end time," she said, "just a start time. When do I need to be home?"

I threw the ball back into her court. "What do you think is reasonable?"

"Eleven o'clock," she said. Interestingly, she phoned right at 11:00 from a girlfriend's cell phone to say that she was on her way home. Did I tell her she had to? No. She did all that herself.

When Sande and I used this technique, our three older children—Holly, Krissy, and Kevin—came up with their own rules regarding the family car. Holly, our firstborn, was the one who started the rules. Sande and I had to laugh—her rules were stricter than ours would ever be!

Children need to know that driving is a privilege—not a right—as a family member. And coming home at a responsible hour without being told is an important part of the road to becoming a responsible adult.

## Defiance/Purposeful Disobedience

"He looked me straight in the eye and said, 'NO!' at the top of his lungs."

"I told her she couldn't go to a movie with her friends. She sneaked out her window and went anyway."

"He's always facing off with me when his father is out of town. He knows better than to do it when his father is home."

Defiance is a mountain—a very big mountain—if you don't conquer it. And the earlier you climb it in your child's life, the better.

Let's say your 3-year-old defiantly stomps his foot and says, "No!" What is he doing? He's challenging you to the nth degree. He has absolutely dug in, and he's not going to do what you've asked him to do. If spanking is compatible with your family values, this is indeed the time for a good swat on your kid's tail, combined with a stern look that says you mean business. This look needs to say, "This is what I expect you to do, and I expect you to do it now." With a younger child, consistency of expectation and follow-through wins the battle. And a period of isolation and think time about his actions is also effective in changing the defiant behavior.

> *What works best with defiance is— all of a sudden, without warning— giving the child vitamin N (No) at every turn.*

If your older child (age 10 and up) is purposefully defiant, then you have a much larger problem. You have a son or daughter you cannot trust.

What's the answer? What works best with defiance is—all of a sudden, without warning—giving the child vitamin N (No) at every turn.

Child: "We gotta go. It's time for basketball practice."
Parent: "No, you're not going. I'm not going to drive you."

Child: "Can I have 10 bucks?"
Parent: "No."

Child: "Can I go to Jack's house?"
Parent: "No."

Here's what's interesting and why this method works so well. These are always things you've let that child do in the past. Now, suddenly, you are not letting her do anything. Sooner or later (and usually sooner) the child wants to know why not. "What's the deal? You *always* let me do that."

How should you respond? Bamboozle the kid. "Why not?" you ask. "Why don't you spend a few minutes in your room thinking about why not? When you come to the conclusion about why you think I said it, I'd be happy to talk to you."

Then remove yourself from the proximity of the child so she doesn't have the opportunity to try to argue and raise your blood pressure.

Most children, when left to themselves, will come up with the reason and will say, "I'm sorry."

But that's when you have to stick to your guns without shooting yourself in the foot. An apology from the child doesn't change the fact that she goes nowhere for the day.

Now, tomorrow? That's a new day, and it should have a new chance.

But for the lesson to stick, the child needs to feel the consequences of defiant behavior. Sometimes it means you suffer too (not being able to go to an event you wanted to go to). However, letting a child do her activity that day, after saying I'm sorry, means she hasn't learned anything (other than to continue manipulating you). And neither have you.

### Disrupting in the Classroom

"Jake's the kind of kid who's always in trouble. He got caught shooting the librarian with a water pistol. Then he let out a mouse from biology into the girls' restroom, and all the girls ran out screaming. Every year Jake spends hours in the principal's office, and teachers groan the following year when they find out he's on their roster."

You know this kid. He seems to make it a goal to disrupt the classroom. He's the one who sets off smoke bombs in the garbage can under the teacher's desk. He's the one who gets out of his desk in the middle of class and starts crawling toward the door like a snake. He's the one with his hand always up, ready to contribute something witty to make the other children laugh. He's the one who simply can't sit still. He's the one that students roll their eyes at, but he always succeeds in being the entertainer.

*All that disruption is for one purpose only: to gain attention. So stop and give him attention.*

He's also the one who drives every teacher on the planet crazy. I know what kids like Jake need, because I used to be one of those disruptive kids. All that disruption is for one purpose only: to gain attention. So stop and give him attention.

"Leman, are you *crazy*?" you're saying. "If I give him attention, he'll only do it more. It'll encourage him."

Ah, but listen to the rest of the story. Jake's behavior didn't change until I suggested this strategy to the parents and teachers. (For those of you parents who are aghast at this one, remember that this book is titled *Have a New Kid by Friday*. We have a lot to accomplish in a short time frame, so drastic measures are needed sometimes.) Every time Jake acted disruptive, the teacher was to stop the class and acknowledge the behavior. "Class, I see today that Jake wants to entertain us. Go ahead, Jake, and do what you want to do, and we'll all watch." This acknowledgment would take all the fun and surprise out of the behavior. After Jake (now not quite so confident) did his little show, the teacher was then to say, "Class, thank you for watching Jake's little show. I hope you enjoyed it. And because we had to take time out to watch his show, we now need to finish math."

There may be a chorus of groans from the class. "But it's time for recess!" someone may say.

"Yes, it is," the teacher was to say. "And recess will be 10 minutes shorter because of Jake's display."

I assured them that peer pressure—having all the kids upset about a shorter recess—would then take over and finish the job.

And it did. Beautifully.

## Driving

"My daughter, who is a really responsible teen, started driving when she was 16. My son is turning 16 in a month, and all of his friends already have their licenses. But I'll be honest. It scares the pants off me to think of Evan driving a car. He's so spacey and can't keep track of anything. His dad is convinced he'll park somewhere and just 'lose' the car, not to mention go through a bunch of gas caps. But he'd be embarrassed if we said no to getting a license, especially since all his friends have one, not to mention his sister did at his age. What should we do?"

"I told her she couldn't take the car to the mall, but she did anyway. Did she think I wouldn't miss it or something? I'm trying to think of an appropriate punishment, but I'm so angry I can hardly think. Help!"

"We were stunned when our son Rick was escorted home by our hometown cop last night. He and three of his friends had been pulled over because the cop saw them cruising the highway and got suspicious. Rick claimed that even though the other kids had been drinking, he hadn't. The alcohol-level test proved him right, but still, he was the driver. He's 17, and his friends are still 16. How could he be so stupid? We are embarrassed beyond belief. If it were up to my husband, Rick wouldn't drive for the rest of his life."

My dad graduated from only the eighth grade, but he was a pretty smart guy. I was a real jerk as a kid, but believe me, I knew Dad's rules that governed the use of the family car. They were emblazoned in black-and-white.

1. You can't *ever* have more than one other kid in the car with you without my express permission.
2. You cannot leave the village and drive in the city without my permission.

The rules were so clear-cut, they were one of the few things I didn't test. I knew my dad would be as firm as cement about them.

Driving is a privilege, not a given. Some teens are ready to drive at 16; others, like Evan, should wait a little longer until their heads are firmly connected to their actions. And a teen who violates a parent's edict about driving the car isn't to be trusted. The keys should be taken away from her, and she shouldn't drive for a set period of time.

> *Driving is a privilege, not a given.*

Her privileges should be suspended for defiance and lack of responsibility.

Am I being too harsh? Think of it this way: if your child defies you on important things like driving a car, would it be smart to let him keep driving? If he defies you, he's saying, "You know, Mom (or Dad), you really don't matter. I don't care what you say. And

I don't respect you." Is that the kind of kid you want driving your $32,000 auto with liability insurance of $100,000?

Certainly not. This is the time for tough love. Give the teen a suspension of privileges and some think time. This is one behavior you need to deal with while the horse is still in the barn.

Should you take away his driving privileges for life? No, that would be impractical. Think about how complicated your life is, then add to it the time needed to drive your teen where he needs to go (such as an after-school job).

But driving is clearly an adult responsibility. If your child is not ready for such responsibility, he should not be driving. If any alcohol is involved (as in the case with Rick), there should be a much longer suspension period, since any facet of drinking and driving is indeed a serious one.

## Drugs and Alcohol

"I couldn't believe it when the principal called to say that he'd caught Seth and some other boys smoking marijuana after school. My son was smoking pot?"

"Anita's always been a good student. Then she entered junior high. Her grades started to drop—not just a little but a lot. Now she's staying out really late with friends, she's mouthy, and she doesn't get up until afternoons on the weekends. Then she still looks bleary-eyed. What happened to my good girl?"

The use and abuse of drugs and alcohol is nothing to mess around with. This is a mountain and a situation you have to address immediately. If your child has been a good or average student, and all of a sudden in seventh to tenth grade you see her grades drop off the table, welcome to the world of marijuana. Smoking pot will rob a kid of motivation quicker than anything else. A lot of kids smoke pot—even teens you would call "good kids." And here's the kicker: once a teen starts smoking pot, his body starts craving that high more and more.

The same thing is true with alcohol use. So many teens start drinking beer at parties to be "cool" and one of the group. Then their bodies and minds start requiring the "relax mode" that alcohol puts them in. As one girl put it, "When I drink, I can escape who I am and be someone else. I'm not uptight anymore. I'm the life of the party, and everyone likes me."

And that's exactly why teens use drugs and alcohol:

1. To escape who they are or their life situation (whether at home, school, or both).
2. To be popular—part of the "in crowd"—and well liked.

But such stimulants are only a quick fix, not the answer to a teen's unhappiness or insecurity. Even worse, drug and alcohol use becomes addicting. Just ask anyone in AA who has struggled for years to come out of addiction.

> *The use and abuse of drugs and alcohol is nothing to mess around with. This is a mountain and a situation you have to address immediately.*

If you find out (or even suspect) your child is drinking or using drugs, ask yourself these important questions:

1. *Where is my child getting the money for alcohol and drugs?* Perhaps he's getting it from you, through his allowance or the extra money he begs from you. If so, now's the time to cut off the supply, since it's only aiding his habit. For a while he may be able to bum money off his friends, but that won't last long.
2. *Do my children know if I smoke pot or do any other drugs?* If they do, they're going to see your use of drugs as the

green light that they can party with their friends, smoke pot, shoot up, snort this or that—whatever comes. By using drugs yourself, you're giving your child blind permission to do so too.

This kind of story happens in homes across America every day. It happened to Danelle, as her story shows:

"My dad had a Scotch every day when he came home from work, and then he had another one after dinner," Danelle told me. "So I grew up thinking that's just what you did when you were an adult. When I turned 11, I wanted to be just like my dad. Everybody seemed to like him because he was fun to be around . . . at least when he was around. So I started taking sips from his Scotch bottle when I got home from school. I'd sneak it from his den liquor cabinet while my mom was making dinner. I just filled it up a little with water so nobody would know I was doing it."

Danelle continued doing so until she became an alcoholic at age 13. It wasn't until she was 15, when she was caught with older friends at a bar, that her family even found out she drank. Her mother was shocked, her father was embarrassed (he was, after all, on the board of their church), and Danelle ended up needing to go to a rehab facility to dry out.

Even more, she discovered at the rehab center that she was pregnant. She didn't know who the father was because she'd had an encounter with him when she was drunk.

The baby was born premature with fetal alcohol syndrome. A doctor and his wife, who knew the complications that could result from drinking while pregnant, ended up adopting the baby and footing the medical bills. Danelle lost a year of high school due to complications with the pregnancy and her resulting depression. She began her junior year in a different high school so she could start fresh and make new friends.

Today Danelle is in her late twenties and works at a center for alcohol-addicted teens (some of whom are also pregnant). "I know where they've been, and I want to see them get to a good place too. I'm a totally different person now because my parents showed me tough love. But the biggest change of all was in my father. He had to own up to his own drinking problem and insecurities, and that has really changed our relationship. When I came home from rehab, he actually *cried* and told me he'd failed me, my mom, and my older brother. And then he hugged me—the first real hug I can remember. He cried too when my baby was adopted, but he told me he was proud of me for doing the right thing."

If you find out your child is using drugs or abusing alcohol, now is the time for tough love . . . to give your child a future. Get your child some counseling. Get her into a rehab program. Don't wait. Far too many teens have overdosed or killed themselves and others by drunk driving. Your child's life is too precious to take chances.

## Earrings

"My daughter is 8 and is dying to get her ears pierced. But I don't think she's quite ready for them . . . the pain or the responsibility."

"My son showed up at the dinner table with a surprise—he got his ear pierced. His mom just about dropped the mashed potatoes when she saw it. He and his buddies did it together on a dare at the mall."

Whether or not to allow your child to have pierced ears is an area where you as a parent simply need good judgment. Would you want your 9-year-old son to have an earring? Probably not. But if my son at age 15 or 16 wanted to have an earring, I guess I'd let him. It would be a molehill in life. Of course, I'd want to talk to my son about it first, since usually the reason children or teens want to get their ears pierced is because all their friends are doing it.

"But do you really want to be like everyone else?" is a good question to ask.

Frankly, I don't, because when I look at "everyone else," I don't always like what I see. Once I went to a basketball game where everyone wore red. You know what I wore? A white T-shirt. I've done major presentations at black-tie events and fund-raisers—and I wore a Hawaiian shirt. Imagine—the only person in the place without a black tie, and I'm the speaker!

> *Whether or not to allow your child to have pierced ears is an area where you as a parent simply need good judgment.*

When our teenage son, Kevin, was talking about getting an earring, I decided to see just how serious he was. So I raided my wife's earring collection and showed up with an earring at the dinner table. Kevin's desire for an earring ended very quickly when I declared that I was also going to enjoy wearing one.

It all comes down to this: are you going to major on molehills or save your big guns for the mountains? If your teenage son is going for a job interview at a more conservative workplace and discovers that he won't get the job because he has an earring, that earring you hate may just disappear for the next job interview (ditto for your daughter who has decided she has to have 3 piercings in both ears).

### Eating (in High Chairs and at Restaurants)

I just returned from having lunch with my 3-year-old grandson, Conner, and my 18-month-old granddaughter, Adeline. Let me just say up front that it's nearly impossible to enjoy a lunch or get a word in edgewise when you take 2 toddlers out to a restaurant. As my daughter Krissy told me, "Dad, you did your good deed for the week."

"I enjoyed this so much," I told her, "that I'll have to do it again . . . *in a year.*"

And we both laughed.

Since I have 5 children and now have grandchildren, I identify with moms in the throes of caring for little ones. When you're a mom, your goal is sometimes simply to get through the day. Asking young children to sit for a period of time—or to sit at all—is a pretty tall task (especially for certain personality types). Every mom needs to know where her child's threshold for sitting is. Pushing it past those boundaries (i.e., doing an hour lunch with girlfriends at a restaurant) is most likely asking for trouble. Getting takeout and going to a park where your children can run is probably a better option. And your girlfriends will thank you.

> *Asking young children to sit for a period of time—or to sit at all—is a pretty tall task.*

Young children especially take a very short time to eat (unless it's turned into a battle and their battle plan is to keep Mom or Dad's attention by dawdling). When they're done, they're done. So if you don't quickly read the message "Hey, I'm done with all this" in your child's eyes, he will do two very natural things:

1. Quickly swipe all his remaining food onto the floor. (Watching it fall and splatter is such entertainment. So is watching Mom or Dad come running! It doesn't matter whether it's at home or in a restaurant. Your toddler isn't embarrassed at all by such behavior. He thinks it's fun.)
2. Remove the tray to the best of his ability and begin to climb out of his high chair.

So what can you do? First of all, realize that children are naturally noisy. Those long dinners where you chatted about the future, held each other's hands, and gazed into each other's eyes are over (except for your date nights). Life has changed.

Second, doing what comes naturally isn't "naughty" to a child. *Hey,* the 12-month-old thinks, *when I throw my Cheerios off my high chair, Mom comes running. Let's see how many times she'll do that.*

Third, we ask too much of children, depending on their age, when we make them sit for long periods in chairs or high chairs. So many parents end up sticking their young children in high chairs and feeding them snacks before dinner, just so they can get dinner on the table for everyone else. That doesn't work. By the time you have dinner made, those toddlers are too full of snacks to eat a real dinner and too itchy to sit any longer in that uncomfortable high chair.

So what's the answer? Feed your children, as much as possible, when you eat, or at least the same food that you eat (even if mushed up and served in installments as you cook it). Also, teach your child something very important: once they get down from that high chair, the meal is over. That means no coming back to the table for another bite. The same holds true for home as for a restaurant.

If you teach your young children this, they will sit for as long as they are hungry and then disappear from the dinner table, leaving you to get a word in edgewise with your spouse or other children.

Of course, this works very well at home, where your child has toys to play with, but is more difficult at a restaurant. That's why, when the children are small, for a while you may want to come up with more creative options than the typical restaurant outing. You'll be happier, your child will be happier, and the patrons of the restaurant you didn't go to will thank you.

## Fears/Fearfulness

It happens in every home, including yours. You sigh with relief after getting the kids in bed . . . but 5 minutes later you see big, expressive eyes peering at you from around the corner. It's your youngest child.

"What are you doing up?" you ask in your sternest voice.

"I'm afraid of the dark," the little voice quivers.

But what's really going on?

Remember, kids are unionized. And if you have more than one child, your children have sent the youngest as an advance scout—as the scapegoat. I know all about that because when I was young, my older brother and sister used to con me into going back out to the living room after we were supposed to be in bed. I was the guinea pig . . . or the sacrifice, whichever way you want to look at it. If they wanted Wheaties cereal for a snack, they'd send me. Why send the youngest out to do the dirty work? As far as siblings are concerned, if he gets killed, who cares? They don't like him anyway.

The truth is, research shows that the child less likely to be punished is the baby of the family. He gets away with murder with Mom and Dad. Your children instinctively know this. They're smart. So the 11-year-old and the 9-year-old tell the 4-year-old to go out there. And the 4-year-old's dumb enough to do it. Once the 4-year-old is out there and successfully negotiating a deal with you, two more shadows will appear in the hallway.

"What are you two doing out of bed?" you bark.

"Corey's out of bed," they say.

And before long you have a nighttime party going on when it's your rest time.

Go back to the purposive nature of the fear. What's really going on with the fear of the dark, things that go bump in the night, and monsters under the bed?

*What's really going on with the fear of the dark, things that go bump in the night, and monsters under the bed? Your child wants you to come into that room.*

Your child wants you to come into that room. He wants your presence. And that fear gives him a reason to cry, scream, and demand your presence with him. So what can you do?

You can go into that room and reassure the child there are no monsters in the house. But as soon as you step into that room, your battle is lost. So try this: at bedtime, put any kind of squirt bottle next to your child's bed. Put water and a bit of food dye in it and say, "Honey, are you in luck! Tonight I've got dragon repellent right here! One squirt, and all the monsters are gone from the area."

The idea is to teach the child how to control his fears.

I remember that as a child when I closed my eyes, I could see little colored dots. I used to call them bugs, and I used to tell my mom and dad, "I see bugs! I see bugs!" and they'd come into the room, night after night, and calm me down. But what was the purposive nature of my behavior? To get to see Mom and Dad just one more time before I went to sleep.

If you're aware of this, you'll come up with creative solutions like the squirt bottle *before* your child is tucked in bed.

## Fighting in the Car

"I told you to stop that . . . *right now!*"

"If you don't stop poking your brother, I'll . . ."

"Just wait until we get home. . . ."

Then there's the parental arm flailing from the driver's or passenger's seat into the backseat. . . .

Why is it that children fight most often in the car? It's because they're in a contained space, and they're jockeying for position to see who is most dominant among the herd—and even to see how they can dominate *you*. It's fascinating how children who are powerful kids select their areas to try to dominate you. Usually it's places where you're a fish in a barrel (like driving a car) and there's no hope of escape.

So what do you do? When siblings are going after each other in the back of the car and you're driving, it can really distract you. Yelling at them and looking in the mirror can distract you even more. Threatening them accomplishes no purpose. They know:

1. You don't mean it.
2. You won't carry it out. Many parents say, "If you don't settle down, we won't get this or go there." But usually those are just idle threats. With a history of those kinds of threats and warnings, no child will pay attention to what you say.
3. You can't reach them (other than the ridiculous flailing arm that only makes you angrier).

So try this first: turn up the music on the rear speakers. Part of their fun is knowing you're overhearing the skirmish. They're waiting for you to step in and settle it. That's part of their unionized plan.

If turning up the music doesn't work and they continue to bicker, calmly pull over the car and stop. Get out of the car, stretch a little, check your tires, open your trunk. If you are going somewhere your children want to be, and they end up getting there late, all the better. Take your time outside that car.

> *Calmly pull over the car and stop. Get out of the car, stretch a little, check your tires, open your trunk.*

When you get back in the car, say something like, "Is it safe for Mom to drive now?"

Try this once and it's usually enough to stop the bickering. If you've been a paper tiger parent up to this point, though, they may need another dose.

And guess what? Your heart rate hasn't gone up either. You've used the principle of "B doesn't happen until A is completed."

Those children are not arriving at their destination until their bickering is dealt with.

### Forgetfulness

"But I just forgot!"

Kids will forget. Everyone does. They'll forget to do homework; they'll forget to bring their clarinet home from school. But don't accept excuses. It only makes the weak weaker.

> *Don't accept excuses. It only makes the weak weaker.*

If 12-year-old Janie forgets her clarinet, the best thing to do is tell her, "Honey, go back to school and get your clarinet. You need it." If you live in a small town or a safe neighborhood and she has to walk half a mile back to school, so be it. If not, you may have to drive her back to school to get it. The point is, don't let forgetting be an excuse for not getting the job done. Your child needs to learn to be accountable for doing what she says she'll do. Don't reward forgetfulness.

Forgetfulness is not an excuse. The only people who gain from it are credit card companies. They make an easy fortune when you're late with a payment because you forget. They just add a $39 (or more) late fee on your credit card and rack up the percentages.

### Going on Overnights

It's so tempting to allow your child to grow up quickly. And that includes overnights. But overnights should be rare, especially when your children are young. Children need to be home, and today's kids are home less and less. It's part and parcel of being a child today, it seems, that by age 3 you have to be in gymnastics, and by 5 you're playing soccer, in swim club, in ballet, etc. That means your children have greater exposure to a wider number of people than ever before.

How well do you really know the family that your child would be staying with? There's a difference between having your 3-year-old at Grandma and Grandpa's for the night (but then, many 3-year-olds aren't even ready for that, since they would miss Mommy too much) and letting your 7-year-old stay at his Little League friend's house overnight. Do you know, for sure, that there is no pedophile in that home? I know that's blunt, but that's our world today. The stakes are very high. And here's the kicker: if a child is sexually abused, the highest probability is that the abuser will be a family member.

> *Today's parents can't afford not to be watchful of their children.*

That means today's parents can't afford *not* to be watchful of their children. So questions you should ask as you consider an overnight are:

1. Has your child been away from home before? If not, will this be a good first experience in a safe environment?
2. Will your child miss Mommy?
3. Is your child a bed-wetter?
4. How well do you know the people your child would be staying with?

For all of these reasons, overnights were very rare in the Leman home. We allowed our daughter Lauren to have a few friends over when she was in junior high. But then we made it a strict policy that Sande drove the girls home (not me, as a guy).

When you send your child on an overnight, you are saying you trust the people in that home with your child's life. Do you know them that well?

### Grocery Store Antics

"But I want it . . . and I want it *now*!"
(the whine)

"Let me out . . . let me out . . ."
(said while wiggling in the cart)

If you have a young child, you would be wise to remember that 3- to 4-year-olds have short attention spans. So if you really want to shop, pick a time when you don't have your children with you. I know one mom who shops at 2 a.m., when her husband gets home from his night shift, just to do it in peace and quiet since she has 4-year-old twins.

> Do not *let your young children make the calls on what you're going to buy.*

If you do have to shop with your children, minimize your list to the essentials. Let your 2-year-old hold something. Make your child part of the experience. "Oh, honey, can you grab a loaf of bread off the shelf for me?" you can say as the cart rolls by the bread. Who cares if the bread gets a little squished? It'll taste the same, and you're involving your child.

But *do not* let your young children make the calls on what you're going to buy. If you do, you'll end up with a cartful of junk, and you'll be setting a pattern for future grocery trips. Remember, children are all about routine, so if you set a pattern, they will insist that it be followed from here to eternity. For example, if every time you go to the grocery store, your child gets a free donut, your child will be like Matlock—she's not going to forget that free donut. So if you pass by that donut counter without getting a donut, prepare yourself for an unhappy time for both of you.

Before you set foot in that grocery store, decide on your expectations for the trip. Make a list of the groceries you need. Decide what you're going to buy and if the children will get a treat or not. (If you set up the treat habit, you might as well buy stock in the Mars company. You'll be stuck buying treats for life!) Tell the child up front what is going to happen—then stick with it. Don't let any pleading, whining, or crying divert you from your plan. If your child fusses, simply remove the child from the store. Immediately. Even if that means leaving your grocery cart, full of groceries, in the store. Remember, B doesn't happen until A is completed. If your goal was to get the grocery shopping done and your child isn't being helpful, even if you promised your child a treat, that treat cannot happen. Otherwise you've put your child in the driver's seat—and don't think he won't want to occupy that spot again.

### Helplessness

"I can't do it, Mommy."

When I was a 5-year-old, I believed that my sandwich tasted better when Mom made it. As God is my judge, I really did believe that. But, looking back now, I realize something else: that I was a manipulative sucker who wanted her to make the sandwich instead of doing it myself. After all, I was the baby of the family and was used to others doing things for me without me lifting a finger.

> *Don't do for children what they can do for themselves.*

Acting helpless is a skillful, manipulative technique, and young children (especially the baby of the family) are very good at it. Many times I set my older brother up for all kinds of grief from my dad because I knew what to say, how to say it, and how to get him in trouble with my dad for not helping me with things just because I was younger and smaller.

The general rule of thumb is simple: don't do for children what they can do for themselves. Young children are capable of making their own sandwiches, even if it means a little extra mess on the counter that they have to clean up. If your child is supposed to phone someone and knows how to use the telephone (or can do it with some simple coaching), there's no reason you need to make that phone call for the child.

Do we do things for our children? Yes, all day long. It's part of being a parent. But the smart parent knows when she is getting worked over by the 4-year-old, 10-year-old, or 16-year-old who just doesn't want to take responsibility.

It's easier to let children not be responsible. It's easier, as a parent, to do it yourself. But did you know that even allowing a child to make a simple peanut butter and jelly sandwich can be an accomplishment she can feel good about?

You are not only a parent; you are your children's teacher. So teach them to be responsible. Do not pick up balls that they have dropped or should be responsible for.

### Hitting

"But she hit me first!"

"He started it!"

Most siblings will think nothing of whacking a brother or sister in the midst of a skirmish. They won't bat an eye or feel bad about it.

Parents spend a significant amount of time sorting out who started it. But consider this: fighting is an act of cooperation. It's not about who threw the first punch. That means instead of you trying to sort out who said or did what, both children involved need to be removed from the scene and taken to a room with the door closed, where just the two of them stare at each other until the problem is worked out.

The amazing thing is that this works with any age, whether 3 or 15. Now, 3-year-olds usually can't work out their problems, but they can have a time-out. Not being where Mommy is and knowing that Mommy is unhappy is bad enough in itself. Did you know that even a minute's time-out can seem like an eternity to a 3-year-old?

I had to laugh (inwardly) the other day when my daughter Krissy sent little Conner to his room for a time-out. He marched up there like a little soldier and sat quietly in his room. After that "eternity" (only 3 minutes) of being separated from his mom, Krissy called up, "Conner, are you ready to come down?" And he said in a very chastened voice, "Yes, Mom."

> *Fighting is an act of cooperation. It's not about who threw the first punch.*

The point is that when the child comes down, he needs to be ready to join the family again. That means treating his little sister with respect even when he doesn't feel like it.

When two children hit each other or fight at the breakfast table, remove both of them from the table, put them in a room together, and close the door. There's a bonus for you: when they come out with their problems solved, breakfast is over. They go hungry until lunch, and the snack counter is not open. Will going hungry for a few hours kill them? No, although they may eat more than normal at lunch. But it will drive the point home that you don't appreciate and won't stand for bickering at the table.

Under no circumstances should you ever allow a child to hit you. I watched once as a 6-year-old smacked her pregnant mom right in the stomach, and her mother only said, "Oh, you're just mad. You don't mean that!"

Many parents think that children—especially young children—don't know what they're doing when they hit you. That's debatable. But whether or not it's true, you cannot allow such behavior to continue. If your 11-month-old hits you in the face, hold her arms down firmly and encircle her arms with yours so she can't hit you again. Reinforce your action with kind but firm words. Softly say to her, "Don't hit. Mommy doesn't like being hit." Draw a line as early as possible in your relationship that hitting is not acceptable. And most of all, never hit back. (Spanking deliberately to change a child's actions, for those of you who are comfortable with that, is a very different action than hitting back as an unthinking response. See "Spanking.")

If you want a perfect child, go find a mannequin. Children don't come in mannequin style. Parenting is all about the relationship you have—one that's built upon love, mutual respect, and cooperation. Allowing your home to be a hit-free zone and addressing hitting when it does happen is crucial in establishing a safe environment.

## Homeschooling

If you're a homeschooler, you may have read the homework section and already be bristling at the thought that someone else would be a better teacher than you. If you're a homeschooler, I applaud you. Most homeschoolers I know are very dedicated and passionate people. It takes a certain type of personality for a parent to be able to homeschool effectively (and also a certain personality of the child).

When Sande and I were in the throes of raising our 5 children, we discussed schooling options. Our "discussion" went something like this.

"What about homeschooling?" I asked.

"What?" Sande said.

That was the end of the discussion.

When you're a homeschooler, you *are* the teacher. But that doesn't mean you should be "on" as teacher 24-7. You have additional challenges because you are both parent and teacher and the classroom is your home. Often you are so close to the situation that it's more difficult to come up with consequences for children not following through on assignments, not getting to the table on time for school, etc. Effective homeschoolers keep to a strict schedule (say 9 to noon for a school day). They have a room of their home set aside for school. The door is open right before school is to start in the morning and closed after school is over. There's no dawdling over breakfast or snack time to delay the start of the school day. If a child shows up late for breakfast and thus is late for school, there's a penalty (such as working longer when siblings are outside playing). The most important thing for a parent is to have an end to the school day. After all, don't teachers in other schools stop working and go home for the day? When your classroom is your home, you can't leave the building physically. But you can leave the classroom mentally and emotionally.

*These simple rules will help both you and your children have a good homeschooling experience.*

It's also important to keep the ball for homework in your child's court. When you're done with school for the day, you're done. Again, if the homework is assigned to the child, who should be doing it? Not you. So don't involve yourself. (Would you phone a teacher from a public or private school for help with homework at night? Then don't make yourself available either.)

If you are butting heads with your son regarding getting homework done, ask another homeschooling parent to work with your child, and do the same for that parent's child. Swapping tutorial skills is a wonderful option for homeschoolers. If one of your children needs extra time to complete a project, walk away and give that child extra time. Let the other siblings play, and take off your schoolteacher hat and put on your mom hat for the rest of the evening. Don't put on your schoolteacher hat until the next morning, when it's time for school.

These simple rules will help both you and your children have a good homeschooling experience.

## Homework

Homework is one of those necessary evils of growing up. If you are a parent, you will, in some way, be involved in homework (whether you choose public school, private school, or home-schooling). The best thing you can do for your children is to provide a quiet, well-lit, consistent place that they can do their homework.

Here's the problem. If you've got kids who are manipulative, they can con you into doing their homework for them. They can con you into setting up your home as a schoolhouse (though it's more like a battle zone with all the emotions flying) for 4 to 5 hours a night. But the reality is that your child's homework is your child's homework. Not yours. There's nothing wrong with checking it to make sure your child has done it and helping by asking questions when a child gets stuck, but no way should you do your child's work for her. In many school systems, you can phone the school, punch in a teacher's code, and get the homework assignment so you know what needs to be done. I have raised 5 children and have never done that. In our home, our children knew we expected them to do well in school—to do their best.

*Your child's homework is your child's homework. Not yours.*

One of the rules in our house is that the computer has to be in one of our central rooms, not any bedroom. So many nights our youngest daughter, Lauren, sits in the same room as me (I'm in my favorite chair) and does her homework by aid of the computer. We're five feet from each other, but I rarely ask the question, "What are you doing?" Sometimes I see her doing math and struggling with it, but I don't intervene. If she asks me for help, I'm glad to help her for a few minutes, but I won't battle homework for hours a night.

Parents shouldn't become the fourth grader or the seventh grader. They've already been there. If a child is struggling in a subject, the best thing to do is to see if the teacher can give her some extra help or to hire a tutor. We've done that with our children on a couple of occasions—once we had a university student help, and another time a high school senior helped.

Do not allow your child to manipulate you into becoming the student and doing what should be her responsibility. (For those of you who are homeschoolers, see also "Homeschooling.")

## Hyperactivity/ADD/ADHD

"Would you just sit still? What's wrong with you?"

People today love disorders and labels. When I speak and later someone comes up to me and says, "I'm an ACA [Adult Child of an Alcoholic]," I'm tempted to say, "I'm into pork bellies, at least in the short term."

What's all the talk about labels for anyway?

"My child has OCD—obsessive-compulsive disorder."

"I think my son's ADD or ADHD."

These days, if children meet any of the qualifications for the 10 symptoms of ADD, the child is labeled—and medicated. It's seemingly an easy fix. But what does that really do for the child in the long run?

What's the purposive nature of giving your child a label? I'm convinced it's not in the child's best interest, nor is it in yours as a parent. Frankly, labeling your child gets him off the hook for his behavior, and it also gives you a convenient excuse for the way your child acts, so you don't have to do anything about it other than agree to medicate your child: "She's not doing well at school because she's ADD, and the teachers don't understand her." Or, "He can't help it. It's just the way he is."

But in nearly four decades of counseling, I've discovered that often the behaviors that are labeled stem from something else entirely. What happens in many families? After countless infertility tests that cost a fortune, 9 months of a difficult pregnancy, the throes of birth, or myriad adoption forms, the baby at last arrives. A few months later the child is sent to the kiddy kennel, where minimum-wage strangers spend their time rearing the child while Mom returns to work. Then, when the child is home, she spends her time vying for her parents' attentions among not only siblings but also her parents' long work hours and subsequent exhaustion.

> *I'm convinced that what children need is not labels but one-on-one attention from Mom and Dad.*

I'm convinced that what children need is not labels but one-on-one attention from Mom and Dad. If a child doesn't receive the attention she needs, she will act out (find ways to get that attention), whether in positive or negative ways.

If you have concerns about your child, don't take a nonprofessional's word for it. Far too many children have been misdiagnosed. Go to a pediatrician who is behaviorally trained or find a true expert in the field. I've been a psychologist for four decades and have never given a diagnosis of ADD or ADHD. Without multiple testing by an expert in that field, I would never hang a label on a child. Instead, I ask the parent, "What do you want your child to be like?" and then I help that parent get the child there. I also gently correct misconceptions parents may have about their children. For example, if your child has an IQ of 85, she won't be a rocket scientist. But she is most likely gifted in other areas that you can encourage.

If you want a responsible child, give him age-appropriate responsibility. If you want a respectful child, show her respect. If you want a kind child, model kindness. If you want a mouthy child, be mouthy.

You see, power doesn't come from thin air; it's modeled. If there's something about your child you don't like, they've probably seen it in action from you and are simply modeling it.

So before you put a label on your child or accept a label about your child from anyone else, why not work on the behaviors you want to see changed?

### Ignoring Parents

"She acts like I'm not even there."

"I have to walk 5 steps behind her, like I don't even exist."

"He never listens to anything I say."

What's going on here? What's the purposive nature of the behavior? Ignoring you is actually a way of getting your attention! *He's ignoring me,* you think. *Something must be wrong.* So you start doing loops around your child, trying to break through to him, trying to get him to talk. And he remains silent. Why? It's a power struggle—to see who is dominant in the home and to see how far you'll go to make him happy.

> *It's a power struggle—to see who is dominant in the home and to see how far you'll go to make him happy.*

If this is happening, the "B doesn't happen unless A is completed" principle works very nicely. If your child is ignoring you, you don't have to take her to a friend's house, do you? If your teenage son is ignoring you and goes to find the car keys in their usual spot, those keys could be "missing"—in your pocket. If your child is ignoring you, there could be one less spot at the dinner table. If you don't exist in his world, why should you cook or provide dinner for him?

Remember, an unhappy child is a healthy child. Your job as a parent is not to make your child happy. It's to raise a child who will be a productive, responsible, and respectful member of society.

The key to the turnaround is your own behavior—your consistency, your follow-through, and your calm, reasonable manner. If you get angry and say, "What's your problem?" your powerful child wins.

## Internet Use

Let's face it. We live in a high-tech world, and a lot of us parents are anything but high-tech. However, computers and the Internet are a fact of life, and every child growing up today will be miles ahead of their parents in computer skills. My children certainly are!

> *Protect your children from Internet dangers. This is a mountain you can't afford not to face.*

That means you'll never be able to keep up with them, but you also need to be savvy about what your children are using the computer for. The Internet is a wonderful source of information for school projects. But it can also be a tremendous danger.

Would you ever let your 13-year-old walk into a strip club or a porn shop? Would you let your 16-year-old take the car and go to the sleaziest part of town to check out the prostitutes? Would you let your 11-year-old hang out with pedophiles? Of course not! But on the Internet, with one click of the mouse, your 13-year-old son can see the worst of the worst photos—and more. Your 11-year-old daughter can email a pedophile writing her under the guise of a 13-year-old boy who is interested in her life. That means right now your child could be seeing some of the most bizarre, perverted material you could possibly view. In fact, www.max.com reports:

> There are 3 facts every parent should know:
>
> - 90 percent of children ages 11 to 17 will be accidentally exposed to pornography on the Internet (without MaxProtect).
> - Children ages 12 to 17 are the single largest group of consumers of Internet pornography.
> - One million predators/pedophiles are stalking our children and teens on the Internet.[5]

If you don't know anything about computers or know just the bare minimum, this is a mountain you have to pay attention to. Go take some computer lessons (or ask your kids to give you some). Find the history button on your computer and use it. Find out what your children are looking at, what sites they've visited.

Move your computer to a central location of the house. Computers should never be in a child's bedroom. They should be in a heavily traveled area where you and others are constantly walking by and can view what's on the screen.

Because of the dangers of the Internet and the fact that children can inadvertently click on a search word and get directly into a porn site, I suggest that you install a safety card that prohibits downloading objectionable material. For further tips, go to www.protectkids.com.

As a parent, your job is to protect your child from danger, and the biggest danger is sitting right in your home. Computers are not going to go away, so it's your job to find ways for your child to use the computer safely. But it takes *your involvement.*

Every child is curious. And it's not just "bad kids" who come across pornography on the Internet and then get hooked. Dan was a straight-A student who had a lot of friends. He loved to play the guitar and was always the child who helped his mother bring in the groceries from the car without being asked. But when his father accessed the history button on their computer, he found out that for the last 6 months, his 14-year-old son had regularly been accessing a porn site. When confronted with the knowledge, Dan said, "I was Googling something else and clicked on it. At first I was shocked, then I was curious. I wanted to go back and see more, even though I knew it was wrong. I just wanted to see what girls looked like." Those wise parents, after they got over their own shock, assigned their son a project—to research and write an 8-page paper about pornography, including how it affects the viewer and how it views women. They also moved the computer to a central desk in their kitchen.

B didn't happen until A was completed either. That meant that before Dan went out with friends, before he even could IM his friends again, the paper had to be completed, turned in to his parents, and approved.

Dan is now in college and says he hates that he ever viewed those images. They still linger in his mind.

Parents, protect your children from Internet dangers. This is a mountain you can't afford not to face.

## Interruptions

Children want your attention, and they want it most desperately when you're on the telephone. You know the drill well. You escape to some far corner of the house to call a friend, and within 25.5 seconds, a child is on your tail and absolutely has to have something at that very moment. So what do you say? "Just a minute!" And you go on talking.

In another 5.5 seconds, there's another tug on your arm and a plea for attention. "Just a minute!" you say again.

Within a few more seconds, you have a whiner or a screamer on your hands.

This behavior is not only annoying, it's a mountain. It may not seem like a mountain, compared to other issues you're facing that bother you more, but it is. Why? Because it's all about respect. If a child continually interrupts you (whether you are working, are on the telephone, or have guests over for dinner), he is not respecting you.

> *If a child continually interrupts you, he is not respecting you.*

Sure, there are times when your kids do need your attention (like when you leave something on the stove and they smell it burning), but many times their interruptions are merely that—interruptions. It's another way to control you, to be boss of the home. You deserve some uninterrupted times—to complete work, talk with girlfriends on the phone, etc.

So what can you do to get your point across, other than yelling (which doesn't get your point across anyway)? As soon as your kids start their dog and pony show, continue talking on the phone, but remove your children from the situation and isolate them (perhaps in their room or even outside the kitchen door). With young children, doing this for a couple minutes will seem like a lifetime. For older children, it can be a longer period of time.

Then after you're off the phone, talk to your children about how their interruption made you feel. "It's important to me to talk to Sandy. She's my friend and I enjoy talking to her. You like talking to your friends too, don't you? When you interrupt me when I'm on the phone, I don't appreciate it. I take it personally. By interrupting me, you're saying you don't care about me, what interests me, or my friends."

In other words, take action, and follow that action with an explanation. But do not interrupt what you're doing.

I got an email from a mom who heard me talk about this in a seminar. She tried it on a beautiful summer day after she returned home, when her children interrupted her as she talked on the phone with her girlfriend. She simply continued talking and ushered them outside the kitchen door into the backyard and locked the door. Forty-five minutes later she said to her girlfriend, "Oh, my goodness! I forgot something—the kids are still outside!" (See "Telephone Courtesy" for the rest of the story.)

Do you think those children forgot that lesson? After that, when their mom was on the phone and they felt they needed something, they merely shrugged and walked away. Most of the time what they needed was something they could get themselves—and they learned to be more independent.

You deserve the freedom to talk on the phone without interruptions. That's your time, and it's all part of the respect issue. Don't let it go unaddressed.

### Irresponsibility with Car, Driving

Driving is a privilege, not a given, in my book. A child's first responsibilities are to home, school, sports practice, music lessons, etc. Driving follows those in importance, but it can become the singular focus in a child's mind once she turns 15.

In order to be able to take out the family car or have a car of her own, a child needs to show a tremendous level of responsibility. Also, it's smart for the child to have taken driver's education classes (it also saves you in insurance money). Some very smart parents I know have rules if the child wants to drive the family car after she turns 16:

1. No more than one friend in the car with you.
2. No talking on the phone or text messaging.
3. No alcohol *ever* in the car.

4. Be home at a reasonable hour.

5. You pay half the insurance every six months.

Do you think their daughter, now 18, is respectful of her parents and careful with the family vehicle?

Just because your child turns 16 doesn't mean he's ready to drive. Driving requires focus, seriousness, and discipline. If your child is irresponsible, why would you want him driving your $32,000 vehicle? And why would you want him to take his life and the lives of his friends and other drivers into his hands? Driving is a mountain, a very serious mountain.

*Just because your child turns 16 doesn't mean he's ready to drive.*

If your child isn't responsible enough to drive, he shouldn't get the keys to the family car. Or if he does, then you or another responsible adult need to go with him as he drives. Is this an inconvenience, since you hoped to be free of all the running to activities when your child turned 16? Of course it is. But so is the majority of parenting. However, the flip side is far costlier.

Recently in western New York, 5 girls who were on the cheerleading squad—popular kids in school, good students who had just graduated from high school and were college bound—were in a tragic, head-on collision. The investigators discovered that, seconds before the crash, the driver had received a text message and that she'd been texting along the way as she drove. When she tried to pass a car, she smashed head on into a semi.

Now, I ask you: is it worth having certain rules that your children must follow for driving the family car? If your child doesn't follow those rules and acts irresponsibly, is it really so bad that she will have to take a 1-month or 3-month time-out on driving? The alternative could be so much worse, as the parents of those 5 girls have discovered.

Taking away the car keys will gain you a temporary earful but will save your child—and others on the road—from tremendous danger.

## Isolating Oneself (in His or Her Room)

"Since Andrea turned 13, I never see her anymore. She comes home from school and goes straight to her room. She spends her time on the phone, text messaging, and changing clothes. It's like she's not even a member of the family anymore."

Let me clarify something from the beginning. It is very *normal* for teens to come home from school, go to their room, and close the door for a while. Talking to friends on the phone, text messaging, etc., is very important to teenagers. And spending time alone helps them process all the changing hormones and resulting emotions.

What I'm talking about is the child who spends *all* of her time in her bedroom. Knowing when the child is spending too much time in her room is a parent's judgment call. Only you know, from your child's behavior, when she simply needs time alone and when she is literally walling herself off from the rest of the family. Some kids become recluses in their own home.

> *You need to ask yourself,* What am I doing to contribute to my child's behavior?

If this is happening in your home, the first place to start is by evaluating your own behavior. When a child separates herself from her family by isolating herself in her bedroom, here's what she's really saying: *I don't like being around you. Every time I open my mouth, you correct me and judge me. Every time I wear something, you look at me funny. You don't like my hair, my clothes, or my music. I'm done with you.*

When a kid is ragged on all the time and told how to do life and when to do it by a hovering parent, that kid will always duck out and head toward her room to escape it. Who can blame her? Would *you* want to be ragged on all the time?

So you need to ask yourself, *What am I doing to contribute to my child's behavior?* If all you do is pry and ask questions, stop! The best way to shut children down is by asking questions. Instead, listen to your children. If your daughter mentions something that happened at school, simply say, "Tell me more about that. That must have been fun/hard." Leave the door open for dialogue, but don't push. When you stop pushing, you'll be amazed what you begin to hear from your child.

At the heart of this behavior is a child's need for acceptance. When your child talks to friends, those friends accept the hairstyle you think is goofy (they think it's cool or at least don't rag him about it), her too-tight shirt, and his baggy pants. When you look at the long term, those things are not mountains, they're mole-hills. (Think about the stupid things you wore in eighth grade. Enough said?)

Your child needs to know you accept and love him unconditionally. That is the foundation for a lifetime of communication.

## Know-it-all Attitude

Children know it all. They're born with knowing it all, and you can't tell them any different.

"The show starts at 6," you say.

"No, it doesn't," your daughter argues. "It starts at 8."

"The program says 6," you say.

And on the debate rages.

You can't tell a know-it-all anything. So why not let reality do the teaching? If you know something starts at 6:00 and your child insists it's at 8:00, follow her

*Reality can be a very wonderful teacher.*

lead. Show up at 8:00, when it's all over, and let your child experience the reality of misinformation. Sure, you attended an event you knew wouldn't be there. But you also let your child experience a very important lesson: maybe, just maybe, she's not always right!

Often we do too much thinking for our kids. We do too many things for them. We're too good as parents. We try to protect them from themselves. But sometimes they need to experience the consequences of their decisions. They need to lose out on something they wanted to do.

Reality can be a very wonderful teacher.

## Lack of Cooperation with Family

"He always refuses to do what the rest of the family wants to do. It's always got to be what he wants to do, or he's a sore loser and makes us all pay for the rest of the day."

I'm not talking about a onetime occurrence here (let's face it: each of us has our moments). I'm talking about the kid who's got attitude. He keeps you running from crisis to crisis. You put out one fire and another one pops up immediately. He makes it clear that his wishes are the ones that are important, and no one else matters.

*Give 'em the bread-and-water treatment.*

What can you do about this? I've got a prescription that works well: Give 'em the bread-and-water treatment.

What does that mean? Your child is used to getting all sorts of things: an allowance, lunch money, guitar lessons, trips to friends' houses. All of a sudden, all of those perks stop. No warning. No fanfare. No anger. Things just stop. Your child heads out the door for guitar lessons and gets in the car. He sits there . . . and sits there . . . and sits there. You don't come out, so finally he's ticked off enough to come in and say, "What's the deal? Are we going to guitar lessons or not?"

Now is your teachable moment.

"I called and cancelled your lesson," you say calmly.

"What?" he says.

"Well, your dad and I have been talking. It seems like you want to drop out of the family, so that's the way it'll be for a while. Being a member of this family has some perks, I think, but you've got to live your life the way you want to live it. I can't force you to do things, but there will be changes on how the family will function. I'll no longer be driving you to guitar lessons, nor will we be paying for them."

This method works very well with older kids. Sometimes you just have to hit kids where it hurts (figuratively speaking, of course) for them to get it.

## Lateness

"No matter what time we start, she's always late for school."

"Whenever we plan a family dinner, he always shows up late . . . just in time for dessert."

Ask any businessperson who hires people and he'll tell you what he looks for in his employees. One of the key qualities is promptness. Why is this? Because business folks know well that the person who is always running late will, in the long run, put himself in a situation in which he'll come up a loser rather than a winner. And that wouldn't be good for the business.

Why would someone always run late?

It doesn't take a psychologist to figure this one out. If a child always runs late, it's because she's stacking the deck against herself. She doesn't feel like she's worth anything. She doesn't think highly enough of herself or believe that she can accomplish what she sets out to do. It's her way of making life difficult for herself.

If you have a continually late child, also read the "Procrastination" section. The child who is always late is, in all probability, the one who is living with a critical-eyed parent (you?) who can spot a flaw at 50 paces. Being late is your child's excuse. She's late so she doesn't have to play her piano solo and hear your critique afterward about her one wrong chord, because the program has already moved on. She's late so she doesn't have to set the dinner table (because the last time she did, you harped on her placement of the utensils).

> *If a child always runs late, it's because she's stacking the deck against herself. She doesn't feel like she's worth anything.*

There's a practical way of dealing with lateness. You can tell your child that you have to leave at 7:30 when you actually need to leave at 7:45 or 8:00. But it won't take long before your child catches on. That's only a short-term solution.

If your child is always late, do a gut-check on yourself. Are you one of those flaw-picking, hovering parents? If so, your child would rather be late and not do the activity than risk failure in your eyes. It all goes back to the fact that your child needs unconditional love and acceptance. And the person she needs it from the most is you, her parent.

This doesn't mean, however, that you don't address the lateness in your child. If you want to curb the lateness in 5 days or less, tell your kids when you need to be out the door. "I have to be out the door at 7:45 in order to go to my meeting. If you are ready, I'll drop you off at Hannah's on the way." If your child isn't at the door at 7:45, leave without warning or fanfare. (This only works, of course, if there is an older sibling or another adult home to stay with a younger child.) Let the child stay behind and suffer the consequences of not being ready.

If your child is continually late in getting out the door for school, go ahead and leave on time with your other children. Let the other child stay behind. It will mean, of course, sacrifice on your part because you'll have to make two trips to school. But welcome to the world of parenting! Sometimes it is inconvenient.

If a child experiences being late and is held accountable by an outside person (maybe she has to go to the principal's office or is given a pink slip she has to give to a teacher), all the better.

If your child has a record of lateness, you may also want to talk with the teacher or principal and say, "We're trying to work on Sarah being on time. Anything you can do to help us on that would be appreciated." In other words, home and school can work together.

Let's say your eighth grader misses the bus, and you have to drive him to school. What would you normally do? Run out of the door in your bathrobe without your coffee to get him there on time, right?

I suggest something different. Take your time. Take a shower, blow-dry your hair, pour yourself a cup of coffee. Quietly make a phone call to the school without your child knowing and tell them why he's going to be late. Encourage the office to give him a stiff warning on that pink or blue slip. Ask the teacher to say something to him in front of the class about his lateness.

Why would you choose to do this to your child? Because the long-term goal is for your child to become a responsible adult. Some children need a little kick-start in that direction, and your child may be one of them.

## Laziness/No Responsibility

"Frank Jr. moved back in with us after he graduated from college and couldn't find a job. Because he was back home and jobless, we continued giving him an allowance. But it seems like all he spends it on is take-out pizza and going out with his buddies. I sure don't see him looking for a job."

"Keri spent her entire summer just lying around on our deck, sun tanning. Now she wants to shop for school clothes. I'd told her at the beginning of the summer that we wouldn't have money for new clothes since her dad's company is downsizing and we don't know what's going to happen. She could have earned some money herself. She was offered a great job. But she just didn't want to do it."

Let me ask you: are you running a home—or a hotel?

If, like Frank Jr., your son is 24, still lives with you, and is bilking you for money and showing no responsibility, then you're running a hotel. And guess what? You're the maid service! Why would he look for a job? Frank Jr.'s got it pretty good right where he is. You do all the work, and he just hangs out eating pizza and not growing up.

> *Are you running a home— or a hotel?*

When I taught at the university, students would come up with all kinds of excuses. One football player—a 6'8" defensive end who weighed 300 pounds—told me one day, "Dr. Leman, this chick was supposed to type my paper for me and she doesn't have it done."

I raised my eyebrow at him. "Well, in *my* class I don't accept excuses. So by agreement with Coach Robinson, I'll just tell him that you won't be ready for practice today." After that point, that big football player would whip into class and lay his homework right on my desk before he even sat down.

Some kids are just lazy by nature. They've got their parents trained to remind them, coach them, and bribe them. But laziness isn't a quality you want to encourage, because your child needs to pull his share of the load as a family member. That's part of his responsibility.

If you ask your child to do something, you should ask only *once*. Otherwise you are being disrespectful to that child. You're saying, "I think you're so stupid that I have to remind you several times to do that."

The next time you want your child to do something, say it once.

"Kenny, I want you to clean out the garage today."

All day you watch Kenny laze around in the hammock, playing on his Game Boy. By nighttime, the garage still hasn't been cleaned. You don't remind your child.

The next morning at 9 a.m. is Little League tryouts. Your son comes out, dressed and excited, in his baseball gear, tossing his baseball. "Come on, Mom! It's time to go!" he says happily.

"Honey, we're not going to tryouts today."

He looks stunned. "Not going to tryouts? Why?"

Here's the teachable moment.

"Your dad wanted you to clean out the garage and I asked you to do it, and I see it's still not done."

At that point, your child will promise you anything—including 30 days of hard labor—if you take him to Little League. But he doesn't get to go to Little League that day. If he misses the tryouts, so be it.

When the garage is clean to his dad's satisfaction, he gets to go to Little League. And chances are, the next time he's asked to clean the garage, he'll do it in record time.

All this was done with no bribing, no cajoling, no reminding.

If this sounds harsh to you, let me ask you, "Do you want your child to be responsible or not?"

If you set the precedent of always reminding and coaxing children, then you'll always be reminding and coaxing. But what happens when they're in college, in an apartment of their own, and with a job in the real world, and you're not there to remind them?

Take the long view. What do you want your child to look like at 18, 20, and 30 years old?

If you want your child to be responsible, give him responsibility. Don't bail him out when he fails to follow through. Don't snowplow his roads in life. Failure and the resulting consequences are good training.

Remember, B doesn't happen until A is completed.

## Lying

Kids lie for two basic reasons.

One is for wish fulfillment. Some kids will come home and tell you they scored three goals in soccer . . . and then you find out they didn't play at all.

The second is out of fear. "Did you break that vase?" you demand. "No! I didn't do it! The cat did it!" your 6-year-old claims.

> *Most children lie out of fear.*

Most children lie out of fear. But lying is a mountain, because in order for there to be a relationship between two human beings, it must be based on trust. Otherwise, you'll feel violated.

So if your child lies to you, he needs to be caught in that lie and told that lying is not acceptable. There also needs to be a second consequence for lying. Let's say that, a couple days later, your child says something innocuous, such as, "Can I go next door and play with Ronnie?"

Your answer needs to be a matter-of-fact "No."

"But why?" your child asks. "You always let me go."

Now's the teachable moment, even more than being caught in the lie.

"Honey, I don't have any assurance that you're going to be where you said you'll be. Remember Wednesday night, when you told me you were going to be at Susan's—and you weren't?"

Do you beat the kid over the head? No. And you don't do it long term. But saying something like that two or three times makes a memorable impression on a child that lying isn't what you do. It doesn't gain you anything, and it breaks down trust between the two of you. Children need to see and feel that immediate result.

There's an age-old admonition: "You won't get in trouble if you tell me the truth." That needs to be true in your family too. If your child does break that vase and comes to you with the truth, she can know that you're unhappy, but she should not be punished for telling you the truth. In those situations, you'll need to think carefully before you open your mouth. How you respond to such a situation directly relates to how comfortable your child is in telling you the truth.

Kids can be as dumb as mud and will do stupid things in life (like hanging a camera out the window of a car and dropping it), but if they own up to them and say they're sorry, they need to know that life will go on. You won't beat them over the head for years for their mistake. The relationship between the two of you will still be okay.

Regarding lying, here's the kicker: parents too have to be careful about their own lies; even those pesky little white lies are still lies. If you say to your child, "If someone from work calls, I'm not here," and it's not the truth, your child is smart enough to know it. And then your child thinks, *If it's okay for you to lie, it's okay for me to lie.*

## Manners

Manners never go out of style. They should be taught to your child from day 1. If you haven't taught them, it's never too late. Any age can learn them.

When my grandson Conner leaves our house with his little duck suitcase on rollers, he says (without my daughter prompting him), "Thank you, Grandpa. Thank you, Grandmama." Why does he, at age 3, do what many teenagers don't do? And without any prompting? Because my daughter has taken time to train him to be courteous.

With all due respect, training a beagle and training a child have a lot of similarities. You have to tell them to do the same thing over and over and over until it sticks.

I'm a car-pool dad, and I really hate it when I'm driving children somewhere and they forget to say thank you. *What's wrong with kids today?* I think. And then I wonder, *And what's wrong with their parents?*

> *Manners never go out of style.*

Common courtesy should be a given that you teach your child. Anything other than saying "please," "thank you," and "you're welcome" is not acceptable.

One little girl I know takes things an extra step. When she has friends over to play and she and her mom take them home, that little girl walks her friend up to the door, and she thanks not only her friend for playing but the friend's mother for letting her child come over. "You ought to see the startled looks from those moms the first time you hear Mei tell them thank you," Mei's mother told me, laughing. "Later they tell me how much they appreciated that, how unusual it is, and that they would love to have Mei over anytime."

Manners will take your child a long way in life. Don't miss teaching the basics.

## Me, Me, Me

"But I want . . ."

"I don't feel like . . ."

Children are naturally selfish and thoughtless until they're trained to be otherwise. You're the parent and the authority over your child, so that's one of your very important jobs. Children need to learn that they are not the center of the universe. They need to learn that there are other people in that universe to think about.

Let's say you have a 12-year-old boy, a 9-year-old girl, and an 8-year-old girl. You have many talks about how you're all a family and you need to share in the fun and the work. Your kids get allowances. You all go on trips together. But your 12-year-old just doesn't get it. He squabbles about helping do the dishes and cleaning the bathroom because he doesn't feel like doing it. He complains about what you put in his school lunches. He critiques everything you do in the kitchen, including the way you cook dinner. And he criticizes everything his sisters do.

> *Children are naturally selfish and thoughtless until they're trained to be otherwise.*

So what can you do? Let's say the next night you're preparing dinner. He's standing there critiquing everything you and his sisters are doing. "You know, girls," you say, "I need your help in the bedroom. Evan, you can go ahead and make dinner yourself. That way you'll make sure it gets done just the way you want it to."

Think you're getting the message across? Ka-ching!

You may also want to assign him to make not only his own lunch but also his sisters' lunches for a week. And if he grouses about cleaning one bathroom, assign him to clean all the bathrooms in the house. He'll get the idea fairly quickly that the world isn't about me, me, me.

The point is, as a parent, you always need to be teaching your children how to be responsible and how to think of others. Children will always have childlike behavior because they're children. But as you take time for training, you'll be fine-tuning their Attitude, Behavior, and long-term Character.

## Messy Room

"I think a sign ought to be posted outside my son's room: *Toxic Zone. Don't enter for fear of your life.*"

I'm not a high-standard guy. I'm a want-to-see-the-floor-twice-a-week kind of guy. But even I have my limits. (My wife, Sande, a firstborn, has a lot less tolerance for mess than I do, as the baby of my family.) Many teen rooms are downright toxic.

Kids are mess makers, and they won't usually have the same standard you do for keeping their bedrooms picked up. And, after all, they have a lot of important stuff in there (like makeup, iPods, rocks), and they only have one room that's totally theirs in which to store their precious belongings. So if you expect them to keep their bedroom as clean as you do the rest of the house, you'll be sorely disappointed.

> *Bedrooms ought to be cleaned at least twice a week so they don't start smelling like locker rooms and looking like the local dump.*

However, bedrooms ought to be cleaned at least twice a week so they don't start smelling like locker rooms and looking like the local dump. That means anything that's been thrown on the floor gets picked up and deposited where it should go, including food wrappers, clothes, and possessions that have been borrowed from a sibling. For a parent to expect pickup twice a week is entirely reasonable.

Parents should decide which two days of the week are cleanup days. And children need to be clear on the definition of what "clean" is. That way, when Mom or Dad walks into the room, it's also clear to the child whether the room is presentable or not. If the child hasn't done a good job and doesn't seem to be willing to do round 2 (if he even attempted round 1), you can assign someone else to complete the cleanup (a sibling, a neighbor . . .) and take the cost out of your child's next allowance.

After all, isn't that what life is like? You pay for things others do for you? Why shouldn't cleaning your child's room be the same way?

Paying someone else to do a job that your child failed to complete and taking the pay out of his allowance is a good way to teach him responsibility. Not to mention that most children would be more than annoyed to find out that a sister, brother, or neighbor was in their space, going through their stuff.

## Misuse of TV or Video Games

"My son lives in two worlds—school and video games. He's in one or the other, but never anywhere else. Is this normal, or am I just being picky? Other than that, he's a good kid."

"My daughter is hooked on all the nighttime TV shows. Sometimes she doesn't start homework until nearly midnight because she's caught up in them."

Let's be honest. A lot of us watch too much TV. When there was a *Mayberry* marathon, I watched 2 hours of episodes, even though I knew every word since I've seen them all over and over and over. (Now that's stupid, but I still did it. It's a great show, but watching that much was a waste of my time.) Worse, there are so many tasteless things on TV. Downright disgusting, in fact. No good for anyone.

> *Let's be honest. A lot of us watch too much TV.*

So why do we allow our children to watch so much TV? Simply said, TV, movies, and video games have become babysitters for a lot of parents. Stick the kids in front of a show and Mom can do dishes and straighten up the kitchen in peace. Dad can get a couple extra hours of work in. If you have a 2-year-old and a portable TV and DVD player, why not take it to the restaurant and let the child watch a movie so you can have a quiet and peaceful dinner? What's wrong with letting a kid sit there, immersed in a DVD or a video game? At least they're quiet!

Using TV, movies, and video games to babysit is functional and very tempting. But is it healthy for children? To stare at an electronic device hour after hour instead of interacting with parents and siblings? Probably not.

There's nothing wrong with TV, movies, and DVDs, if used sparingly and screened for objectionable material and age-appropriateness for children. Some programs, like *National Geographic* and *Kiddy Planet*, are educational. The problem is that most parents don't set reasonable limits for the use of these items. Why not ask your child what a reasonable limit is? Interestingly, children usually give stricter limits, when asked, than adults do. If they help to come up with a reasonable limit, they'll be more likely to follow their own rules—and you won't have to be the watchdog.

One last note: do not allow children to have a TV in their bedroom. TVs should be in a central room in the house, where anyone walking by can see what is on the screen. Putting a TV in a child's bedroom, especially if you have cable service in your home, is just asking for trouble. Would you ever allow your child to walk down the sleaziest street in your local city? Then why allow your child access to all the sleaze that comes through cable and late-night television? You have a responsibility to protect your child's mind.

## Musical Influences

We all have our likes and dislikes when it comes to music. Chances are good that you don't like your child's music. (Hey, did your parents like what you listened to? Does your child like listening to the Eagles or U2? Point made.) But do you really gain anything by putting yourself in direct opposition to your child over music? Your child's musical tastes will change rapidly. The group you can't stand that's hot now will, within 6 months, most likely be pushed aside in her repertoire for the next popular group (which you probably won't like either).

You don't have to like your child's music. But you can always find something good about it—you might as well, since you'll be surrounded by it, especially during your child's teenage years.

"Great beat."

"What's the name of that song?"

"Who's performing that?"

At age 15, my daughter Lauren can fly like a mad woodpecker from one radio station to another in the car. "Oh," she coos, "I love that song. It's my favorite song," and then we're flipping through four more stations to find her other favorites.

Why not have fun with your child's music? Get to know her world?

But there's also a place to draw the line, and that's at the lyrics. Some lyrics are downright repulsive, vicious, and demeaning to ethnicities, men, and women. If your child is listening to such lyrics, it's time to throw up the red flag. "Honey, let's stop a minute. I want to hear those lyrics better. Would you mind turning that up? Do you hear what they're saying? Do you agree with that?" Eminem comes to mind, with his violent lyrics about a young man dreaming about slashing his father's throat. What parent in his right mind wants his child to go to sleep with that image in her brain? There's no way you should pay money for that CD or allow your child to listen to it.

You may not like the music, but it's the lyrics that count. So listen carefully.


## Music Lessons

"My daughter was so sure she wanted to play the clarinet. So we bought her a clarinet for sixth grade band. Then, about 2 weeks into it, when all we'd heard were squawks, she stopped practicing. She said she didn't want to play the clarinet anymore. And we'd spent all that money. . . ."

"Rob is 12. He plays the piano beautifully and has played for 6 years. But lately his practicing has been in a slump. When I asked him about it, he said, 'Mom, it's not cool to play the piano anymore.'

But I hate to see all his talent go to waste. How can I encourage him to keep it up?"

Any music lesson has to be contracted in minimum bites of a semester. In other words, it's not fair for your child to say she wants to try something, then quit 2 weeks into it when things aren't as easy as they seem. Every music teacher I've talked to says you need at least 4 to 6 months to begin to understand an instrument (and for it to not sound like something from a horror movie). But today's instant-breakfast, microwave kids want things to happen quickly and automatically. They get discouraged when they don't (and, you have to admit, so do you).

> *Any music lesson has to be contracted in minimum bites of a semester.*

But if you want to teach your kids diligence, insist that they stick out their lessons for at least a semester, no matter how much they hate it (this is true with sports too, by the way). If you start to feel sorry for your child, keep in mind that she is the one who said she wanted those lessons. If you were the one who insisted on the child getting lessons, the same principle of sticking it out for a semester holds true. You just have to battle the guilt and disappointment that all parents have when they discover that little Buford is not going to become Franz Liszt.

What about the child who really has talent, who has taken 4 years of violin and wants to quit? To that child I would say, "Listen, honey, I understand what you're saying. But I've talked to your teacher, and she says you really have a gift for playing the violin. She says what you're doing at this stage of your life on that instrument is highly unusual. We've invested 4 years in this instrument and all your lessons, and we're not going to quit now. You deserve more. Your talents deserve to be fine-tuned. So we're going to continue your lessons until the end of the school year, then review all this again."

Waiting until the end of the year gives you a chance to investigate getting your child involved in some group of like-minded students (i.e., a Suzuki group, a jazz ensemble for piano, a local youth orchestra) to see if having friends who like doing the same thing will help extend your child's interest.

Many children who are talented decide, between ages 10 and 13, that they no longer want to pursue their instrument. Often the reason is because their friends aren't interested. Ashley had played flute for 7 years. She had won multiple awards for solo work through state music festivals. But when she turned 13, all her friends started getting interested in soccer. Going to support Ashley in concerts by listening to her play songs by Handel and Bach wasn't big on their priority scale anymore. Her practice hours started to dwindle, and finally she told her dad she wanted to quit.

Ashley had a wise father. He encouraged her to hang in there, attended all of her events, and came up with special father/daughter surprises after every performance. Behind the scenes, he did a lot of research on music opportunities for flutists. That summer, instead of quitting, Ashley got involved with a new jazz group—all junior and senior high students—in a nearby town. They played at a lot of summer festivals, and Ashley's interest in music expanded. At the last performance of the summer, the group played an unusual piece of music, featuring Ashley as the soloist. It was a piece that Ashley had written herself, then adapted for the other jazz musicians who played with her.

Guess who had the biggest smile and clapped the loudest in the crowd? Ashley's dad.

## MySpace.com/IM-ing

Every teen on the planet loves IM-ing, if given the chance. It's instant contact with a friend. And MySpace.com is built to attract kids. To give them a forum to talk about what they love, what bugs them, how rotten their parents are, etc. Since these things are a fact of life, check them out for yourself. Sign up on MySpace.com as a member. It's a great way to quietly get access to your child's friends and to look at what they post.

My son-in-law Dennis, a middle school principal, was amazed at what he found. He looked for children who were sixth graders, keyed in their names, and was stunned how many times the children used their real name (a no-no in computer land).

*Looking at the topics posted and what kids say is an eye-opener for any parent.*

Looking at the topics posted and what kids say is an eye-opener for any parent.

If you want to enter your child's world, MySpace.com gives you such a window. And chances are, you won't like it. But it will give you a gritty look at what your child is up against every day she's at school.

Remember when you used to call your friends at night and jabber on the phone, and your parents rolled their eyes? Then they looked at the phone bill and restricted your minutes? Internet usage has made it even easier for your children, at no cost to them, to contact their friends in private (no one overhears a typed conversation), as well as to make new friends (who may not be who they say they are—for more on that, see "Internet Use"). That's why it's so important to have the computer in a central location in your house, where you and others can walk by at any moment and see messages that are typed. Does this mean you hover protectively over your child? No. No child would like you intruding on her friendships. Would you? But let's just say that a child will be less likely to get on an objectionable topic if she knows that a parent could walk by at any moment.

Then again, every computer has that history button. Smart parents will use it to protect their children.

## Name-Calling

"The playground monitor called me at home because my third grade son called another boy 'fatso' and made him cry. I was so embarrassed I didn't know what to say. Why would Luke say that? Luke's no skinny kid either!"

"I spent my entire childhood with kids in the neighborhood who called me names because I was a different race than everyone else. So it really got to me when my daughter went to kindergarten and came home saying, 'Mommy, what's a spik? Some kid called me a spik.'"

Why do kids call each other names?

People who label others do so to feel better about themselves. Name-callers may look big and bossy, but underneath, they're insecure. Still, they can do a lot of damage to other children unless they're stopped.

If your child calls another child a name, you can't afford to let that behavior slide. You need to bring your child to a screeching stop.

> *Name-callers may look big and bossy, but underneath, they're insecure.*

"Do you feel bad about yourself?" you need to ask.

"What are you talking about?" the kid sputters.

"You just put your brother down. You called him a _____. People who do that don't feel good about themselves. It bothers me that you apparently don't feel good about yourself."

Kinda takes the fun away from the kid's name-calling, don't you think? All of a sudden it registers in the child's mind, *If I put my brother down, I'm telling people I don't feel good about myself? Huh?*

Children in general are blunt. They will sometimes say things that hurt others out of ignorance or naïveté. But any parent knows the difference in honestly speaking out of turn just because you're curious ("Mommy, why is that woman's face and body all black?

Is she black on her belly too, or white, like mine?") and choosing to name-call and hurt another person. It's all in the attitude.

Kids can be especially hurtful when it comes to race, ethnicities, and physical characteristics. One little girl was told she couldn't play with her classmates because she didn't have blond hair like them. Another boy was told that his ears were "funny," and he spent the next 3 years begging his parents for surgery on his ears so that he could look normal.

When I was a kid, there was a girl in my class whose nose closely resembled a pig's. Everyone called her "pig face." Can you imagine? That poor girl! I cringe today when I think about what she went through. What her classmates said in jest must have driven her to despair. Kids can be downright cruel. Don't allow your child to be! And if he is a name-caller, you have to address it now. Don't wait and let your child prey on someone else.

If your child is the one on the receiving end of the name-calling, encourage her. "Honey, I know that what she said had to hurt, but I'm proud of the way you handled that situation. What you chose to say and the story you told that girl really painted a wonderful picture of what friendship should be like." Saying that you are proud of the way your child responded will outweigh the hurt of the name-calling and does more to restore your child's self-concept than anything else you can do as a parent (as much as you want to stomp over to the other child's house and let her have it).

By doing so, you're teaching your child that, yes, sometimes people will mistreat you. But it's how you react to that situation that makes you different. If you take the high road, you'll win out in the long run.

### Not Getting Up in the Morning

This is the biggest mountain of all in the life of a family. It's a Mount Saint Helens, ready to blow your family sky-high.

Everyone who is part of the family has responsibilities. You're living in a home, not a hotel with wake-up service. Children have responsibilities to get themselves up.

My daughter Lauren is now 15. In all the time she's been growing up, I can remember only one time when she didn't get up for school. She had forgotten to set her alarm clock. I woke up at 8 a.m. and was startled to see she wasn't yet up. For Lauren, that was a big surprise, since she always set her alarm and got herself out the door on time. So did I make a big deal of it? Of course not. It was a onetime event. I just drove her to school.

In many families, however, it's a battle to get the kids up and out the door in the morning. Parents cajole, bribe, threaten, and yell, and children go running out the door without breakfast to get to the bus—just as it pulls away. And what do the parents do? They drive the children to school and risk getting a traffic ticket to make up the time the children lost by not getting up earlier. Now that's crazy!

And how do you as the parent feel when it's all over? You're breathless from running around, and you feel like a lousy parent because you spent the morning yelling at your children.

If you want to see this end in your family, try this. Don't be your child's alarm clock. Let the child sleep in tomorrow morning. She's going to wake up at 10:00 very unhappy because she overslept.

But that's not your fault. You're not the one who overslept.

The good news is that your child will require a note in order to return to school. And you get to write the note.

*Dear So-and-so,*
*    Sally has no reason to be late. She simply chose to sleep in. Do whatever you do with children who are tardy.*
*    Many thanks,*
*    Mrs. Anderson*

Young children hate to go to the office. They fear the pink or blue slips. Older kids don't fear the slips as much, but they fear the embarrassment of the peer pressure when they're noticeably late. If you have to drive them to school because they missed the bus, they might try to pick a fight the whole way.

Your response should be this: "I'm tired of what we do every morning, so you're going to have to figure out mornings."

Your calm words, the child's fear of going to the principal's office, and the child's embarrassment of being late in front of peers—all these will help you turn around the situation.

## Nursing a Child

Every woman and expert you talk to will have a different opinion on this one. But in this book, I'm sharing my opinions. You don't have to agree.

I encourage moms to nurse their babies. A mom who nurses her child builds in all kinds of positive health safeguards. (La Leche League has a lot of great information about this that is worth checking out. When my little grandson was born 3 years ago, Krissy received a fact sheet and immunity sheet from them.) So when you have a choice, I encourage breastfeeding. Even some adoptive moms have tried breastfeeding, with help from La Leche League. Is breastfeeding natural? Yes, but lots of moms struggle with nursing in the beginning because both the new baby and Mom have to learn how to do it. (That's why there are lactation consultants in hospitals.)

My rule of thumb has always been to nurse a child for one year. This arbitrary year came from the suggestions of many pediatrician friends I have—a consensus of the medical community.

Some of you, just hearing that, are ready to go for my throat. Since a lot of mother's needs (psychological and emotional) are met through nursing, it's not uncommon to see children nursing at the ages of 3, 4, or even 5. But I think, when a child can say to you, "I'm ready," he's too old to be nursing. A year is plenty!

## Obsessive-Compulsive Disorder (OCD)

When I was in Atlanta for a seminar recently, a lady came up to me afterward and told me that she'd diagnosed her son as OCD, an anxiety disorder in which a person must go through certain rituals in order to curb their panic or irrational fear. She told me about all the procedures that have to be performed before he does something. Like the fact that she has to use an imaginary eraser in the bathtub to go through all the motions of cleaning the bathtub before he'll get in. And that she has to fold his blanket a certain way when he's tucked in at night. He certainly sounded like a perfectionistic child. But all people have their quirks. And children are lovers of routine. They insist that certain procedures in the home are followed (most notably, the bedtime routine). So what made her think her child was OCD? Because she'd read a book about it, and her neighbor had confirmed her thinking over coffee.

> *Far too many children have been misdiagnosed with OCD when they are simply powerful children who want you to approach them in a certain way.*

If you're concerned that your child may have OCD, get an evaluation from a professional in the field. Far too many children have been misdiagnosed with OCD when they are simply powerful children who want you to approach them in a certain way. What is the purposive nature of the behavior? To get your attention. To control their world. To dominate and control others.

And they will do a very good job because they are doggedly perfectionistic. However, the important thing with these children is helping them understand why they have to have rituals. Is it because of a deep, underlying fear that things will change? That you will go away?

Before you put a label on your child or accept a label about your child from anyone else, why not come to understand the purposive nature of the behavior, then work toward changing the behavior?

## Overeating

Take a look around, and you will see a lot of overweight children in America.

I watched poolside at a hotel as a family of four ate lunch. Their son, who looked to be about 10 years old, was grossly overweight. His belly hung way over the waist of his swim trunks. Long after the other 3 family members had left the table and started swimming, he remained in his chair, shoveling all the leftovers from others' plates into his mouth. What was on the table? Hot dogs, chips, and brownies. No sign of veggies anywhere, unless you count the pickles on the hot dogs.

Finally the father seemed to notice his son wasn't swimming. "Leave it!" he ordered, then went back to soaking in the hot tub. When the son ignored the dad's orders and ate some more chips off his sister's plate, the father got out of the hot tub, marched over to the table, and grabbed his son's arm.

"I said, leave it! And since you can't seem to listen," the father said, clearly angry and red-faced, "you can walk around the pool 20 times."

Each time the boy did a lap, he noticeably began to breathe harder when he got close to his dad in the hot tub. After the boy had done 3 loops around the pool, his father said, "Okay, now that you've cooled off, you can stop." (I had to wonder, *Which of the two needed to cool off?*)

What did the boy do? He smirked, sat back down at the table, and proceeded to eat 3 more brownies off the serving plate.

I couldn't help but think, *How dumb is that dad anyway?*

What did the boy really learn? A lot more than his father, that's for sure. *Hey, if I just pay attention to Dad and do what he says for a minute, he'll let me do what I want.*

Sometimes we parents are dumber than mud.

When children struggle with weight and overeating, junk food is the #1 cause. I know parents who actually have big straps around the refrigerator to keep their children away from nighttime raids. But the real answer is having smaller, well-balanced meals and no junk food, including sodas. Weight that is lost gradually is weight that can be kept off long term. Most important is a change of lifestyle, not diet plans or fasting.

If a child eats a well-balanced meal for dinner, he may still overeat. But the extra food won't do terrible damage because what the child is getting is complex carbohydrates and proteins.

The real trouble is the junk food—overeating on sweets. And who brings the junk home? Usually the parents! Part of the problem is that fewer and fewer families are eating dinners at home anymore. Everyone's in a hurry, so food has to be fast—but very little "fast food" is healthy. So many families eat on the go, but there's a lot more fat content in that food. Packaged lunches may be quick and easy, but they are mainly fat and sodium.

To prevent overeating and to provide balanced meals for your children, get back to family dinners. Serve healthy, nonfried food, and downsize the amount of food you prepare for dinner. Then, after dinner, close the kitchen to snacks and nighttime raids.

In the mornings before school, make sure that your child has a healthy breakfast. Often children dash out the door without breakfast because the bus or carpool is waiting. Or they grab anything junky that's easy to take on the road. Then what happens? They get to school, they're hungry, and they find the vending machines and fill up on Oreo cookies! Add to that the fact that phys ed classes are often being removed from the school curriculum (they're the first thing to go when there are budget cuts) and that little attention is paid to physical fitness, and you've got a weight problem in today's youth. Even 18-month-old children sit at a table and eat breakfast with a DVD propped in front of them to keep them from tossing food and throwing a fit. Do they really know what—and how much—they are eating? Are we priming our kids to overeat, even from a young age?

> *To change a child's overeating habits, you need to change your lifestyle.*

To change a child's overeating habits, you need to change your lifestyle. Sit down for dinner together as a family (this often requires the biggest change in the parents' schedule). There's nothing like a home-cooked meal for satisfaction, for lower fat content, and for bonding conversation. So don't miss out.

There's another aspect of overeating: bulimia. Ninety percent of the children who struggle with bulimia (overeating, then throwing up to purge the food from their system) are teenage girls. The underlying, driving reason is perfectionism. Teen girls see "perfect" bodies all around them on television, on billboards, in movies, and even within the "popular girls" group. In order to be accepted, they assume they have to be stick thin. If these girls don't feel supported by their parents, they may find another way to control their world—by binge eating a whole pan of brownies, then gagging themselves in the bathroom so they throw it up. If you suspect or discover this is happening with your child, please get help immediately from a professional. Bulimia is a serious condition that needs to be addressed by health-care providers because of the long-term impact it can have on your child's overall health—physically, mentally, and emotionally.

## Overcautiousness

"Mindy is afraid to try anything."

"Before Dave turns his homework in, he checks it over and over and over."

It's good to be cautious but not overly cautious. The key word is *overly*. When kids are overly cautious, perfectionism is in full bloom in your house.

A lot of children who don't start projects fear that if they do start, they might do them wrong. They fear criticism more than anything else, so the worst thing that parents can do is criticize them. These children live life with a boulder around their neck: *I have to produce . . . or else.*

> *These children live life with a boulder around their neck:* I have to produce . . . or else.

How did these children develop this fear? Because parents have used praise rather than encouragement. (For more on this, see the chapter "Thursday.") They have overused praise with everything the child has done until the child tells himself, *I only count in life when I do things perfectly. If I don't, I'm nothing.*

Here's the surprise. You may have a child who doesn't look like a perfectionist. He may be always late, his room may be a mess, and he may look like a mess, but underneath it all, he's a perfectionist. He may get his homework done and get it done right, but then a month later the teacher finds it in his desk at school.

"Why didn't you turn that in?" you ask. He has no answer, because he doesn't know how to voice his fear that if he had turned it in, someone would evaluate it. Someone would give it a star or a black mark. And what if it was the black mark? How could he live with that?

If you are constantly praising your children for what they do, giving them the rah-rah treatment, and rewarding them with a prize every time they get a good grade or win a speech meet, then perfectionism will run its course and make your child overly cautious. You may not see it come into full maturity until your child is in his late teens or early twenties, but it will be there.

Interestingly, this type of perfectionism happens especially with firstborns and "only" children in a family. It makes sense if you keep in mind that their models in life are adults. Just Ma and Pa are around. No younger siblings.

What is the purposive nature of the behavior of being overly cautious? To get out of a task the child doesn't want to do for fear of failure. In overcaution, as in all things, your relationship with your child is what makes the difference. So tell your child what you do well and where your blind spots are. She needs to see you laughing at yourself instead of taking yourself seriously and getting upset when you make a mistake. Then, when she needs to get a task done, take her by the hand and do together what needs to be done. Don't let overcaution be a deterrent to completing that job or task.

As you work through overcaution together, your child will gain confidence. Then her fear of failure will be dimmed, with some successes under her belt.

### Parties (Birthday Parties/Teen Parties)

Do you feel like you have to give your children to-die-for birthday parties? Why exactly is that? Do you fear your child will miss out on something? That you won't be labeled a good parent if you don't deliver—and deliver big?

Whatever happened to "invite the kids over after school for cupcakes in the backyard"? In the quiz in the preface, I mentioned these over-the-top parties:

> *Whatever happened to "invite the kids over after school for cupcakes in the backyard"?*

• Seven-year-old Rosa's parents chartered a bus and took her and multiple friends to a city 115 miles away so they each could "Build a Bear"; then they celebrated with cake and ice cream at an ice cream parlor.

204

- Five-year-old Mikey's parents rented the stadium club that overlooked an athletic field.
- Marti, a single mom, spent a whole month's income on her 10-year-old daughter's birthday party.

Oftentimes I've found that it's the *parents*, not the children, who up the ante on themselves. Under the surface is the drive to prove themselves as good parents in keeping up with the Joneses. But is that really what children want? Most young children I know just want to run around the yard, have fun, maybe play in the sprinkler or with water balloons, and eat ice cream and cake. To them, that's a party they can enjoy.

The Lupkin family has a birthday party rule that everyone in the family follows. Other than immediate family members, each child can invite one additional special guest each time he turns a year older. That means the 6-year-old can have 6 friends over for an at-home party. The 15-year-old can have 15 friends over. That has kept this family of 6 children out of the craziness of inviting an entire classroom over for each child's birthday.

For teen parties, why not offer to have the party at your house? You don't need an expensive limo for prom—and who really wants their child off somewhere with a date you barely know and a lot of pressure to drink and have sex? But you do need to know exactly what is going on (you don't have to hover, but a few well-timed and well-placed walk-throughs are important). Even better, your child will be home and in a safe environment, and you don't have to be up late worrying about who is driving her home (or if that person is drunk). When you weigh the food bills against the worry and safety issues, who cares about buying some extra party food?

The most important thing to decide is what kind of parties you will do and not do—and then stick with that decision, even if you're challenged by the child or a well-meaning friend or relative, who thinks you ought to do more than you do.

## Peer Group/Friends

Peer influence is extremely important in your child's life, and it only ramps up as your child reaches the adolescent and teen years.

Years ago a classic study of peer pressure was done, in which groups of 10 children were brought into a room. Three lines were drawn on a board, and the children were asked to identify which line was the longest. The first line the experimenter pointed to was definitely the *second* longest line, but when he asked, "Is this the longest line?" 9 children shot up their hands. Why was this?

Those 9 children were actually in cahoots with the experimenter. They had been told to vote for the second longest line. The subject being tested was actually the remaining child. Would the child cave in to peer pressure when his peers were undoubtedly wrong?

Well, you can guess what happened. An expression of disbelief would cross the face of the child. Then, in three-fourths of the cases, even though the subject child could plainly see with his own eyes that the 9 other children were absolutely wrong in their vote, he would raise his hand to vote with the peer group. Why? Because he didn't want to stand out as different from the others in the crowd. Is it any wonder, then, that teens do really stupid things sometimes when they're together? No one wants to be the naysayer.

There's nothing you can do about the strength of peer influence. It's a part of life. But what you *can* do is to be aware of your child's activities and who her friends are. That means having the peer group over at your home as much as possible. Make your home the hub of activity—the comfortable hangout place. Rent a movie, buy pizza, invest in a good CD player, whatever it takes. If you do, you'll have the home court advantage (for more tips, see my book *Home Court Advantage*). It will give you an up-close and personal chance to see who your children are hanging out with.

You can also get to know the parents of the children your child hangs out with. In today's world, it takes effort to do that. It's not like the old days, when children mainly played with other kids on the block, and you just walked over to your neighbor's for coffee. Why not call the parent of your son's friend and say, "Hey, I just got a Starbucks gift certificate for a present. My son talks a lot about your son, and I've never had a chance to meet you. Want to meet me for a cup of coffee—my treat?" That's a simple way to open the door for communication. And it also gives you the heads-up about what kind of person that parent is.

For example, when my friend Mike was 16, he smoked openly in front of his parents. So I knew I could go to his house and smoke cigarettes, and no one would say anything. But at my house? My dad would have had my hide for even trying them. It's pretty obvious, even in one conversation, which parents would buy beer for the kids and rent hotel rooms for prom. That kind of information is very important for you to know so you can encourage your kids to spend time with those who share similar values.

> *There's nothing you can do about the strength of peer influence. It's a part of life. But what you can do is to be aware of your child's activities and who her friends are.*

Sometimes your child will have a friend that you really disapprove of for one reason or another. My advice? Have the friend over to your house. The best time to do that is when your very stiff, blue-blood, conservative aunt Sally is coming from out of state to stay with you. Just say casually to your child, "Aunt Sally is coming into town. I'd love for her to get a chance to meet Philip." That ought to make your child think.

Although your child's peer group will have a tremendous pull on her, you want your child to be able to think for herself. Sometimes she'll make mistakes—big ones. The most important thing for you to do is to stay part of her world. And, at times, you'll need to enter her world, unbeknownst to her, in tough love. Like the dad who decided to go view the same movie his daughter and her boyfriend were supposedly seeing—he didn't see them at the movie, put two and two together, and showed up at the town's local make-out spot. Neither of those teens will forget the flashlight beam he shined into the backseat that illuminated exactly what was going on.

When a university student insisted on dancing topless at a local strip club, her parents were nearly apoplectic. However, when they confronted her about it, she said vehemently, "You just don't understand like my friends do. It's artistic expression!" But the picture changed when her two older brothers decided to go and view her "artistic expression" on stage, and her parents joined them. When the girl spotted her family midway through her act, her gyrations came to an abrupt stop, and she ran offstage. As hard as it was for those family members to show up, they did so because they knew it would bring reality into the situation—and show the act for exactly what it was.

I applaud all of you parents who take the extra time to enter your child's world and show tough love when it's called for.

### Pets (and Caring for Them)

Whose pet is it?

If you're one of the parents who bought a pet for your child because (1) you thought it would be good for your kid to have a pet or (2) your son really wanted that fuzzy little puppy, then I suggest that pet belongs to you. If you buy a pet for a youngster under 5, it's definitely your pet. Between the ages of 5 and 10, it's principally your pet. After age 10, it's more likely to be your child's pet.

Should children take care of their pet? Yes. If they want to claim ownership—"that's *my* dog"—then brushing and walking the dog, feeding the dog, and doing dog poop control need to belong to them. Even a 5-year-old can use a little shovel to pick up dog poop and hurl it into your neighbor's yard. If your older child—say a child over 8—has campaigned nonstop for a dog, make sure you go over these things with your child: "This will not be my dog. It will be your dog. And I expect you to feed it and clean up after it! There can't be any poop or pee on the floor either."

The problem is, as soon as you take on a pet, everyone in the family is going to have some responsibility for that pet. At first everything is rosy. That cute little puppy will get a lot of attention. Soon, however, it will become more and more evident that your child isn't planning on doing a lick of 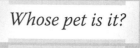 *Whose pet is it?* work. If this happens in your home, here's what I suggest: stake the dog in the front yard with a FOR SALE sign. Or put an ad in the paper or on the Internet to sell the dog. That ought to get your child's attention.

In other words, don't give your child wiggle room or any gray area here. Either he steps up to the plate and takes care of that dog or cat or guinea pig, or he doesn't—and the critter goes to someone who will. I like goldfish because they teach kids a lesson about caring for pets, but you're not stuck with them for years. They certainly teach kids about death and burial at sea. That's always been my job: the grand flush down the porcelain canyon. Recently, though, I've been stumped by a black fish that won't die. Every time we travel from Tucson to New York for the summer, we expect to come back to Tucson and find that fish dead. But the fish must have 9 lives. . . .

I love pets. We've had our laughs and tears over them (and lots of funerals in the backyard). I adore our dog, Rosie. She's got a great personality. She even sleeps with Sande and me. She's an integral part of our family.

But all 5 of my kids, while growing up, knew that pets were a responsibility. That once you got 'em, you didn't take 'em back

. . . until they went down the porcelain canyon or out under the tree in the yard.

Don't get a pet just because it's cute or you think it will help your child be responsible—unless, that is, your children aren't enough for you to take care of and you're craving something else to do. If you buy your child a little chick at Easter, you're nuts. (If you live on a farm, I withdraw my diagnosis.)

## Picky Eaters

There are three things in parenting that you don't need to spend a lot of time worrying about—eating, sleeping, and going potty. All those things take their course quite naturally, believe it or not, if a parent stays out of it.

Eating is way too big a thing for many parents. They turn a molehill into a mountain by constantly harping on eating habits:

> "Eat your veggies. They're good for you. If you do, you'll grow big and strong like your 143-pound father."

> "People who are starving across the sea would love to have that food."

> "Eat it. You'll like it."

> "Just take a bite, and I'll give you some candy for dessert."

Those kinds of comments were around when I was a kid too, and they didn't work for me either. But here's the truth: if eating is in a mountain category, it's because the parent is dumb enough to bring home all the sugars and fats that the kids are eating. If parents are smart, they start early in getting children interested in eating real food rather than the sugar-carb crap that serves as baby and toddler food.

Many studies have been done that show that children, if not pushed by their parents, will eat what their bodies crave. For example, children who are in a growth phase might require a lot more protein. Who cares if a child eats fish, fish, and fish for a week, then eats veggies the next week because that's what she craves? She's still getting an overall balanced diet.

When eating becomes a battle with children, it's because the parents are too pushy. They hover, they overcontrol. And every child has a built-in antenna that's aimed toward identifying what's important to Mom and Dad. That's the way your kids keep you over a barrel and controlled—at least in their thinking. So if you make eating an issue, they'll say, "Hey, let's give Mom a run for her money and see how far we get."

One key to good nutrition is preparing well-balanced meals. Dishes should be passed, and children should use a serving spoon and put the food on the plate themselves (rather than being served a certain amount). Emphasize that trying things is good. Acknowledge that not everyone will like the same thing, but everyone needs to try it. Don't force children to finish what's on their plate. Studies have shown that your child can eat in one sitting only the amount of food that is the size of his fist. Any more than that can stretch his capacities and lead to struggles with overeating. Also make it clear that when dinner's over, it's over. There's no going for the snacks in the cabinet an hour afterward.

> *When eating becomes a battle with children, it's because the parents are too pushy.*

Another key is not having junk food in the house. If you have it in your house, who is bringing it in? The next time you go to the store, check out the fat and sodium content in Lunchables and Goldfish crackers—two items many parents consider standard kid food. Then there's McDonald's and pizza day at school. The American diet, in general, is horrible and life-shortening. So many of the things our children consume are actually horrific to eat.

And with our on-the-go American lifestyle, the average American child ends up eating out at least one meal a day!

Recently Lauren, my teenage daughter, and I went to a basketball game. Neither of us had eaten before the game, so we were really hungry afterward. "Where do you want to go to eat, honey?" I asked her. Well, guess what? She didn't say McDonald's or Burger King. Good for her. You know what she wanted? Salmon! Yup, salmon. A whole lot more expensive for her thrifty father, but a whole lot healthier for her. And you know why Lauren said that? Because Sande, my dear wife, spent her time at the food processor when Lauren was a baby, making her own baby food without all the preservatives and junk that go into the Gerber variety. What we ate at the dinner table, Lauren ate in mushed-up form. And it taught her to enjoy the taste of real food, healthy food.

That's a taste she'll have for a lifetime. Well worth the extra work, I'd say.

## Pornography

All the mom had intended to do was change her adolescent son's stinky sheets, but she got much more than she bargained for. Just as she pulled the sheets off the bed, something else peeked out from under the mattress: *Penthouse* and *Playboy* magazines.

Stunned doesn't describe how this mom felt. What should she do? She had filth in her house, and her young son was not only looking at it but had brought it in to the house!

Here's what I suggested she do. Rather than confront her 13-year-old and get into a yelling standoff, the mom quietly placed the two magazines on the coffee table in the living room, along with her *Good Housekeeping* and *Self*. Then she waited for her son to come home from school and discover them.

Sure enough, he did—within minutes, as he plopped down to watch TV. He nearly choked on his Coke. Then he turned bright red. "What are these doing there?" he finally managed to say.

"Oh," the mom said glibly, "I found these magazines with beautiful women in them under your mattress. I thought I'd just place them out here, where your sister and your dad can enjoy the pretty pictures too."

At that point, the son looked like he was going to puke. He'd been caught red-handed.

"Or maybe there's a better place for this stuff," the mom continued matter-of-factly. "Like tearing it up and putting it in the trash. But I felt like that's something you should do, rather than me doing it for you. After all, you're the one who brought it into the house."

The mom sat down with the son, talked with him about what the magazine was all about and how it depicted women, and asked, "Is this really what you want to spend your time looking at? Pornography is highly addictive."

And that's true. Addictive long-term behaviors start with brief encounters with such material.

Is it natural for an adolescent or teenage boy (11 to 14 is the age at which 9 out of 10 boys view pornography) to want to see what a woman's body looks like? Yes. But there are healthy and unhealthy ways of viewing a woman's body. And pornography is definitely unhealthy because of its lewd poses, raw view of sexuality, and degrading perspective of women.

Every boy since the beginning of time has been interested in and fascinated by a woman's body. But today's culture ups the ante of parental watchfulness because of the types of objectionable material that are so readily available. When I was a kid, porn wasn't easily available like it is today. My buddy Moonhead and I got our sex ed from his father's subscription to *National Geographic*.

With the Internet, pornography steps right into your living room . . . if you let it. Did you know that Internet pornography is a $12 billion industry?[6] Wise parents set up blockers for objectionable material and periodically check the history button on their computer. You would never let your child wander through an adult bookstore, right? Well, I've got news for you. Your child can see a lot worse than that on the Internet with just one click of the mouse. Wise parents need to become savvy about everything their children are viewing—whether in magazines or on the Internet. Stats say that 9 out of 10 children will view pornography on the Internet. Will your child be one of them?

> *Stats say that 9 out of 10 children will view pornography on the Internet. Will your child be one of them?*

There's also an additional danger—adults whose mission and business is preying on unsuspecting children and teens. According to Donna Rice Hughes of Enough Is Enough, an organization that has been working hard to make the Internet safer for children and families, "Child pornography has become a multi-billion-dollar commercial enterprise and is one of the fastest growing industries on the Internet. And 90% of youth receiving sexual solicitations are teenagers ages 13–17."[7]

You can't always protect your child from every danger, but setting up safeguards in this area is extremely important. Once pornographic images have been viewed, they are hard to erase from your child's brain. And you certainly don't want to give a sexual predator an easy way to get to your child.

### Potty Training

There are three basic things that your child will do, no matter what—eating, sleeping, and going potty—and parents make a bigger deal out of them than they should.

Have you ever seen a second grader who isn't potty-trained? A fifth grader? An eighth grader? Potty training will happen. Some kids are merely on a faster timetable than others.

Numerous people have written books about potty training, but the basic gist is this: look for signs of "I'm ready" in your child before you begin the toilet-training process. Otherwise you're fighting an uphill battle (and a trail of pee down the hallway to the bathroom). Then ramp up your rewards. Get some new Thomas & Friends underwear for the big boy or some special My Little Pony underwear for the big girl. Buy one of those little potties where your child can sit close to floor level and be comfortable trying it out. Or some parents simply get a padded smaller seat that can fit on top of the big potty (but be aware that some little bottoms can still slide through that space).

Of course, these little tools won't potty train your child. But they'll be good aides along the way. Make the case to your child that he'll be a big boy and can do it "by self" (very important to a toddler). The important thing is that the child needs to be responsible to feel those urges of when he needs to go instead of Mom asking him every couple minutes, "Do you need to go?" If Mom tries to help too much, she'll weaken her child's self-confidence. Will you have accidents along the way? Sure. But as the child has an accident and helps to clean up the mess (instead of Mom racing to do it for him) he realizes, *Uh-oh, I waited too long. Gotta get there when I first feel I gotta go.*

Some parents use pull-ups at night. They see it as a progression. But if you really want to potty train a child, I would say, "If he's old enough to say 'I want a pull-up,' he should be toilet trained." If you tell the child, "Honey, we ran out of pull-ups and don't have any more," most children will accept that. By not having the pull-ups available, you make it incumbent on the child to take charge of his own bladder.

A talk show host once said to me about his son, "Hey, Doc, little Jake won't do #2 unless we put a Pampers on him. Then he does it in his Pampers. What can I do about that?" That's simply crazy, to put it bluntly. If the child can ask for a Pampers in order to do #2, he can get himself to the potty in time. That child is manipulating you and enjoying every minute of it. He's in charge of the house, not you. And that's not good for the child or for you.

My wife made a colossal mistake with the firstborn of our brood of 5. She decided she was going to pick the day Holly would be toilet trained. She had read a book by two psychologists about toilet training and was determined to do it by the book. I reminded her that I was a psychologist too, and I saw things differently, but that didn't matter. My firstborn wife, who knows how things are, banished me from the house for the day and demanded no interference. With potato chips and M&Ms—things that would clog your veins and kill you 20 years down the road and weren't normally in our house—she proceeded with "the plan." By the end of the day, Holly was patting the potty and saying, "Potty, potty"—as the "potty" ran down her leg.

We parents often think we know what's best for our kids, but the reality is that all children have a time clock implanted in them for potty training. It's called readiness, and you can read the signs. The child begins to mimic your behavior of going potty, asking questions and wanting to follow you into the bathroom. So you take the next step. You buy the Kmart plastic potty, put it on the floor, and let it become a fixture in your bathroom. You don't make a big deal out of it, so the kid doesn't think it's a big deal (and thus a way to control Mom or Dad).

When the child sees that potty, you explain calmly that it's her potty, one she can use. It's low to the ground and easy to sit on. With this method, many moms are pleasantly surprised at how easily potty training happens when they're not pushing to get the job done. Often the curious child will be found in the bathroom, trying out that new potty for herself!

When the child hops on that potty and goes #1 (the easier of the two), *then* make a thing of it (but not a huge thing). "My, look at that. You did that all by yourself!" are encouraging words to a child. If you want to back it up with a treat, you can do that. But I don't think it's a good idea. Why not? If you surveyed all your friends and asked them, "How many of you have gone potty today?" the majority would look at you like you were crazy and say, "Of course I've gone potty." Well, did anyone give *them* an M&M for going potty? No. So why would you do that with your children?

Going potty is one of the most natural things in the world. We're the ones who make it into something big and complex. It doesn't deserve to be. If your child doesn't respond to potty training within a few days, don't make a big thing of it. Just put away the potty for a short time and then bring it out again. Sometimes 1 to 2 weeks is enough time for the child to decide now is the time.

> *Most children are prepared to potty train at age 2 or 2½.*

When your child goes #2 in the potty, you can say, "Oh, look at what you did; that's great!" But as excited as you are for such an accomplishment, don't make too big a deal of it. One mom I know "saved" the poop to show her husband when he got home from work. That night she, her husband, and the two other siblings gathered around the porcelain throne to worship the doo-doo. They thought it would encourage the little nipper to go more frequently. Instead, all they did was show the hedonistic little guy, *Hey, this is a big deal. Mom really likes it when I go poop. Hmm . . . I wonder what she'll do if I refuse to go. What will she give me?* So that mom's good intentions actually backfired on her. All of a sudden, that child couldn't create a 4-inch Picasso without her or someone else sitting in the bathroom with him.

Most children are prepared to potty train at age 2 or 2½. If a child is developing normally (and isn't developmentally delayed), there's no reason for a child not to be toilet trained by age 3. If your child isn't toilet trained by 3½, you've made far too big a deal of the job with rewards and punishments. That kid's got your number, and he's in charge of you.

Keep in mind that even when a child is 4 years old, he can wet his pants. "But, Doc, he's been potty trained for 2 years. What's the deal?" you ask.

What will that kid tell you? "I forgot."

The child didn't forget. He has the same feeling in his bladder that you and I have when we have to go potty. He simply got so involved in playing that he got lazy and wet his pants.

The law in the Leman house has always been that there is a certain number of underwear you can wear in a given day. If you took a poll of people in your community, you would find that the mean, median, and mode are one pair of panties a day. That means if a child forgets to come in to go potty and wets his pants outside, he comes into the house, and his day outside has come to an end. It's a simple cause and effect that makes a child responsible for his own bladder. If that child's day with friends ends because he wet his pants, do you think he'll remember next time to come in and go?

## Power Games/Domination/Power Struggles

The key question is, who's the parent in the relationship—you or your child?

I was standing in the store the other day, and a teenage girl was definitely calling the shots. In no uncertain terms, she was telling her frazzled-looking mother exactly what to buy and what they were going to do when they left the store. And you know what? That mother was falling for it!

This is a mountain, one that you need to climb as early as possible in your child's life. Does that mean you dominate your child? You act as an authoritarian figure that orders your child around? Someone who projects the view "I'm better than you are"? Certainly not. We're not better than our child; we simply have different responsibilities. And one of those is to be a parent. We are the ones who need to decide what's best for the child—and the family.

Instead, what happens? A child becomes the deciding factor just because she whines, complains, cries, and screams. Or she may also dominate by being shy and quiet and not saying anything, thus putting the parent in the role of always prodding. Let's say a parent is concerned about her 3-year-old's language development. If a powerful child gets wind of that, she'll just shut up and not say anything. Before long she's only using motions to get people to do what she wants—and everyone is feeling bad and concerned for her and goes out of their way to help her.

How does powerful behavior develop? It doesn't come out of thin air. When I teach about power games in seminars and someone tells me, "Dr. Leman, I have an extremely powerful young daughter," my first response to that parent is, "Which one of you is the powerful one—you or your spouse?"

Children learn their behavior from somewhere. It's modeled for them. That means parents need to be very careful about how they express their frustration.

I understand how tough it is to be around young ones all day. I've had 5 children myself. So when my daughter Krissy phoned me one day and said, "Dad, I just need to get out of the house," I could relate. "Sure," I said, "I'll meet you." Being around children all day is exhausting. There are constant demands, and they take their toll on you. But if your frustration with those demands you chose when you decided to become a parent is taken out on your children, then you've got a problem that needs to be addressed. After all, you are the adult.

If you get into a power struggle with your child, you are destined to lose. A child can hold out much longer than you can; she's singularly focused on that one thing she wants, while you have multiple things you're thinking about. You'll give in every time just to have the power struggle over. And then the child wins.

> *If your child is trying to draw you into a power struggle, the solution is simple: don't go there. Don't get drawn in.*

If your child is trying to draw you into a power struggle, the solution is simple: don't go there. Don't get drawn in. Don't fall for it. Instead, calmly begin withdrawing the norm—no fanfare, no threats. If your child says, "I'm not going!" in no uncertain terms, leave the child at home. But then when she wants to go a friend's house, *you* don't go. If your child says, "I'm not doing my homework!" drop the matter. Then the next day write a note to the teacher:

*Elizabeth refused to do her homework last night. Would you please give her an F on this assignment and do whatever you need to do to encourage her to do her homework from now on? Many thanks.*

What's important is that your child learns she is accountable for her behavior. "I don't want to" and laziness are no excuses. Is this tough to do as a parent? Sure. It's easier to just drive the kid where she wants to go for a few hours and do her homework yourself. But what are you teaching your child in the long run? *Hey, if I don't do something, no worries. Mom will do it.*

> *Children need to learn that the jig is up. If they don't do what they're supposed to, there are immediate consequences.*

It comes back to this: are you running a home or a hotel? If it's a hotel, most likely you're the maid. Is that how you want to spend your days?

It's time to get tough. Children need to learn that the jig is up. If they don't do what they're supposed to, there are immediate consequences relating to that behavior.

## Procrastination

If you've got a kid you always have to push to get anything done, there's one thing I'd bet my paycheck on: your child has at least one perfectionistic, flaw-picking parent. Is it you or your spouse?

Kids who procrastinate do it for a reason. What's the purposive nature of procrastination? It protects them from criticism because you can't criticize what's not done. Are they capable of doing that job? Yes, in most cases. But they fear criticism so much that they will fail to complete the task. They might even run right up to the finish line on the project, but just before the end, they'll make an abrupt right turn and involve themselves in something else. They run in spurts: when they're hot, watch out. But then they hit a cold streak and stop. If you find this to be true in your home and family, I've got a great book for you: *When Your Best Isn't Good Enough.*

These children love piles. They surround themselves with books and papers. They have multiple projects that are unfinished. Why do they love mess? Because procrastinators are stacking the deck against themselves. They feel they don't measure up, so they'll draw a picture, then say it's no good and tear it up in front of your eyes. They'll do their homework but not hand it in. They'll stop short of completing nearly every task.

All these behaviors stem from fear. Procrastinators fear evaluation because their parents are perfectionists who have set standards so high that the children can never meet them.

In many families, firstborns are the achievers—the ones who are born to fly high in their adult life. They're the adults who always hit the home runs and become airplane pilots, civic leaders, surgeons, etc. But let's say that the firstborn has an overly perfectionistic parent. Then the firstborn will become a procrastinator. There's a role reversal that happens as the firstborn takes the initial emotional hit from a perfectionistic parent. Then it's the secondborn who becomes the superachiever—the self-motivated, mature, in-control-of-life person who proceeds through life with great skill and ability—while the firstborn flounders in expectations. This phenomenon plays itself out in life, especially when there are 3 years or less between the firstborn and the secondborn.

If your child thinks he can't measure up to your standards, he won't try. Or he'll try only so far and won't get to the finish line.

This is why it's so important to know the difference between praise and encouragement. (Refer back to the chapter "Thursday" for more specifics.) When you praise a child, it's analogous to sticking a carrot on a stick in front of a donkey and letting it swing. "If you're a good boy, I'll give you a carrot." The problem is that every time the donkey tries to get a bite of that carrot, it moves! If you're a perfectionistic parent, your child knows he can jump higher and higher for you . . . and never win your praise.

Praise focuses on the actor: "You're the greatest kid in the world!" Encouragement focuses on the act: "Thank you so much for doing that. That was very helpful." "Oh, that's terrific. The extra studying really paid off, didn't it? Great job!"

The perfectionistic parent who says, by his own words and actions, "You better jump—and jump higher—to measure up in my book," has a high probability of creating a carrot seeker who will always be looking for an emotional star.

In contrast, children who grow up with encouragement rather than praise feel a sense of support, rallied trust, and confidence all throughout life. They are finishers rather than procrastinators.

## Punching Holes in Walls

This is one of the most common behaviors I'm asked about in counseling, and usually it's boys doing the punching. Girls tend to slam doors and yell, "I hate you!" Guys are more likely to lose it and punch holes in the walls (hey, even adults do it—dads especially). One dad told me shamefacedly that he was so mad at his teenage son that he himself smacked the car window, broke it, and had to take himself to the hospital for stitches. (And he wondered where his son had learned to punch walls.)

When your child is punching walls, he's most likely a child who has been angry for a lot of his life. I've got news for you. This type of behavior isn't an easy fix because the anger has been brewing for a long time. Oftentimes embarrassed parents try to deal with this situation at home. But what that child needs is some professional help. (And I'm not just saying this because I'm a psychologist and I need to make a buck. I'm saying it because it's the truth.) These are the children who are so angry and volatile that they could go off the deep end and hurt someone else. You read about them in the news, and if you don't handle the situation appropriately and immediately, your child could be making his own news.

> *When your child is punching walls, he's most likely a child who has been angry for a lot of his life.*

Does this mean that you don't do anything at home with the situation? Of course not. First you need to say, "We are not tolerating this behavior in our house." The problem is that the behavior is so fixed by now that it's like the grain in a plank of wood. It goes one way and can't change. You can wax it, polish it, or paint it, but the grain stays the same direction. That's why it's so important to train a child to love, respect, and be a member of the family when he's young.

So please get some professional help for your child to work through his anger issues. But don't let him get away scot-free at home either. Your child should be working to make the money it will take to repair the holes in the walls. If he doesn't have a part-time job to do that, then suspend his allowance until the repairs are paid out of it. Also remember that "B doesn't happen until A is completed." That means you don't drive him to a friend's house when he says, "I'm not going to counseling." Counseling is the one thing you need to insist he goes to, for his sake—and for the rest of the family's.

Don't back down on this mountain.

## Putting Each Other Down

"You're a—"

"No, you're a—"

"I'm telling Mom!"

Does this sound familiar in your house?

Children will put each other down. What's the purposive nature of the behavior? To make themselves look better—and to get your attention. As children get older, sometimes the put-downs are more subtle, but they're put-downs all the same.

> *Do not tolerate put-downs in your family. Period.*

Put-downs are a form of fighting. In order to fight, two people have to be involved. To end the put-down game, take both children to a room and tell them that neither of them is coming out until this thing gets worked out *to your satisfaction.* That means the children don't exit that room until they show that they've reached an agreement and apologized to each other. Then life outside that room can go on.

What are you teaching those children? That they need to resolve their own battles; you are not going to be Big Mama Gorilla, who sits on her youngsters to solve their skirmishes. Your children need to learn they are responsible for their actions and their words.

You're saying, "In this family, we're not going to tolerate put-downs or name-calling. We're a family. That means we support each other. That means when you want to be in a play, we support you and go see you in that play. When your sister plays soccer, we support her and go to her games. That's what family is all about. When you put each other down, that hurts everyone. And it breaks down our family."

Do not tolerate put-downs in your family. Period.

## Respect

This is a fundamental issue for all families. Without respect, there is no family. You're simply people living together in one building and doing your own thing when you want to do it. Responsibility, accountability, and respect are what make a family a *family*.

When you hold a child accountable for being respectful of you and other members of the family, you are being respectful of him. After all, if a young man doesn't learn to respect his mother, who is he going to bring home to marry someday? A woman he can dominate and wipe his feet on. And if a daughter isn't respectful of her father, what kind of view will she have of the other men in her life, including her boss at work?

> *Attitudes, Behavior, and Character are caught rather than taught. Your child is watching you. What is she learning?*

She'll marry a guy she can push around. Her disrespect for her male supervisor will not only get her in trouble; it may get her fired.

A parent's outlook on life is transmitted to the children. That means we as parents need to think about our words before we say them. Are they ones we'd want our child to remember? Or are they words spoken in haste that aren't respectful? We need to remember that every member of the family gets a vote on family activities. That doesn't mean your child runs the family, but part of being a family member is the perk of getting a say in things.

When you listen to your child's opinion and care about the things she values, you're saying, "I value you and respect you. I care about what you think and feel."

Respect is a two-way street. If your child isn't respecting you, take a look at yourself first to see if you're a part of the problem. Most of the time, respect issues stem from the Attitudes, Behavior, and Character of one or both parents.

I know you don't want to hear that, but it's the truth. I said up front that there will be times in this book when you won't like what I have to say. This is one of those times. But please hear me out, for your family's sake. *You* are the key to your child's behavior. In order to move your child toward respecting you, you have to be willing to make changes in the respect area yourself. Are you, through your words and behaviors, respecting your child? If not, why should she have respect for you? (The old adage is true: would you treat your boss at work the way you treat your spouse and child?) Remember that Attitudes, Behavior, and Character are caught rather than taught. Your child is watching you. What is she learning?

Parenting is a tough job. You can do eight things well and blow two of them, and those two things take you back to square one with your children. This is when you have to work hard at being carefully consistent—not overreacting, not blowing it. You need to stay the course, to act in a respectful, responsible manner yourself. For example, what is your child learning if you bark out, "You have to go to church. It's good for you!" but then you drop the child off at church and go out for coffee?

Your child is watching your Attitude, your Behavior, and your Character. If things aren't in line at home with the image you project to others, your child will be the first one to spot the dissonance. Saying one thing and doing another will set up the framework for disrespect in your home. Strive for consistency and calm, rational behavior. No yelling, no "I told you," no "If you don't . . ." Your children need to see by your actions that things are different in your life. That you are changing for the good. Yes, you still may mess up and blow it at times. After all, you're human. But when you do, you need to go to your child and apologize for your behavior.

If you want a respectful child, you need to be respectful.

## Retention in School (Kindergarten through Third Grade)

For years, parents have looked down on the notion of holding kids back in school. Somehow we're worried it'll damage their psyche—their self-concept, their self-esteem. That doing so will embarrass the child.

All of this is a pack of lies. The reality is that all kids grow and learn at different rates. Two 5-year-olds who start kindergarten can be completely different physically, psychologically, and education-ally. One could be 28 pounds; the other could be 50 pounds. One could look forward to starting school; the other might still be clinging to Mama. One could know her ABCs; the other might not have a clue.

*All kids grow and learn at different rates.*

We parents are funny creatures. We don't have a problem if a child is able to excel in baseball or draw a horse at 5 years old while another is not. But we do have a problem when a child doesn't learn her ABCs at the same rate as another child.

Just as there needs to be readiness for potty training, there needs to be readiness for school. Some 5-year-olds are ready for kin-dergarten both academically and socially. Other children should wait until they are 6 to start kindergarten. Some children are ready to go on to first grade after a year of kindergarten. Others need another year of kindergarten.

It's important for parents to take the long view. We retained our youngest, Lauren, in kindergarten. By seventh grade she was way past high school level on the standardized tests.

Over the years, there have been many critics of retention in school, mainly because of the fear that a child will be embarrassed or lose his friends. But such concerns do not register highly for a child at a young age—unless the parent makes them register. Explaining to a child the decision to retain him is all in the pre-sentation. "You know, Andy, how you're frustrated with learning how to write your letters?" (Child nods and starts to look sad.) "Well, Mrs. Miller and I were talking. She'd love to have you again next year. In fact, she has plans to teach the ABCs in a different way. She's going to have a jungle theme, and each child will get to be a different animal. Doesn't that sound like fun?" If a child hears a positive interpretation from you (and not your mutterings and fears behind the scenes), he'll be positive about being retained in school.

When you retain a child in school, you're doing him a great service. You're giving him a chance to learn the basic academic behaviors required for a certain grade level. If you pass that child on to the next grade level and he doesn't have those skills, you're being disrespectful of him (and setting him up to fail). The respectful thing to do is to hold a child accountable for where he is in the learning process.

A special note for those of you who are parents of boys: in general, boys tend to grow up slower and often need that extra year to mature and grow up before going to kindergarten. When does this really pay off? In their junior year of high school, when they're in competitive sports and at the top of their game! I always pointed out to Lauren that she'll get to drive when she's a sophomore in high school. Most of her friends will have to wait until they're juniors. And that's something a teenager can smile about.

If you have a later-born child (born anytime from August through December), you're much smarter to wait a year to start kindergarten. Lauren's birthday is August 22, so she was very young going into kindergarten the first go-around. That's why she needed another run.

If you're worried that your child will look like a failure, then your thinking is all about you (you're afraid of what your friends will say about your child and your failure in child-rearing) and not in your child's best interest. Karen, a single mom, threw a fit in the principal's office when he suggested that her daughter, Mandy, be held for another year in first grade. But then the principal said to her, "How would you feel if you were taking a course where everyone else knew the basics, but you didn't? Wouldn't you feel a little lost and scared all the time? Like you couldn't measure up?"

Yet that's what some parents do to their children all the time. They push them forward, even when they shouldn't, and call it social promotion. That's what happened to me in school and why I'm such a strong advocate for holding children back when they need it. If I would have been held back in one of the first grades, I would have done much better in school. I would have been more ready for it.

To 5-year-olds, repeating kindergarten is no big deal. They get to play for a year longer!

It's all in your perspective. Wouldn't you rather retain your child at a younger grade than watch him struggle through school with concepts he's not ready for?

If your child needs to be retained in a grade level past third grade, it's best to look for another school for your child. It softens the blow and the peer pressure for your child to be somewhere new.

### Rolling Eyes

Children can be so dramatic, can't they? Especially preteens and teens. They're masters at the rolling-eye syndrome. It's their nonverbal way of saying, "Please, not again!" "Dad, you're embarrassing me. I can't believe you did that!"

When your children roll their eyes, it's not a mountain. All children roll their eyes. (You do too sometimes!) It's like saying, "What you just said/did is completely out to lunch. I can't believe you said/did that." Rolling your eyes is an attitude, yes, but it's not the end of the world and won't affect long-term character. (But talking back and being a smart aleck is another story.)

> *The next time you see the eye roll, say, "Oh, that was great. Would you do it again? In slow motion?"*

Parents, this is not an issue to go to war on. So why not have a little fun with it? The next time you see the eye roll, say, "Oh, that was great. Would you do it again? In slow motion?"

Treating this attitude and behavior in a lighthearted manner will downplay it when it happens . . . and it might just give you both a well-needed laugh.

## Rudeness

Children are blunt, and sometimes they can be rude without meaning to. "Why is that lady so fat?" your daughter asks you in the grocery store line . . . and the lady is standing right behind you.

So when your child makes a rude remark, before you react, ask yourself, *Did she really mean to be rude?* If it was just an honest, blunt question, say, "Honey, what you just said sounded rude, but I don't think you meant it that way. Sometimes we say things that are rude and don't mean to. I just thought you'd want to know."

> *Before you react, ask yourself,* Did she really mean to be rude?

If the child really was being rude (and you as the parent can usually tell the difference), pull the child aside and say, "What you said just now was rude, and you need to apologize immediately. It was very disrespectful of that person, and in this family we do not show disrespect." Do not snowplow your child's road by assisting in the apology either. You may need to walk the child over to the person, but you shouldn't "help" your child apologize. Your child needs to feel the weight of her rudeness so she'll think before she says something rude next time.

## Saying Thank You

Saying thank you is a common courtesy. Everyone should say thank you. That includes parents and children. But saying thank you doesn't come naturally. Every 2- and 3-year-old couldn't care less about others unless a parent teaches him to do so. And if 2-year-olds are not taught to say thank you, they won't automatically learn to say thank you as teens either.

It always annoys me, as a car-pool dad, when children in my car don't even say thanks for the ride or for the little surprise treats I sometimes bring them.

Contrast that to the little girl who was chosen as 1 of 10 children to play as a guest violinist with a local college orchestra. After the performance, that little 6-year-old, of her own accord (no prompting from Mommy), walked up to the director of the orchestra and said, "Thank you for giving me the opportunity to play with you. I loved it. I hope you enjoyed it too." The orchestra director was stunned. He waved the mom over and asked, "Do you know what she just said?" After repeating it to the mother, he continued, "I've been directing an orchestra for 12 years, and we've invited scores of children to play with us for special events. But not one child has ever said thank you . . . until yours."

> *Saying thank you is a common courtesy. Everyone should say thank you.*

See the impact that a simple thank you can make?

Don't be remiss in teaching your children the basics of manners, including saying thank you. That means that until your child says thank you for a gift, life doesn't go on, and she doesn't use that gift either. If your child forgets to say thank you for playing at a friend's home, the answer is no the next time he asks to do so.

Insist that your child say thank you, and hold him accountable to do so.

## Screaming

"Her screaming is driving me crazy. I jump up every time I hear it and run out into the yard because I think something's wrong."

You need to understand something basic about child development: young children scream. That's a given. Children are beginning to explore life, and that includes not only their surroundings but the way their bodies work. Children from 14 months old to 2 years old discover that they have voices. Even more, these delightful voices can create wonderfully high-pitched noises that bring a parent running. It's quite a game to try it out! It's like a new toy, and they have to see how it works. So a child tries out one kind of scream to see how his parents will react. If they overreact to the scream, the child will say to himself, *Hey, that was fun. I scream and they come running. They do that funny little hand motion and get a funny look in their eyes, and those veins on their necks pop out. Ah, so that's the game we play and how we play it. Oh, I get it. Let's do it again. . . .*

> *Children will scream. But they won't continue to scream unless that behavior has paid off.*

Two of the parents I counseled were at their wits' end with their young child. The kid woke up screaming in the middle of the night and disturbed the entire household of 6 people. The parents had tried everything to keep the child from screaming, and nothing worked. One day the siblings said, "What would happen if we screamed back?" Well, they did just that. The kid looked so startled that the screaming ended in a gurgle. And that was the end of the 3 a.m. screamings in that household. Sometimes unorthodox things work.

The point is, children will scream. But they won't continue to scream unless that behavior has paid off. Rushing over to hush them is a way to reinforce that negative behavior because it gives them attention. Unless you overreact, your child won't see the screaming as a negative behavior.

That's why it doesn't bother me if I see a child 2 years and under screaming. That's part of his development and body exploration.

But if a 9- or 10-year-old is screaming, he's doing it for a specific reason. He wants to show you who's in charge. That needs to be nipped in the bud because it has moved from experimentation with how the body works to a respect issue (see "Respect").

## Selfishness

Kids, by their nature, are selfish, having little "social interest" in anyone else. We parents ought to take a clue from the first thing they say when they're born: "Waah!" All they care about is themselves—and whether they're warm, cuddled, and fed. Life is truly "all about me." The human species is interesting and different from most other species because it takes a while for a young child to become fully functional (versus this happening much faster in the animal community). For the first year, the child doesn't usually talk, feed herself, etc. She is completely dependent on Mommy (Dad doesn't quite have the body parts needed).

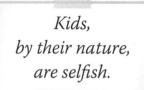

*Kids, by their nature, are selfish.*

When the child begins to get mobile is an important time for training, especially in the area of sharing (more on that in "Sharing"). You see blatant examples of kids' selfish natures all the time. When this happens, say to the child, "That was a selfish thing to do. Did you mean to be selfish?"

Many times the child will say, "No."

"Can you think of a better way to handle the situation?" you ask. "Why don't you call your friend back now and suggest something different?"

In this situation, your responsibility is to be the shepherd guiding the sheep. Like a good shepherd, you sometimes have to guide them gently in the right direction with your staff (even when you feel like whacking them over the head).

Every parent has a responsibility to guide their child toward selfless behavior and thinking of others.

In my seminars, I ask parents, "Why do we stop at stoplights?"

"Because it's the law, and you don't want to get a ticket," they usually say.

"The best answer," I say, "is that we stop so we don't hurt someone else."

Note the difference between the answers—and the fact that the unselfish answer isn't the first one that came up. All of us are selfish. We live in a self-driven society. There's even a magazine called *Self*.

When you teach a child not to be selfish, you're actually teaching him to be antisocietal, to be unlike everyone else. But why do you want your child to be like everyone else anyway?

Learning to be selfless is an important trait for a healthy child. We've worked hard at instilling that in our children. From age 10 on, Lauren has taken the time to write to the child we sponsor in El Salvador. It's good for her to understand and see that the majority of the world has far less than she does. We also deliver groceries during the holiday to needy families.

Modeling giving as a family and as an individual to those who are less fortunate than you is very important. Friends of ours volunteer on Saturday mornings in a soup kitchen. Their teenage children go with them. Funny thing is, before they started serving in the soup kitchen, those teenagers were always bugging their parents about getting another car so they wouldn't have to be inconvenienced when their parents' car wasn't available. After 3 weeks in the soup kitchen, the request wasn't mentioned again.

When your children show selfishness, they need a little dose of reality, like the teenagers who served in the soup kitchen. Or like the "only child," whose mom decided she wasn't going to share her treat with her child since her child had refused to share *her* treat with a neighborhood child earlier that day.

Teaching selflessness pays off down the line. I've always seen that character trait in our fourthborn, Hannah. Ask anyone who knows her, and they'd say selflessness is the way she lives her life. Last winter, one of Hannah's classmates needed a winter coat and didn't have money for it. Hannah, who heard of the need, just quietly bought the young woman a coat and gave it to her.

Trust me, it's not because her father is a well-known psychologist. It has everything to do with how Hannah was reared—how her brother and sisters interacted with her, how we interacted with her—and that she saw her home as a loving, giving place where she thought about the welfare of others. Do I say this to pat the Leman family on the back for being so great? No, I use that example to explain a simple principle: children model what they've experienced at home. If you create an environment where children feel loved and accepted for who they are, and they are a part of giving back to your family, then when they leave your home and go out on their own, guess what happens? They do what they've been doing in their own home!

What's the alternative? Look through your city's paper tonight. You'll see all kinds of cases of people who didn't grow up in that kind of environment. Their crimes are documented in newspapers and on news reports across the nation. Prisons are full of people who never learned selflessness.

Teach your child selflessness. Then she'll emerge into society as a giver, not a taker.

### Sharing

Children don't understand sharing. They don't have a capacity to even contemplate it when they are 14 months old. If they're holding an item, there's no sharing. They own that item. It's theirs. And no one can tell them any different. It doesn't matter if they can break it or it's worth 5,000 dollars or 50 cents.

However, with each passing month after that age, children become more acutely aware of others, so they must learn how to share. However, young children will not share unless sharing is modeled for them. Role-playing sharing is important. "Okay, it's your turn. . . . now it's my turn." Or, "You take a bite. Then I'll take a bite."

> *Young children will not share unless sharing is modeled for them.*

When young children willingly share with others, parents need to reinforce that behavior by saying, "What a big girl you are! You shared that with your brother!"

Three- and 4-year-olds can be extremely territorial. They have a difficult time sharing because everything is "mine." But does that mean they can't learn? Absolutely not. Let's say 4-year-olds are playing and arguing over a ball. The best way to teach sharing is to take the ball away. "If you can't share this ball," you tell them, "no one will play with it. I'll put it away for now." By taking away the object, you are holding the children accountable for learning how to share it. You can also add, "When you are ready to share, let me know."

With such words, young children will quickly figure out that sharing can be to their advantage. Otherwise, their fun disappears with that ball!

To reinforce the concept, later that day you can sit down with an aromatic bowl of popcorn. When your son comes up and asks for some, simply say, "No, I'm not sharing my popcorn tonight. I don't feel like it."

You're not being mean. You have a level tone. Then you explain the importance of sharing and how you felt about what happened earlier that day. "We're all part of one family, and we share things. But if you choose not to share, I can choose not to share."

Let's say older children are fussing over the last piece of cake. Just hand a knife to one child and say, "I'll tell you what—you cut it." To the other kid, say, "And then you choose which piece you want."

236

That keeps the ball in the court where it belongs and doesn't get you into the discussion of who had the bigger piece last night. One kid cuts; the other chooses the piece. And you stay out of the Judge Judy role.

Ditto with the skirmishes between teenage girls over a sweater. If your child bought it with her money, it's hers. If you bought it with your money, sharing would be in order. If they can't share it, simply take the sweater and add it to your own wardrobe until the girls can come to an agreement. The skirmishes over clothing may still go on behind the scenes, but there's less likelihood they'll draw you into the midst of them.

Something that can help children understand sharing and how each member of the family contributes is helping you pay bills online or writing checks for bills. Younger children can even put stamps on the envelopes and see how many bills go out and come in. When children understand the costs of running a family, they are even more thankful for the privileges of being a member of the family.

## Showing Off

Boys will always be boys. They're forever flexing their muscles in front of each other. But there's a difference between flexing in a group of boys on the playground and doing it in front of your business guests who are over for dinner. There's also a difference between boys having a burping and farting contest among themselves and doing it at the family dinner table. Kids are kids, and they'll do dumb things. And the dumbest of all are boys who are trying to show off for girls. But eventually they too will grow up, become adults—and still do dumb things.

Let's say you have company over, and your daughter runs into the room, trying to do somersaults to get your attention. What should you say? "Would you come back and do that again so I can give it my full attention?"

That would stop most children in their tracks, because most kids, contrary to how they act, shy away from the spotlight.

You could also say, "Honey, would you mind showing off outside?"

By saying either of these things, you're acknowledging to the child that you know she is trying to get your attention. However, the way she's doing it is not appropriate in the situation.

"Dr. Leman," some of you might be saying, "how could I do that? Why, it would embarrass my child to say those things."

> *When kids show off, you can surprise them by saying, "Would you mind doing that again?"*

Now, let me ask you. You came to this book because you wanted to see things change in your home. I'm telling you how, in 5 days, you *can* change them and not let these behaviors linger. Will one embarrassing comment ruin your child—or propel her into behavior that will make her acceptable in society for the rest of her life?

If you are the kind of parent who says, "Well, I could never do that to my child," you'll be facing these same sorts of dilemmas—and many more—down the line because you didn't follow through on disciplining your children earlier in life. And later the stakes will be much higher than doing somersaults in your living room.

For a number of years I taught teachers who were enrolled in grad courses. I told it to them straight: "If you have a child who is disrupting your classroom, ask everyone to put down their work and stare at that child for 5 minutes so he has the entire room's attention. When the bell rings, children are conditioned to run out the door. That's when you say, 'Now we're going to make up the 5 minutes we wasted watching Timothy today.' Hold the class in for 5 minutes from recess. Let the peer pressure take over."

A lot of tree-huggers and social do-gooders got mad at me for saying this, but the teachers who tried it raved about how well it worked. And amazingly, it took only *one time* to curb the behavior.

When kids show off, you can surprise them by saying, "Would you mind doing that again? I can tell you're looking for attention, so I want to give you my full attention."

I was a child who loved getting attention, but that approach would have stopped even me in my tracks.

## Shyness

> "She doesn't have any friends because she won't talk to anyone. She's really shy."

Did you know that an extremely shy child is an extremely powerful child? Shyness becomes a way of making sure the adults in that child's life do things the way the child wants to do them. It's actually a form of manipulation.

Perhaps little Annie says she's too shy to go over and play with other children at the park's sandbox. What is she really saying? "Dad, I don't want to go over there by myself. I don't know what to say, and I

> *An extremely shy child is an extremely powerful child.*

don't want to go out of my way to even try it. I want you to walk over there and break the ice for me." But does that do any good for little Annie in the long run?

To become healthy adults, children need to learn how to relate to others. That means communicating with others. Your child will never learn to do that if you're always putting yourself in the middle and snowplowing her road in life.

What should the father do with his little Annie at the park? "Oh, that's too bad, Annie. I thought it looked like a great day to play, and those children look like they're having fun. I brought you here so I could get some work done while you have fun, but I guess we just need to go home. I can work from there too."

In 95 percent of the cases, that remark would prod little Annie to become more proactive about going over and starting to play with those children. Why? Because in her heart of hearts, she really doesn't want to go home. She wants to play with those children. She just wanted everything her way, the easy way.

The wise parent won't fall for it.

The other day I overheard an interesting conversation between second graders who were on their way to visit a retirement home for their school field trip.

Kimmy, the first little girl, declared, "Well, I'm not going to talk to those old people. I'm shy."

Kayla, the second child, paused. "You know what shy is? My mommy says that being shy is thinking about yourself instead of thinking about others. It's being selfish. It's saying, 'I'm more important than you.'"

I wanted to cheer Kayla on. Especially when I saw the look of utter confusion on Kimmy's face.

What Kayla said was entirely true. Shy children are saying "me, me, me"—but in a way so quiet that oftentimes parents miss it. The wise parent, however, will see shyness for what it really is: a manipulative tool for a child to get her way. (See also "Selfishness.")

## Sibling Rivalry

Years ago I wrote a book on birth order and how it affects children in the family. My working title was *Abel Had It Coming*, but my publisher said we couldn't have a title like that. So they sloughed it off and came up with a more provocative title: *The Birth Order Book*.

Sibling rivalry has been around forever, ever since Cain and Abel duked it out in the backyard and Abel lost. If you have more than one child, you will always have sibling rivalry in your home. But if you want to keep it to a minimum, make sure the children are accountable for it.

Let's say your daughter complains, "She wore my sweater and left it in a pile. Now I want to wear it, and it's dirty!"

If you as a parent get in the middle of that battle, you'll get chewed up and spit out. What is that saying—"where angels fear to tread"? You don't get between warring siblings.

Since fighting is an act of cooperation, both siblings need to be held accountable. Get them in a room together and let them duke it out. I can guarantee that one of them will end up washing the sweater so it's wearable again.

> *When the rewards stop, the behavior will stop.*

If your children start fighting in the car (see "Fighting in the Car"), turn the car around and go home. Then don't go anywhere the kids want to go for the rest of the day. Once you do that, your children will think either, *Mom's losin' it,* or, *Guess we got her attention. But it didn't work out quite the way we thought it would, that's for sure.*

Either way your smart kids will figure out that it doesn't make sense to do things that don't get rewarded. Too many parents unknowingly reward the negative things their children do as a result of an immature personality. When the rewards stop, the behavior will stop.

I guarantee it.

## Slamming Doors

*Bang!* There it goes again—another slammed door down the hallway.

Slamming doors gets old, really old. Even worse is the attitude that's implied by the behavior.

The attitude is saying, *I don't like you. I don't want to talk to you. I don't really want to be a part of this family.*

If this is happening in your home continually (I'm not talking about a onetime situation—who hasn't let a door slam just a little louder than needed when ticked off?), you have a kid who's got attitude with a capital A. He keeps you running from crisis to crisis. His mood controls the rest of the family's moods, including yours.

> *The attitude is saying, I don't like you. I don't want to talk to you. I don't really want to be a part of this family.*

That child needs the bread-and-water treatment. I talked about this in "Lack of Cooperation with Family" in more length, but let me summarize here. Everything stops. That means you do nothing that he wants to do until he stops slamming doors. When he wants to know, "What's the deal?" you answer calmly, "Rob, you don't seem to want to communicate with us anymore, other than saying you're mad about something by slamming your bedroom door. Part of being in this family is communicating with us. So since you're choosing not to communicate, you're losing your perks as being a part of this family. Dad won't take you to your baseball games; in fact, you won't be going at all. And you also won't be going over to Jason's for that computer game night you planned either. Nothing happens until we get the problem of the slamming doors solved."

There it is again: "B doesn't happen until A is completed."

It's amazing how quiet your house can get when you take this tactic. And how respectful your child can become in a hurry.

### Smoking

Smoking is a mountain. I ought to know; I used to smoke. At age 7 I tried out my first cigarette—a Viceroy—on the back of my friend Eddie's bicycle, and I thought I was cooler than cool. I smoked all the way through high school and into college. A few months after I met Sande, who has now been my wife for 4 decades, I quit cold turkey because she hated it. For those of you who have struggled with smoking, that says a lot about my wife, doesn't it?

I also know some parents today who think that smoking's no big thing. They even allow their 15- to 16-year-old kids to smoke in the house and endure the secondhand smoke. They don't even have a standard that says you can't smoke in the house because they don't want to offend their children or take away their rights.

That's crazy, in my view. Do you know how bad secondhand smoke is for you? Not to mention that those parents are allowing their children to run their home— and ruin their own and others' health.

When you catch a child smoking, have him do a 5-page research paper on the ills of smoking. The paper has to be handed in to you before the child can do any other activity he wants to do. In other words, life doesn't continue until he's done with the paper and you've had the time to read and approve it.

> *Psychologist Alfred Adler said that people who smoke do so for one of two reasons: (1) they're trying to draw attention to themselves, or (2) they're stupid.*

Why are some children drawn to smoking and others aren't?

Psychologist Sigmund Freud had an interesting perspective on smoking. In summary, he said that people who smoked cigarettes were fixated at the oral stage of development. They didn't get enough stimulation through nursing from their mother.

Psychologist Alfred Adler, whose thoughts were westernized by Rudolph Dreikurs in *Children, the Challenge*, said that people who smoke do so for one of two reasons: (1) they're trying to draw attention to themselves, or (2) they're stupid.

Whatever the reason, smoking is harmful to your body. If you think your child is smoking cigarettes, smoking pot, or doing drugs, it's time to take action. Some parents I know wiretapped their own home to find out what was going on while they were gone for the weekend. Other parents checked the history button on the computer and read their child's comments on MySpace. com.

"But, Dr. Leman," you might be saying, "what about my child's privacy?"

When it comes to the safety of your child, there are no privacy rights. If there is something going on, you are responsible to find out. You're the parent.

If you believe that your child is smoking dope (meth/crack cocaine is very big today, and so is heroine in affluent neighborhoods), set up a doctor's appointment for your child. Do it without any fanfare, but make sure the doctor knows (out of the child's hearing) that you want a urinalysis done to see if there are any illegal drugs in her body.

If the results come back positively, you need to take action. Drugs are habit forming, so some kind of intervention might be necessary. Get a few key people together that your child respects, sit down with the child without any warning, and lay your cards on the table. Tell her that you know what is going on in her life. If your child drives the family car or her own car, all privileges are rescinded immediately because it is clear she is not responsible.

Where are the finances coming from that are supporting the smoking or drug habit? If from an allowance, discontinue that allowance immediately. If your child works a part-time job, go to that job and disengage your child from it. Tell the employer that your child no longer has your permission to work there. It's hard to support a drug habit when there's no cash coming in to pay for it. Bumming money off friends for cigarettes or other drugs goes only so far.

A wise parent will take a hard-line approach to get the behavior stopped immediately. There is far too much at stake.

## Spaceyness

"Oh, she just forgets to do it. She's kinda spacey."

Most parents live in La-La Land. They have a ready excuse for their child at every turn. What are they really saying? "Oh, my child's accountable for nothing."

Well, what happens later when your child is 21 or 22 years of age and still isn't held accountable for anything? How will his employer (if he has one) feel about that? What about when he wrecks your car and still isn't accountable?

Why is it that we feel we must project our children as winners at every turn? That we must make up for what they don't do? Why can't we hold our kids accountable?

*For every action there is a consequence, and the sooner children learn that, the better.*

I'm convinced it's because many parents today are too lazy to parent. They take the easy way out. They've grown up with the "me, me, me" view too, and life is still all about them, so children run amok without parental supervision. The parents do this all in the name of letting their child be an "individual," I might add.

If your child spaces out on his homework, let him suffer the consequences the next day. If your child forgets to bring in his bike from the driveway and someone steals it, don't buy him a new bike. That's a good lesson on taking care of your possessions, one that he'll remember for a long time—especially when his buddies want him to go biking and he has to explain why he doesn't have a bike anymore. (Sometimes peer pressure can be very useful in changing behavior.)

It is through failures that children learn diligence and discipline so that they can become successful later in life. Excuses regarding their spaceyness will only weaken their development.

Children will be spacey. They will be daydreaming sometimes and not hear your instructions. Other times they'll simply forget. But for every action there is a consequence, and the sooner children learn that, the better.

## Spanking

This is a hot topic, and parents are polarized on their perspectives. But you're reading this book to see what I think as a psychologist and an expert, so I'll tell you.

There's a time and a place for giving your child a whack on the behind as the most appropriate discipline you can come up with. That is when your child is defiant.

What do I mean by defiant? Let's say your child is playing with an electrical outlet, and you tell him, "No, I don't want you to play with that. It's dangerous." But then he looks at you, narrows his eyes, and does it again. That's defiance. It's an active choice that says, "I am not going to obey you. In fact, I'm going to do exactly what you say not to do. I'm in charge."

Now don't you think that deserves a swat on the behind?

But let's also define what a spanking is. Spanking should never be done when you, the parent, are angry. You need to remove your child from the situation and calm down first if you are angry. You won't act rationally if you don't. A swat on the behind needs to be preceded with an explanation of why you are spanking the child and should not be done simply as a knee-jerk reaction. "I don't appreciate what you did just now. It showed me that you are choosing to disobey me and to do exactly what I'm asking you not to do. That is not respectful of me as your parent." Then proceed with the swat.

246

Let me clarify what I mean by a swat, though. A swat is an open hand on a kid's tush. It's a onetime shot.

That is very different than a prolonged, angry spanking that whales on the child. Using your hand (so you can feel how hard you are swatting your child) is also different than hitting a child with a belt. Many angry parents, sadly, proceed to abuse their children instead of disciplining them to correct a behavior. If you were physically abused as a child, you should never use spankings as discipline for your children. There is too much baggage attached to it for you—and too many emotions. It would be very easy for you to lose control and do what your father or mother did to you.

> *A swat is an open hand on a kid's tush. It's a onetime shot.*

Some children are so sensitive that one spanking will do the trick for a lifetime. Other children will need more frequent reminders.

But if you choose to spank, you have to keep the goal in mind: to correct the child's behavior, not hurt the child. For example, if you tell your child he cannot play in the street, and he continually runs out into the street, a swat is in order. His behavior is dangerous. What happens when that car comes around the corner and doesn't see the child, who is the height of a yardstick?

Discipline should always be for the child's best, not an angry response that makes you temporarily feel better—and guilty later.

## Spitting

This is one of those habits that a lot of folks find repulsive. Little boys spit, and sometimes little girls do too. Some adults are also spitters.

I'm a spitter myself. I'm one of those guys who just generates a lot of saliva. It's all this postnasal drip. I can either hawk it out, as gross as that sounds, or, worse, swallow it back down. For years if I had to spit to clear my throat in the car, I'd roll down the window and pop one out, yelling "Fore!" (as you would in golf), then, "Look out below!" One day 3-year-old Lauren, who was always so serious, was in the car with me, and I proceeded to pop one out the window. A calm voice said from the backseat, "Uh, Dad, you forgot to say, 'Fore!'" Another time when Kevin II was little, I had to spit out the window. I heard a little "aargh" from next to me. Kevin had attempted to model his dad's behavior, and guess where it landed? Right on my neck.

> *For years if I had to spit to clear my throat in the car, I'd roll down the window and pop one out, yelling "Fore!"*

Don't think spitting comes from thin air. The humor is that we get what we deserve. Our kids model themselves after us. What are you going to do about it? Your child is watching what *you* do and say. If you have a child who's a spitter, there's often a parent who's a spitter.

Is this a mountain? Nope. It's a molehill. Chances are, your son won't be hawking out a big one in front of his girlfriend in a few years, nor will he do it down the road in front of his boss. Some things are taken care of with maturity. Spitting is one of them . . . unless you're me, of course.

### Sports Activities

"He said he wanted to play soccer. We went twice, and he already wants to quit. He says he's no good at it. But we spent so much money on the equipment, we don't want him to quit. What should we do?"

My rule with sports activities is the same as my rule for music lessons. If your child insists on trying a sport, he keeps with that sport for at least a quarter, a semester, or 6 months (in other words, a full season for that activity). Nothing is easy when you first try it. It's like the old adage: "Nothing ventured, nothing gained."

Don't allow your child to be a quitter. Don't allow her to hop from activity to activity. If she wants to try something, make sure she knows the rule up front: "You're welcome to try anything, but then you have to stick with it for 6 months."

> *Nothing is easy when you first try it.*

I also suggest that children try only *one* extracurricular activity at a time. Today's families spend so much time running from activity to activity that they never have any family time together at home. The family dinner is just about null and void . . . unless it's McDonald's in the car.

If you have three children and each of them chooses one sports activity, you'll be more than busy, especially if the activity has a schedule of multiple practices a week. If this is making your family too crazy and not allowing you home time as a family, then you all need to make some sacrifices. Perhaps your high school daughter will play volleyball in the winter, your son will play baseball in the summer, and your kindergartener will do ballet in the fall. You may need to limit yourself to one outing with your friends every two weeks or once a month, rather than once a week.

Part of being a family is sacrificing for the good of the whole. What will last down the road? Your child will most likely change his interests multiple times. His friends will change. Your friends will change. But your family relationships are for a lifetime. Don't set them on the shelf because of busyness.

## Stealing

It doesn't matter whether your child was caught in the act of stealing or not. What matters is that your child stole something. That behavior needs to be addressed immediately.

Whether it was an 89-cent candy bar or a pair of designer jeans, the item needs to be returned as soon as possible to the owner, with the child in tow. But the fact that you walk the child into the store doesn't mean you do the talking for the child. The child herself needs to hand the item to a store clerk (or a neighbor or whomever she stole from) with an apology: "I'm sorry I took it. I know it was wrong, and I am returning it to you."

> *Ownership should be firmly implanted in a child's mind.*

Please, parents, do not sweep stealing under the rug because you're embarrassed. If you discover, for example, that your son took a candy bar, march the child immediately back into the store, find the clerk, and hand the candy bar over with an apology from your child. You'll probably notice that most times the adult tries to talk to you. Refocus the attention instead on the child, and make your child speak for himself.

If you find out after the fact that your child has stolen (i.e., you're back at home later in the evening or a day later and see the surprise item), call ahead and find out if the manager of the store is available so the child can apologize in person. Again, make sure the manager knows that he should address your child, not you, and that you want to make a point that stealing is not appropriate.

Even though stealing is a very embarrassing situation for the parent and for the child who gets caught, there is no more need for discipline other than to return the item and face up to any action that the store (or the neighbor) requires. Stern words coming from an authority figure outside the home are usually enough to curb the behavior.

One local store owner asked a boy who had stolen a watch to come in after school and sweep the floor for a week. Another asked a girl who had stolen a purse to pretend like she was a shopper and to keep her eye on other teens who might be possible shoplifters—intriguing punishment for the crime.

Many children steal from stores. Other children steal cookies out of a cookie jar or take quarters off dressers at home. The location isn't the issue; the important thing is that the stealing is addressed and the child is told that such behavior is not honest or appropriate. Unless he has been given something or paid for something, it is not his and should stay with the owner.

Ownership should be firmly implanted in a child's mind.

## Stomping out of the Room

"It was such a grand performance—a dramatic stomp through the kitchen and up the stairs—that I could have laughed . . . but it made me too mad."

Children definitely know how to make statements, and stomping out of the room is a good one. It's often paired, seconds later, with the slamming of a bedroom door (or the front or back door).

What is a stomper saying? The same thing as a door slammer: "You are absolutely the stupidest parent I could have.

> *You're the parent and the adult in the situation, so you apologize first.*

I'm so mad I don't know how to deal with it so I'm just going to show you. Take this!"

The stomper has no idea how utterly ridiculous he looks. The wise parent will allow the child to finish the stomp through the house and exit out the door or to his bedroom. As mad as that stomp makes you, you'll be smart to find something else to do for a while before confronting the behavior. If you go charging into the bedroom or run out the door, saying, "Let me tell *you* something, young man!" you'll only make things worse. It'll escalate the battle further. In power struggles with children, you'll never win, so don't go there. You have a lot more to lose than the child does in a power struggle, and you don't have the single-minded focus that a child does. You have other things to get done.

So wait until your child calms down, then go into his room (or wait in the living room for him to arrive back home) and say, "You seem mighty upset, and I've been thinking that what I said to you was inappropriate (or wrong), and I need to apologize."

Such an approach will startle your child. *What? She's gonna apologize? To me? This is new....*

When you say to someone, "I was wrong," and you apologize, most of the time that person will soften toward you. You're the parent and the adult in the situation, so you apologize first. Then say, "Hey, listen, can we start over again? Before you stomped through the kitchen and I made a fool of myself by yelling at you and then following you down the hallway? Can we take a few minutes and talk about this? How do you feel?"

Now who is going to argue with a speech like that?

And what are you doing? You're modeling an alternative way to respond. Getting mad, stomping through the house, slamming doors, and running away isn't the way to respond. Instead, you're saying, "Okay, we're both mad. But we love each other, so let's face this thing together. I want to know how you feel and what you think."

If you can get to that point with a child, you are establishing equality. You're not projecting the "I'm holier than thou" approach. You're meeting your child on even turf. Just about any child on the planet will respect that—once he's cooled down.

## Stubbornness

Children don't come out of the womb stubborn. They learn to be stubborn—because it pays off.

Let's say a child refuses to go with you to see his grandparent. So what do you do? You dance around the child. "Oh, come on. It's not that boring at Grandma's. And she'd love to see you."

The child still refuses. He shakes his head stubbornly.

"But, Daniel, she hardly has any company. It would mean so much to her if you come. Please do it. If nothing else, for me?"

By now, you as the parent have adopted a wheedling tone. What's the next step when the child refuses?

"Okay, I know you don't want to go, but if you go with me to Grandma's sometimes, I'll buy you that skateboard you wanted."

Aha, now your child's interest perks up. He agrees to go. He got that skateboard without much trouble, didn't he?

You walk away thinking you won, but did you really? Your son has learned that if he holds out for a while, you'll offer him the moon—and he'll get it too. Your child has you wrapped around his finger, and you're allowing it.

What's the purposive behavior of your child's stubbornness? To get what he wants. So don't give him the satisfaction of getting anything. Otherwise every child on the planet is smart enough to know that if he stalls long enough, you'll go to Grandma's without him, you'll do the task yourself that you asked him to do, or you'll completely forget your request in the first place.

It's a game of trial and error. Your kid's got your number. Are you going to let him win? Or are you going to hold him accountable for his responsibilities?

> *Children don't come out of the womb stubborn. They learn to be stubborn—because it pays off.*

If you want your child to go with you to visit Grandma at the nursing home once a month, that's not an over-the-top request. If he refuses, go without him. But then don't drive him where he wants to go the next time.

Remember, B doesn't happen until A is completed.

## Talking Back

Nothing ticks off a parent more than a child who talks back. Who disses you right to your face. Who has attitude, and then some.

Most often this happens after you've given the child a command to do something she definitely doesn't want to do.

What's your first gut reaction? To engage that child in battle, to show her exactly where she's wrong. You want to outpower her, outargue her. But guess what? Parents never win in the "sass 'em back" game. Parents have too much to lose, and every child is smart enough to know it.

Opening your mouth in response will only escalate the battle further. The best thing to do as soon as her mouth gets going is to shut *your* mouth, walk away, and get busy doing something else.

> *The best thing to do as soon as her mouth gets going is to shut* your *mouth, walk away, and get busy doing something else.*

Her jaw will drop. She'll think, *Huh? How come that didn't work to get Mom riled? It sure used to. . . .*

All of a sudden you've taken the wind out of your child's sails, and the sails deflate a bit. Not only that, but the direction of your child's boat begins to flounder. She isn't quite sure what's going on.

Your role? Just sit back and wait for that teachable moment. It may not come for 6 hours, depending on what day of the week it is. But there will come a time when she wants something from you, when she needs you to do something— that's the time you're waiting for. The fact is, your children need you all the time; they just don't realize it. You hold the keys to everything in their life and about their life, and they can do little without a parent's cooperation. You, by nature, are the powerful one. Not them. Yet so many parents give up that position of power to their child by giving in to the child's mouthiness and demands.

When your child needs something and asks you, your answer, no matter what the request is, has to be no. Your child will get agitated. "But, Mom, you always let me do that. What's the deal?"

Now's the time to let your child work through the problem a little. "I don't like the way you talked to me this morning, so I don't feel like doing anything. So no, you can't do that."

Some children, especially powerful children, will try to argue you out of your decision. They try to hit you from every angle, including the guilt one: "But, Mom, you know I didn't mean what I said. . . . Everyone gets angry sometimes. . . . Don't you love me?"

Other children will say, "I'm sorry." Some will mean it; others will say it just to get you to do what they want you to do.

But the scenario doesn't stop there. Now tell your child how what she said made you feel. "When you talk to me like that, you're basically saying I don't count in your life. My existence doesn't matter. You don't value or respect me. You don't want me involved in your life. So I'm choosing not to be involved right now."

Takes the fun out of talking back, doesn't it?

This is a huge mountain between parents and children. You have to deal with these things as they come up, because without respect, there can be no relationship.

It may take several days of you saying no for the child to fully get the picture. After those days have passed, to clinch the deal, you can add, "You've treated me like I'm your slave for a long time. But I am *not* your slave—someone you can use and abuse. I'm your mother, and you will show me the proper respect due a parent. This week you got a taste of what it feels like to not have a relationship. Is that really what you want?"

Your responsibility is to put the ball back in your child's court so she has to "own" her mouth. Talking back is never acceptable. Homes need to be built on love, respect, and accountability. There is no relationship without these important cornerstones.

## Tattling

"Did you know what Katherine did?"

"Sam got in trouble at school today. . . ."

"I saw Damon over at Jason's tonight. Wasn't he supposed to be at the library?"

Tattling—just like sibling rivalry—has been around since Cain and Abel first walked the earth. It'll continue to be around, so you might as well get used to it. The reason it continues to linger is that parents find it convenient to listen to the tattler.

> *Chances are, everyone in the family would be better off if the little narc kept her mouth shut.*

The tattler is the narc (often a quiet whisperer), the person in the family who loves to give insider info about what other children in the family are doing. Often she's right about the information, but does that make what she's doing right? It's so tempting to listen to a little narc. After all, as a parent, it's good to have info about what your kids are up to. But, chances are, everyone in the family would be better off if the little narc kept her mouth shut.

The wise parent will say to the little narc, "I don't want to hear it. If you have a problem with your brother, go talk to him. If there's something that he did, then he should be the one to tell me, not you."

That will take the wind out of any narc's sails because narcs love to dish about others. Did you know it's a way to make the narc feel better about herself? Most often when children tattle on siblings, it's because the tattler is jockeying for position as to who is the better kid in the family. It's a put-down in the guise of "something you oughta know." Frankly, it's also another form of name-calling, only this one is often said with a whisper.

Three-year-old Annie was a beautiful child with naturally curly blond hair—the kind of child who would look great in an angel costume. But she was far from an angel. She used to constantly tattle on Michael, her big brother. It drove her parents up the wall. When they talked to me, I gave them a simple strategy: "Just tell her you don't want to hear it."

Her mother took the advice a step further. The next time Annie wanted to tell her a tale, she said, "Annie, I don't want to hear it. Tell it to the tree in the yard."

A week later her mother looked out the window and laughed. Little Annie was standing out there, talking and gesturing to the tree!

## Tattoos and Body Piercings

Long ago, when I was growing up, the only people who had tattoos were Harley drivers. They were tough guys who made it clear that no one was going to mess with them.

Today's world is very different. The young moms who come to hear me speak about marriage and family issues are well dressed, they're educated, and they have one or more children. And some of them are also tattooed—on a shoulder, a leg, an arm, and who knows where else.

> *Allowing tattoos and body piercings is a judgment call every parent has to make.*

It's obvious that tattooing is popular. Some of you reading this book will have tattoos and wonder what the big deal is. Why would I even include this in my book? Am I an old fuddy-duddy or something?

The point I'd like to make is that people have a love/hate relationship with tattoos. They either love them or hate them. Frankly, allowing tattoos and body piercings is a judgment call every parent has to make.

For some parents, tattooing isn't a big thing. "So he got a tattoo. It's not the end of the world," they say. "He's a good kid."

Most children who want to get tattoos or body piercings (nose, eyebrow, belly button, ears, tongue) want to do it to make a statement about their uniqueness. What's funny about that, though, is that they also want to do it because their friends are doing it. So what's unique about that?

I fall on the side of those parents who wouldn't encourage their kids to distinguish themselves as being unique by the tattoos or body piercings they have. I'd rather challenge them to be the meanest clarinet in the band or the surest-handed tight end on the football team. There are lots of ways to be unique—by playing the trumpet, being a voracious reader, or being a killer chess player. The more confident a child is about herself, the less likely she'll be tempted to get some body part pierced to fit in with the crowd.

Lisa got a tattoo when she was 13, with her parents' approval. Fifteen years later she became a mom of two and moved to a very conservative neighborhood in an affluent section of town. That's when she decided to go through the pain of having the tattoo removed. "I was uncomfortable wearing any sleeveless shirts because I was afraid of what other moms would think. Especially after a mom talked vehemently about a woman who got a tattoo and how loose her morals were, etc. Last month my daughter turned 16 and wanted a tattoo. I explained to her why I didn't want her to get a tattoo. It was a different perspective from what she'd heard, and she didn't totally understand it, but she honored my request."

I also fall on the side of the parents who don't believe in tattoos or earrings for young children unless they are a part of the ethnic culture (i.e., Indian or Hispanic). Why put pressure on your young children to be like everyone else? "Well, Susan down the street has her ears pierced. Don't you want yours pierced?" (Susan is 5 years old.)

Parents today seem to be racing to give children everything as fast as they can in life. That's why first graders are walking around with cell phones at school. If this is your perspective as a parent, don't you think your child will catch on?

If your child is older, you can always tell him what you think. But it's his decision. When he's 18, he can tattoo his nose, cheeks, and neck and end up looking like Michael Tyson. (His body will pay for it, but it's his body.) However, if you take the time to tell your children what you think and why, the majority of them (even older children) won't act against their parents' wishes.

What about body piercings? I talked about earrings earlier (see "Earrings"), so I won't discuss that again, but I will discuss other body piercings.

Recently Jeff, a dad I know, was shopping at Best Buy. He's an early-thirties hip dad. But after spending 20 minutes in the store, trying to decipher what a clerk was saying, he asked to see the manager. You see, the young clerk had a pierced tongue, and as hard as Jeff tried, he couldn't understand what she was trying to say. His point to the manager was that the store should at least hire clerks who could communicate with the customers.

I'm not making any moral judgments about nose, tongue, eyebrow, belly button, or other piercings. I'm simply saying that allowing your 14-year-old daughter to "express herself" by allowing her to get her tongue pierced is plain stupid. It's gross. It's sanitarily unsafe, with all those germs in the mouth. And it certainly isn't going to help her socially to be trying to talk to others with slurred speech and clicking—especially to those who don't have pierced tongues (the majority of the population).

Also, a parent would be wise to keep in mind that what a child wants to do at 14 isn't necessarily what she wants to do at 17. A lot of maturing happens during those years. Any kind of piercings that take place on nontraditional parts of the body (i.e., other than the earlobe) are really acts of silent rebellion. They're done to show the whole world "I'm not like anyone else." I go back to my view that there are better ways of showing the world your uniqueness than harming your body.

I think it's okay for a parent to say no to tattooing and body piercing. After all, the parent is usually the one who is paying for it. Why would you pay to harm your child's body? Give the kid vitamin N (No) if tattoos or body piercings don't square with your values and your belief system.

## Telephone Courtesy

How do your children answer the phone?

"Yeah? Who's calling?"

"This is Megan. Who's calling, please?"

"Yo! What's up?"

"This is the Leman residence. May I help you?"

Have you taught your child proper telephone courtesy—how to answer a phone? Have you taught your children not to admit to any callers when they are home alone? They should let the answering machine pick up the call (unless it's someone who lives in the house who is calling) or simply say, "I'm sorry, she isn't available right now. May I take a message?"

When someone asks for you, do your children say, "May I tell her who's calling?" (the proper etiquette instead of the demand, "Who's calling?"), or do they yell, "Ma!" at top pitch from across the house?

How do your children respond next? It should be whatever you prefer as a family, such as, "Hang on, I'll get her for you."

If you think this isn't an important enough thing to bother with, consider this. When I speak to businessmen, I ask them: "Who answers the phone for your auto dealership?" It's the receptionist.

She's the first person who has contact with the outside world of that business. So that receptionist is the one who represents you as the CEO. Similarly, you need to be sure of who is answering the phone and how, because it reflects on you and the way you do business in your home.

If your child needs to ask for something on the phone, teach him to start with a statement: "I need your help. Could you help me?" If you start by such a statement, it's hard for the person on the other end to say, "Hey, drop dead." Usually, asking for help sets up the listener on the other side to say, "How can I help you?" The difference is subtle but effective.

> *You need to be sure of who is answering the phone and how, because it reflects on you and the way you do business in your home.*

I've already talked about what to do when children interrupt you on the phone (see "Interruptions"), but I'll summarize it here. Most parents cover the phone and hiss or yell at the kids, "Would you please hush up! I'm trying to talk!" But it makes a far greater impression on your children if you remove them from the room. Put them in a room away from you, or, depending on your children's age and the weather, put them outside and close and lock the door. Show them by your action (without interrupting what you're doing) that you expect them to be respectful and quiet when you are on the phone. After all, when they are on the phone with their buddies, you don't put on a dog and pony show in front of them.

In "Interruptions" I talked about a woman who, while talking to her girlfriend, put her children outside the door and didn't realize until 45 minutes later that they were still outside! When she went to let them back in, the children had found an old paper bag and written a note on it: *Mom, we love you. Can we come back in?*

That mom certainly made her point! It's all about action, not words. And her actions said, *I am to be respected in this house, and you are to be quiet when I'm on the phone.* Do you think those children did a dog and pony show in front of their mother when she was on the phone the next time?

## Temper Tantrums

I hear these sorts of things over and over from frustrated parents:

"He explodes every time I ask him to do something he doesn't want to do."

"I don't take her to the mall anymore because she throws a tantrum if I don't take her to McDonald's. And sometimes I don't have the time or the money to do that."

"When he has to share with his brother, he starts screaming, kicking the floor, and throwing things."

> *If throwing tantrums has worked in the past, your child will continue to throw them in the future.*

Let me ask you: when your child is throwing a tantrum, what's the purposive nature of the behavior? To get attention. To exert authority over you. And if throwing tantrums has worked in the past, your child will continue to throw them in the future.

If your family is one of faith, you might be interested in what St. Paul said in Ephesians 6:1: "Children, obey your parents. This is the right thing to do because God has placed them in authority over you." That means you are to be in charge of the home, not your child.

Two-year-olds will throw tantrums, and those tantrums need to be addressed. My favorite suggestion to deal with tantrums is to step over the child (reigning in the temptation to step *on* her), totally ignore the behavior, and move on with whatever else you were doing. If it happens in the mall, just ignore her and move on ahead. (For those of you who are worried, I can guarantee you that any 2-year-old who sees Mommy or Daddy moving away into the crowd will stop the fit she's throwing and *run* to follow her parent. She won't be out of her parent's sight because she's not that confident.) And without an audience there, there's really no need for the temper tantrum to continue.

If you handle the tantrums when your child is age 2, you'll change the behavior, guaranteed, by using my tried-and-true method:

1. Say it once.
2. Turn your back.
3. Walk away.

You won't be dealing with the behavior down the line. But this method requires consistency, follow-through, and no looking back to see if the child is following. Otherwise she gets clued in: *Hey, Mom is nervous about this. She's checking to see if it works. Aha! That means she doesn't want me to be out of her sight. So she'll come back. I'll just continue this fit thing a little longer.*

If children are still throwing tantrums at age 8 and up, however, they've got your number. They know what it takes to win the fight because they've always won in the past. They are going to show you in full, bloomin' color just how unhappy and miserable their life is because you haven't given them a toy or a treat, let them go somewhere, etc. With older children, the same holds true (no matter where you are):

1. Say it once.
2. Turn your back.
3. Walk away.

If you're not in the vicinity, it's less likely your child will continue the tantrum (especially if you're in a public place). What's the purposive nature of the behavior? To get your attention. It defeats the point if you're not there!

If you've allowed tantrums to control your actions in the past, you'll need to hold especially firm. Now is the time to stop the power tantrums. (Power is really what they're about, isn't it?) Do you really want your child to grow up to be a 13-year-old who's kicking the magazine rack in Wal-Mart, or an 18-year-old who has poor impulse control and a bad temper and throws tantrums when he doesn't get his way?

After a temper tantrum is over, the child must apologize before life moves on. And that doesn't mean you say, "Young man, I want an apology out of you." It's like asking for a hug. That hug doesn't mean very much because you had to ask to get it. Asking takes all the emotional fulfillment out of it. In the same way, making a child say "I'm sorry" doesn't carry the same weight as a heartfelt response without the prodding.

Remember that in all things, "B doesn't happen until A is completed." Until you receive a real apology (and you know the difference!), life doesn't go on.

## Thumb Sucking/Blankies

How many junior highers have you seen sucking their thumbs in public? How many take their blankies on field trips?

So many parents get hyper about a child sucking his thumb after a certain age. They hear all the horror stories about how it'll ruin the child's teeth and he'll have to get braces. They worry about how babyish their child will look. They wonder why their 4-year-old still sucks on a blankie during his nap.

But what harm will it do to suck on a blankie? Will it hurt the blankie to get wet? Will it make the blankie gross? Gross never bothered a kid yet. I know that from personal experience. When I took out my cell phone this morning, it was a mess. My granddaughter, Adeline, had her sticky fingers all over it at lunch yesterday. Sticky and gross certainly didn't bother her.

What I'm trying to say, parent, is that if you pay attention to all these little things that will change anyway as kids grow and mature, you'll drive yourself completely nuts.

> *How many junior highers have you seen sucking their thumbs in public? How many take their blankies on field trips?*

Everyone has a different view of thumb sucking and blankies or certain stuffed animals as psychological crutches. But will any of this mean a hill of beans to you or your child in a couple of years? Most likely not.

Then don't make a mountain out of a very tiny molehill. If your child is still sucking her thumb in kindergarten, just let a little peer pressure take over. The minute she's called a baby for doing so, her thumb sucking might just stop by itself (at least at school).

## Undereating

There's a big difference between the way young men eat and the way young women eat. It's not uncommon for a 14-year-old boy to come home from school, take a serving bowl (not a cereal bowl), fill it with half a box of cereal, cut up 2 bananas on it, and chow down the whole thing. In 2 hours he's ready to eat a big dinner. It's that time of life where he's growing by leaps and bounds and expending a lot of energy, so no wonder he comes home hungry.

Young women are much more mindful of what they put in their mouth. It's not uncommon today for 8- to 11-year-old girls to tell their parents, "I'm too fat" or "I don't like my body." If you are hearing such words from your child, that's a sign your daughter might be headed in the wrong direction because she's becoming preoccupied with how she looks.

Take a look at billboards, movies, and magazines, and you'll see in a second that those of us in America put a premium on how people look at a very early age.

Years ago, Charlie Gibson, Joan Lunden, and I did a *Good Morning America* show on Barbie dolls. They asked me to comment on them. "Notice how perfect and thin they are," I said, then proceeded to talk about the pull of anorexia, a disease that strikes young women primarily in their teen years (90 percent of the time), when looks are becoming so important. When young women who are perfectionists see how perfectly thin all the models are on television, in magazines, on billboards, and in the movies, they want to be like them. That drive to be perfect begins a downward spiral into anorexia (undereating or not eating) and/or bulimia (binge eating, then throwing up to purge the system).

> *Let your imperfection show. Even flaunt it at times. It will give your child the freedom she needs to be imperfect—and healthy.*

Anorexics believe that, in order to be accepted by others, they must be stick thin. Oftentimes they don't feel supported by their parents in their ventures, so they feel alone. Feeling out of control, they secretly find a way to control their world—by not eating or eating very little. By doing so, they feel they will be able to reach perfection, and everyone will like them.

If you suspect or discover that this is happening with your child, get professional help immediately. Some symptoms include sneaking into the bathroom immediately after eating to purge the food she has eaten, claiming "I'm not hungry" meal after meal, excusing herself from the table and saying she doesn't feel well, and losing weight unnaturally quickly. Both anorexia and bulimia are serious conditions that need to be addressed by health-care providers because of the long-term impact they can have on your child's growth patterns, overall health, teeth, stomach, mind, and emotions.

If your child talks a lot about her body and not liking it, show your own imperfections. (Children rarely realize just how air-brushed the photos of models are.) I like to pull my sweater up and show people a side view of my gut—now there's perfection! And then I tell them the story of how I ate a whole pumpkin pie, slice by slice, out of the refrigerator; then I had to hide the pie plate from my wife so she wouldn't know I'd gotten a 2-for-1 deal at the pie shop and eaten a whole pie by myself. Children love to hear stories about you and how you fell short. It gives them the freedom to also be imperfect.

So tell your children (especially your girls) how you fell short. About the time you got a bad grade. When you got into trouble with your parents for lying. When you did something really stupid. Believe it or not, children still see parents as model-like. To children, parents can do no wrong. Explaining that you have done some dumb-as-mud things shows your child that everyone does goofy things sometimes. No one's body is perfect. By showing your imperfections, you give your children the courage to be imperfect in an imperfect world. That's why I applaud the cover model who insisted, "Don't airbrush my wrinkles out. I've earned every one of them. They're a part of me."

Let your imperfection show. Even flaunt it at times. It will give your child the freedom she needs to be imperfect—and healthy.

## Unkindness

Children, by their nature, are very unkind. They're all about "me, me, me" and "gimme." Unless they are taught by their parents to be kind, they're not going to do so on their own.

When your child speaks or acts unkindly right in front of your eyes, the best thing to do is pull her aside and say, "That was a very unkind thing to say. Is that really what you meant to say? Did you mean to be unkind?"

After the child has a chance to respond, then say, "That made me feel [used, taken for granted, etc.]. Is that what you wanted to communicate?"

Such wording brings the situation to an immediate head so the child realizes that what she said was unkind. It also sets up the possible response, "Mom, I'm sorry. I shouldn't have said that."

If you get that kind of positive reaction, life goes on. If you don't get that kind of reaction, then life doesn't go on for long. Remember, "B doesn't happen until A is completed." And A demands an apology and a removal of privileges until the point is made. *Then* life can go on.

> *Some children are mean without knowing it, and some are mean because they want to be mean.*

If you're a person of faith, you are bound by the command in Ephesians 4:31–32 to be kind to one another. How is your family doing in that aspect of life?

I guarantee that, as you go through life as a parent, you'll have hassles. If you are truthful, you'll lock horns with some people. Jill, the mom of a kindergarten daughter, had to confront continual unkindness in another kindergartener by talking to that girl's mother. "Oh, no, my child would never say that," the defensive mom claimed. "Your daughter must be lying."

"I can understand your initial response," Jill said, "because I would have done the same thing—defended my daughter—if someone told me that. But I want you to know that I heard your daughter's remark with my own ears. Your daughter did say that, and my daughter was greatly hurt by it."

All Jill could do was state her case. Then it was up to the other adult to continue to live in La-La Land (thinking her perfect daughter could never do such a thing, or hiding from Jill so she didn't have to meet Jill's eyes after that point) or to confront the behavior in her daughter. If she chose to pretend the event never happened, she would continue being a weak parent. And her daughter would someday make a statement even less kind in an audience that might react more vociferously.

The wise parent addresses the behavior when it happens—no excuses. And life doesn't go on until a heartfelt apology is made.

Should you always fight your child's battles for her? Certainly not. But sometimes, as in this case, the stakes are high. Jill was defending her child against a racial slur that was deeply hurtful—even more so because Jill's child was the only ethnic child in that class.

Some children are mean without knowing it, and some are mean because they want to be mean. Everyone will say dumb things sometimes. But whether it was meant or not, if your child says hurtful words to someone else, she deserves to know the truth about how she hurt that person. And life cannot go on until the apology is delivered to the injured party.

No exceptions.

## Wardrobe Issues (Clothes, Hair, Makeup)

Did you know that children wear costumes every day? They may look like clothes, but they're actually carefully thought-out costumes. The way your child walks, talks, and acts is all part of her persona. Each time she switches clothes, she's trying on a new personality. No wonder she spends so much time in front of the mirror!

From day 1, children will always express themselves differently than the main culture (their "parentals"). When I was dean of students at the University of Arizona during the Vietnam War, a Marine Corps colonel asked me how to get his teenage son to cut his hair and stop wearing T-shirts that said, "We don't want your freakin' war."

"Well, sir," I told him, "the hair part is easy. Just grow your hair long and he'll cut his. As for the wardrobe . . . give it a couple months past graduation."

Every child wants to be different from his parents. Interestingly, when that colonel's son started to get job interviews, the antiwar T-shirt got packed away, his hair was clipped stylishly short, and out came wingtip shoes and a fine business suit. Within months after graduation, that young man was absorbed into adult culture as he began earning his first check in corporate America.

*The way your child walks, talks, and acts is all part of her persona. Each time she switches clothes, she's trying on a new personality.*

Children will go through different stages, and most of them will be fairly harmless. The important thing is to stay tuned to the inner workings of your child. What's going on in your child's heart? Is she compassionate and kind? Is he responsible? These are the things that will endure, not the wardrobe.

Fashions change. Just look at the history of any young society in America and you'll see that young people have always distinguished themselves from older people by the way they dress. So why are we parents making mountains out of molehills? Did your parents always like what you wore? I noticed recently, when I was at a college basketball game, how baggy the shorts are today—going way below the knees. I figure if I just wait a few years, the regular shorts I always wear will be back in style.

So what if your 14-year-old son wears baggy pants that two people could fit into? Just make sure he's got a serviceable belt so no one de-pants him, I say. But if all of a sudden your child is dressing only in all black, wearing Goth makeup and leather, then clothing is becoming a mountain. Why? Because with that clothing, your child is trying on a persona that could take her into dangerous territory.

As the parent, you have every right to exercise vitamin N (No) in your child's life, and those decisions need to be based on your belief system. However, I urge you not to make the small things a battle. If your child feels she needs a $60 pair of jeans to fit in with her peers, let her spend the money from her allowance for them. Or give her a certain budget for school clothes every year and let her spend it as she wishes. That means she may buy 2 designer-label shirts, 1 pair of jeans, and 1 jacket instead of a whole wardrobe from Old Navy, but who cares in the long run? That's the small stuff . . . she's the one who will have the diminished wardrobe and will have to keep up with the laundry to have those precious items clean for school.

It's no sweat off your back, and *you* don't have to wear the clothes, so why not let your child be a little creative and learn from the experience?

## When Life Isn't Fair

Whoever said life would be fair was lying.

When your child gets bullied, picked on, or put down, the best salve is to say to your child, "You know, honey, that really must have hurt. But as your mom/dad, I noticed how you handled that, and you handled it really well. You didn't strike back, and you didn't call him names, even though he was thoughtless and mean-spirited. There are a lot of people like that in life, unfortunately. I'm proud of how you handled the situation."

> *With any bully, what goes around eventually comes around. Even if you aren't around to see it.*

If you say such things to your child, you'll be giving him the inoculation that says, "I can weather this thing. My parent believes in me."

With any bully, what goes around eventually comes around. Even if you aren't around to see it.

And sometimes it comes around creatively.

Karyn, a first grader, was continually bullied by Tyler, another first grader. Day after day he'd get in her face, and they'd go at it verbally. One day her mom asked, "What do you think he'd do if you didn't fight back?"

Karyn decided to try that. Three days later, she came running to her mom's car after school. "Guess what? Tyler says he wants to be my friend now. He says I'm no fun to pick on anymore because I don't fight back."

It takes two people to fight. Fighting truly is an act of cooperation. When one quits the fight, the other often does too.

## Whining

"But, Da-ad . . ."

"Mommy, he saaaaaaid . . ."

My favorite one-liner on this topic is: when you get too much whine, you need to build a whine cellar.

The truth of the matter is, there are whiners in this world for sure. I've seen far too many of them, and they're not pleasant people. The whiner only continues because whining has paid off in the past. Whiners know that whining keeps Mom or Dad over the proverbial barrel and the child in charge. And we parents are dumb enough to fall for it. As soon as we give in to the child's demand, we've added fuel to the fire of the whining. It'll ramp up the next time.

*Never* **ever** *pay off whining with any kind of reward.*

Children are addicted to routine. So don't start a habit with them that you don't want to continue. Never *ever* pay off whining with any kind of reward. A whine fest always starts meekly, then crescendos into a "But, Mom . . . !"

The smart mom or dad will pick up the child and say, "If you want to whine, whine outside. I don't want to hear it."

What's the purposive nature of the child's behavior? To get your attention and to get what he wants. When both purposes are removed, as well as the audience (you), whining isn't fun anymore.

### Youth Activities/Church Youth Activities

"We go to one church, but my son wants to go to youth group at another church. How should we handle that?"

Lots of children (especially teens) want to go to youth activities at another church. Usually there are good reasons for that. Some churches have really cool youth groups; others are stodgy and old-fashioned and plain uninteresting. Or just maybe there's some cute girl or guy who seems awfully interesting at the other church's group.

Parent, if you are going to pick a fight because your child wants to go to someone else's church, there's a clinical term to describe you: nuts! Be glad your child at least wants to go to church! Would an alternative—sitting on the corner smoking crack cocaine—be better?

Encourage your child to do that kind of thing, if he's interested. It might mean an extra drive, but happily agree to get your child there. Ask him if his buddy's family could get him home so you could get his younger siblings to bed on time. That way there is some give and take in the relationship, and you're not the one doing all the running.

> *If you are going to pick a fight because your child wants to go to someone else's church, there's a clinical term to describe you: nuts!*

Part of developing good Attitude, Behavior, and Character in your child is for him to associate with other children who think along the same lines—children who aren't clones of each other but whose families have an interest in the spiritual side of life. Some children who go to youth groups will have a personal relationship with our Creator; others go just for the fun time.

Just because it isn't *your* church doesn't mean it's not a good church—and a welcoming place for your child to be with peers of like mind.

# Epilogue

## Fun Day

You're now equipped with the *Have a New Kid by Friday* strategies and ready to tackle those things about your children and your relationship that drive you crazy. In fact, you're just sitting back, relaxed, waiting with a smile on your face for your kids' next move. You now know why they do what they do, and what the volume and continuation of their war whoops has to do with you and the kind of parent you've been. And that little secret puts you front and center to win *big* on your home turf.

Also, you're smart (a lot smarter than your kids give you credit for). You're more convinced than ever that Attitude, Behavior, and Character are the three most important things your children need not only to learn but to carry with them for the remainder of their lives. You, of all people on the planet, are in a unique role to teach those aspects—because you're continually on display in front of your kids. It's like the bumper sticker I once saw and chuckled about: "Being a parent is like being under a microscope 24-7." And that's the truth. Values are caught rather than taught. No matter the age and stage—from tiny toddler to exasperating preadolescent to rambunctious middle teen to questioning young adult—your kids are learning how to live life by watching *you.*

How you cope with anger, sadness, and disappointments.

How you acknowledge accomplishments and celebrate joys.

How you prioritize.

How you treat others and yourself.

> *Being a parent is like being under a microscope 24-7.*

A little intimidating at times, isn't it? But it can be stimulating too, if you know how to use that natural human tendency to watch others. Okay, let's call it what it is. We're all just plain *snoopy.* And you can use that to your best advantage with your children.

You've also had the eye-opening opportunity to view a neighbor's or co-worker's experience and decided you don't want to be in their shoes down the road. You're more determined than ever that *now* is the time for a change.

For some of you, sparking that change using the *Have a New Kid by Friday* game plan may be fairly easy. Five days in the saddle and your children will be so bamboozled by the change in you that their jaws are agape. *Why doesn't that work anymore?* they'll wonder. *It always used to get me what I want. . . .*

For others of you, *Have a New Kid by Friday* will set the stage for how your family will now be run, but your child may be more resistant, more set in his ways. The younger the child, the easier it is to mold that wet cement, as we discussed earlier. Usually the older the child, the more difficult it is to shape him because some of the prints of Attitude, Behavior, and Character have already begun to harden.

Parent, as you've read this book, some of you have had great successes. Your son or daughter is now mostly grown or out of the home. You've seen the tremendous power you can have as a parent in creating the kind of environment that encourages your child to reach his or her true potential.

Others of you have battled difficult situations with a child who was extremely rebellious and gave you all kinds of worries and sleepless nights. At last your child has turned the corner. Let me issue you a few words of caution. Don't get smug or think you have all of life's answers in your back pocket. Don't be a bone digger. Don't rub your child's nose in her mistakes. Just be thankful that both you and your daughter have a new grasp on life.

I realize that some of you who read this book are not people of faith, so I'd like to share a story with you from the Bible.[8] It's for those of you who have had (or currently have) a prodigal, a child who has blown off your family beliefs and values. Perhaps he's left home and lived in undesirable surroundings, engaged in things you never thought you'd see your child do, and embarrassed you in front of the whole neighborhood, not to mention all your friends and relatives.

The prodigal in the Bible was tired of the way things were at home. He was restless. He went to his father and said, "You know, this place is Dullsville. I'm out of here. I want my fair share. I'm history. I'm leaving."

> *When he saw his son, he ran to him!*

And the child did exactly that. He went and lived life the way he wanted to. He spent all his money—wasted it on wine, women, and song. Finally he came to his senses and realized that even his father's farmhands were better off than he was because at least they had something to eat. So he went home to his father.

One of the most moving parts of the whole story is when the father saw his son coming from afar . . . coming back home.

What did that father do? When he saw his son, he ran to him! He embraced his son. He was absolutely delighted that his son had come home.

I need to point out to you a couple of things he didn't say.

He didn't say, "Well, look what the cat dragged in. Had enough of the independent life?" or "Oh, I suppose you've learned your lesson." Not at all.

That father embraced his son and loved him.

It's a great reminder for anyone who has a prodigal.

Yes, you wish you could relive those 3 years your son was absent from you and got himself in so much trouble. But you need to rest in the fact that your son is now safely home. You need to start a new chapter in both of your lives. You need to love him and move on.

> *Sometimes your child will misbehave . . . and in colorful, exasperating, and embarrassing ways.*

Let's just say it boldly. You're not perfect. Your kid isn't perfect. Sometimes your child will misbehave . . . and in colorful, exasperating, and embarrassing ways. Like the little girl whose parents asked her to lie down for a nap in her room on a Sunday afternoon while the pastor and his wife were over for dinner. "Mommy," the little girl yelled out when she was supposed to be asleep, "guess where my fingers are?"

Sometimes *you* will be the one who gives in when you know you shouldn't . . . or the one who reverts to the old authoritarian ways you grew up with.

None of us is perfect. Your children need the three-pronged foundation of Acceptance, Belonging, and Competence in order to become healthy, functioning members of society. They also need the character building of truth-telling and encouragement, rather than the false and empty platform of praise. Most of all, they need consistency. They need a mom and/or a dad who will stand up and be a parent. Even if that means being Public Enemy #1 of the kids for a while.

Today is *your* day. Fun Day. The reward for your work and determination. The day you get to sit back and watch the fun! The look of absolute confusion on your child's face when you launch your action plan will be priceless.

Remember little Matthew, the 4-year-old in the "Monday" chapter, who dissed his mom in the car, then wondered why he wasn't getting his usual milk-and-cookie snack after preschool? Who couldn't understand his mother's "no" until he was so desperate for his routine snack that he was finally willing to listen to the reason she refused to give the snack to him?

Ah, but next came the very hardest part for any parent. That mother had to lean down and look that red-eyed, tear-stained, humbled 4-year-old in the eyes and *still not give him what he wanted*!

How tempted do you think she was to give in? How tempted would *you* be? But what would have happened if she had? Would she really have won anything, for all her effort?

Without determined follow-through from Mom, Matthew would have had no idea how serious she was or how much he had hurt her feelings. Most of all, that little ankle-biter, no taller than a yardstick, would have remained in the driver's seat of that relationship.

The old adage is right: sometimes love has to be tough. And sometimes you have to be the one to deliver that type of love. But if you do, the payoff will happen right in front of your eyes. You'll be amazed!

You too can experience what thousands of families already have: a complete revolution of their relationships and family life. Just read this story from a mother of three. It sure made me smile.

EMAIL

TO: Dr. Kevin Leman

FROM: A no-longer overwhelmed mom in Texas

Dear Dr. Leman:

I attended the seminars you taught last weekend in Dallas, Texas. Thank you so much for the practical, easy-to-implement ideas. I put them into practice immediately.

After the talk on Monday morning, I gathered up my 3 children (ages 6, 4, and 3) and started home, which was about 30 minutes away. Since it was lunchtime, I decided to stop at McDonald's to eat. While waiting in line to order, my 4-year-old started whining and tattling. I told her we were leaving, and as I walked to the exit door without any food, all three of my lovely children started screaming, crying, jumping up and down, etc. People were looking at us like we were a bunch of lunatics. I loaded them in the van and started home. They all continued screaming and crying, so I turned the radio on as loud as it would go. The oldest and youngest finally quieted down, but Emma, the 4-year-old, continued to pitch a fit. When we arrived at home, I didn't say a word, just picked Emma up out of the car, walked in the house, and went straight to the back door. I put her outside, closed the door, and locked it. She continued crying for another 10 to 15 minutes, while I proceeded to fix lunch. Once she quieted down, I let her in to have lunch, and all three behaved quite well the rest of the afternoon.

My husband and I attended the Monday night session as well. Emma used to be a good sleeper, but a switch was flipped when she turned 2, and bedtime has been our battleground for 2 years. We've tried just about everything we could think of to get her to go to sleep without a fight. Although we had tried the isolation technique, it was usually paired with talking, a lecture, yelling, etc. As we listened to her screaming in her room that night after the session, I looked at my husband and said, "I think I'm going to put her outside." He replied with, "I think I'll help you." We went upstairs, and without saying a word, I pried Emma's fingers from her covers and carried her, kicking and screaming, down to the back door. She even began screaming, "I want a spanking; I want a spanking; don't put me outside." I set her down outside, closed the door, and locked it. Within 10 seconds, I heard three little knocks on the door, followed by a very calm voice saying, "Mommy, I stopped my crying." When I opened the door, she headed upstairs, and we didn't hear a peep out of her the rest of the night. Needless to say, my husband and I were amazed.

To speak plain English, this mom and dad decided they were no longer going to put up with little Miss Emma's power plays. So they decided to take action.

They are not alone. Others who have tried the *Have a New Kid by Friday* strategies have said the following about their effectiveness:

"Try these principles—they *really work*. But no wimps are allowed. I took the chaos out of my home, and now everybody—including me—loves living there a lot more."

Wilma, South Carolina

"I was dubious at first when I heard about this as 'the miracle cure,' but it is. I've been a single dad for 5 years, and I've always felt bad that my 2 girls no longer have a mother. So I gave them everything they wanted, even when I couldn't afford it and had to do without some basics myself to provide the latest toys for them. Then one day, when they were 12 and 13, I realized, after they threw fits over not getting designer jeans, that I'd raised a couple of brats. I was stunned. I felt even more inept. It wasn't until a friend of mine talked about what she'd learned at one of your parenting seminars that I started to say no to their whining. I did like you said—I said no and stuck to my guns. After 5 days, my older daughter came up to me, gave me a hug, and said, 'Dad, I love you. You've made a lot of sacrifices for us.' It was the first time she'd hugged me in over a year since she'd become 'cool.'"

Stan, New York

"My youngest daughter, Mary, has always been a challenge, but her behavior ramped up a notch when she turned 4. Nobody wanted to babysit for me anymore because they said Mary was impossible to control. I knew I had to do something. I was letting a 4-year-old rule our home. My husband and I couldn't even go out for our once-a-month date night anymore because she was such a handful. We tried your strategies, and they work! After she threw a screaming fit, Mary spent 20 minutes outside our kitchen door, peering in while the rest of the family ate chocolate cake, her favorite dessert . . . and there wasn't any left over when she was finally done with her power tantrum. I waited 3 days, then made chocolate cake again. This time Mary joined us with no fussing and even said 'please' when I asked if she'd like a piece! That's incredible in our home. My other children just looked at me with big eyes. My oldest child winked and said, 'Guess it's working, Mom.'"

Betty, Iowa

"Devin was always a great kid. Then he turned 14. All of a sudden he started wearing black all the time, got his entire arm tattooed without our permission, refused to participate in family activities, wouldn't go to church with us anymore, and was surly every time I asked him a question. I finally sighed and gave up, figuring it was just a phase. I hoped he'd outgrow it. But it bugged me just the same. He always expected us to be there for him when he wanted something—like to be driven to a friend's house—but he never showed us any respect. Finally I decided I'd refuse to drive him anywhere after school. It took 3 days of him calling me 'stinkin' crazy' and telling me it was my problem before he finally got quiet and asked why . . . but what followed was the first good conversation we've had for nearly 6 months. That was last night, and tonight he not only showed up for our family dinner, he asked what he could do to help. I know the fight isn't all over, but at least now we're talking."

Jane, Illinois


"Dinnertime was always a big battle zone. Neither of my kids ever liked what I cooked, and they always complained. Based on your principles, I decided that I'd make dinner for my husband and myself and just serve my kids empty plates. They couldn't believe it! But they got the message. I'm not on this earth to be a short-order cook for them. And guess what? Last week they even offered to cook dinner for all of us . . . and they cleaned up too!"

Amy, Texas


"My son didn't find a job after college, so he settled in back at home. Two years later, he was still at home, and it didn't seem like he was making any effort to find a job. I work full time and take care of my aging mother, so I'm gone from home a lot. I'd come home to stacks of dirty dishes and Nate sitting on the couch, eating pizza. It wasn't until I took your principles to heart and got tough that things changed. I told him that to earn his keep, there were certain things he'd have to do around the house—and I left him a big list. I also stopped paying for cable TV and his Internet service, and I bought only the food I needed and took a stash from my pantry in to work and over to my mother's. His first response was shock, then anger. But after 3 weeks, he knew I meant business. I was asking him to stand up and be a man instead of a baby. Two weeks after that, he started job hunting and now has a job that pays for his own apartment."

Kari, Indiana


"I can't believe I'm writing a letter to tell you this because I'm not a letter-writing kind of guy. In the last 3 years, my wife and I have felt exhausted constantly because we couldn't get our 6-year-old, Jessie, to stay in bed. She's always roaming the house all through the night, asking for drinks of water and snacks. We took your advice and insisted she stay in bed. When she didn't, we firmly closed the door and ignored her crying. (She didn't know it, but we had a baby monitor hidden in the room so we'd know if she was really in trouble.) After 3 nights of this, Jessie was exhausted. She fell asleep. Ever since, she has stayed in bed on her own! Thank you for giving us our life and some private time back! My wife would thank you too . . . but she's sleeping."

Martin, Oregon

You've read the emails. You know the principles work. But what if they don't seem to be working in your home? What do you do then?

Perhaps you can identify with this parent:

EMAIL

TO: Dr. Kevin Leman

FROM: Exasperated in Michigan

Dear Dr. Leman:

I've followed all of your principles, and I still have a 4-year-old with a mouth. Recently we were on my uncle's boat, and Christopher began to fuss and complain about everything. I told him if he didn't settle down immediately, there would be no amusement park tomorrow. (Wednesday is Kiddie Day, so we save by going then.) He kept whining. I got really embarrassed and angry and told him we were not going to go to his favorite restaurant— across the lakefront—for lunch. Still no results.

He finally settled down a half hour later in the restaurant, after my husband gave him a swat on his behind.

I need more help in a hurry. If there's any way you could email me back some advice, I'd be glad to pay for it.

Here's what I said:

EMAIL

TO: Exasperated in Michigan

FROM: Dr. Kevin Leman

Dear Exasperated:

Let's review the principles in light of your email.

1. When Christopher fussed, you told him to stop
   *immediately.* Basically that's never a good idea
   because most 4-year-olds aren't good at stopping
   anything immediately.

2. You threatened Christopher twice. First you told
   him there would be no amusement park tomorrow
   unless he settled down. Then you told him you were
   not going to lunch at his favorite restaurant unless
   he settled down. Nowhere in my speech did I ever
   say to threaten your child. In fact, I pointed out that
   threatening a child is counterproductive to what
   you are trying to accomplish and not respectful to
   your child. Threatening never works. Telling a kid,
   "If you don't do this, I'm not going to give you . . . "
   never works. You, as parent, will always lose in that
   situation. Your child understands you well enough to
   know, from past experience, that you'll give in if he
   just fights or whines loudly enough.

3. "Tomorrow" means nothing to a 4-year-old. It's too
   distant. An eternity away. So threatening him with not
   going to the amusement park didn't even register on
   his radar screen.

4. When you told him you weren't going to take him to
   lunch, I bet your uncle and the other folks on that boat
   were happy to hear that.

5. Even when you said you wouldn't take the child
   to lunch, obviously you took him. Two of the most
   important principles in parenting are consistency
   and follow-through. You need to be consistent in

your actions all the time and follow through on what you say you will do. If you say something is going to happen, it should happen.

I applaud you and thank you for being honest. You showed yourself to be human and used the terms *angry* and *embarrassed* to describe yourself. Those are probably good reasons your husband decided to give Christopher a swat on the behind in the restaurant.

What you need to understand about kids is that they will get attention. And they will get it in either a positive or a negative manner. Your time on the boat was a power struggle in which your son was determined to make you pay attention to him. After all, it's hard to ignore a 4-year-old who is misbehaving on a boat.

However, if you were doing things according to my principles—and you were out on the lake and your 4-year-old started to misbehave, you would ask the captain of the boat if he would mind dropping you and your 4-year-old off at the dock. You wouldn't threaten your child with missing the amusement park. Your child would miss lunch, so it would be a consequence for both your son and you—hopefully one that both of you would remember in future exchanges. There would be no power struggle, because you would remain calmly in charge and your son would experience immediate consequences.

If you use these principles consistently and always follow through on what you say you will do, you *will* have a different child on your hands by Friday. And you will have a smile on your face most of the time. I guarantee it!

The key to any action plan is consistency and follow-through. So many parents I've talked to say they've tried everything—spanking, taking away allowances, withholding privileges, etc. They've read all the books and consulted a bunch of experts, and nothing works.

But what they've been trying to do is similar to a frog jumping from lily pad to lily pad and never landing on any particular one for long. Is it any wonder that both children and parents are exasperated? So much confusion is created by the parents "switching the plan" continually to try to find something that works better. The Leman strategy is simple. Say it once. Turn your back. Walk away. Let reality be the teacher. Learn to respond rather than react. B doesn't happen until A is completed.

It'll win the game every time. Guaranteed.

# The Top Ten Countdown
## to Having a New Kid by Friday

10. Be 100 percent consistent in your behavior.
9. Always follow through on what you say you will do.
8. Respond, don't react.
7. Count to 10 and ask yourself, "What would my old self do in this situation? What should the new me do?"
6. Never threaten your kids.
5. Never get angry. (When you do get angry, apologize quickly.)
4. Don't give any warnings. (If you warn your child, you're saying, "You're so stupid, I have to tell you twice.")
3. Ask yourself, "Whose problem is this?" (Don't own what isn't yours.)
2. Don't think the misbehavior will go away.
1. Keep a happy face on, even when you want to . . . do something else.

# Notes

1. Anne Ortlund, *Children Are Wet Cement* (Backinprint.com, 2002).
2. "Mountain or Molehill?" quiz answers
   *Randy—molehill
   *Jennifer—molehill
   *Sam—mountain
   *Mandy—mountain
3. The points for these three types of parents are taken from Dr. Kevin Leman, *Making Children Mind without Losing Yours* (Grand Rapids: Revell, 2000), 127.
4. J. Neusner, quoted in Malcolm Stevenson Forbes Jr., "As Undergraduates Recommence Their Efforts," *Forbes*, October 1981.
5. "Facts Every Parent Should Know," Max homepage, http://www.max.com/site/maxprotect.shtml.
6. Donna Rice Hughes, Enough Is Enough homepage, http://www.enough.org (accessed August 20, 2007).
7. Ibid. For further information and valuable resources, go to http://www.protectkids.com.
8. Luke 15:11–32.

# Index of A to Z Topics

# About Dr. Kevin Leman

An internationally known psychologist, radio and television personality, and speaker, Dr. Kevin Leman has taught and entertained audiences worldwide with his wit and commonsense psychology.

The bestselling and award-winning author has made hundreds of house calls for radio and television programs, including *The View* with Barbara Walters, *Today*, *Oprah*, CBS's *The Early Show*, *Live with Regis Philbin*, CNN's *American Morning*, and *Life Today* with James Robison. Dr. Leman has served as a contributing family psychologist to *Good Morning America*.

Dr. Leman is also the founder and president of Couples of Promise, an organization designed and committed to helping couples remain happily married. He is a founding faculty member of iQuestions.com.

Dr. Leman's professional affiliations include the American Psychological Association, the American Federation of Television and Radio Artists, the National Register of Health Services Providers in Psychology, and the North American Society of Adlerian Psychology.

In 1993, he was the recipient of the Distinguished Alumnus Award of North Park University in Chicago. In 2003, he received from the University of Arizona the highest award that a university can extend to its own: the Alumni Achievement Award.

Dr. Leman attended North Park University. He received his bachelor's degree in psychology from the University of Arizona, where he later earned his master's and doctorate degrees. Originally from Williamsville, New York, he and his wife, Sande, live in Tucson, Arizona. They have 5 children.

For information regarding speaking availability, business consultations, or seminars, please contact:

Dr. Kevin Leman
P.O. Box 35370
Tucson, Arizona 85740
Phone: (520) 797-3830
Fax: (520) 797-3809
www.lemanbooksandvideos.com

# Resources by Dr. Kevin Leman

## Books for Adults

*The Birth Order Book*

*Sheet Music*

*Making Children Mind without Losing Yours*

*Sex Begins in the Kitchen*

*7 Things He'll Never Tell You . . . But You Need to Know*

*What Your Childhood Memories Say About You*

*Running the Rapids*

*What a Difference a Daddy Makes*

*The Way of the Shepherd* (written with William Pentak)

*Home Court Advantage*

*Becoming the Parent God Wants You to Be*

*Becoming a Couple of Promise*

*A Chicken's Guide to Talking Turkey with Your Kids about Sex*
(written with Kathy Flores Bell)

*First-Time Mom*

*Keeping Your Family Strong in a World Gone Wrong*

*Step-parenting 101*
*Be Your Own Shrink*
*Single Parenting That Works*

## Books for Children, with Kevin Leman II

*My Firstborn, There's No One Like You*
*My Youngest, There's No One Like You*
*My Only Child, There's No One Like You*
*My Adopted Child, There's No One Like You*

## DVD/Video Series

Making Children Mind without Losing Yours (Christian—parenting edition)
Making Children Mind without Losing Yours (Mainstream—public-school teacher edition)
Value-Packed Parenting
Making the Most of Marriage
Running the Rapids
Single Parenting That Works
Bringing Peace and Harmony to the Blended Family

Available at 1-800-770-3830 or www.lemanbooksandvideos.com

# Have a New Husband by <u>Friday</u>?
## *Is that even possible?*

Dr. Kevin Leman says it is. The *New York Times* bestselling author and relationship expert shows you how with his easy and accessible principles.

# Change your life with these great resources
## from Dr. Kevin Leman

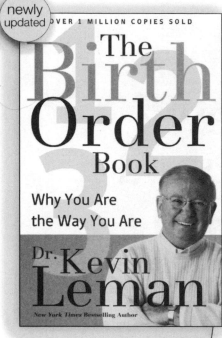

# Kid-tested,
## Parent-approved

If anyone understands why children behave the way they do, it's Dr. Kevin Leman. In this bestseller he equips parents with seven principles of "Reality Discipline"—a loving, no-nonsense parenting approach that really works.